The Languages of Psychoanalysis

John E. Gedo

Routledge
Taylor & Francis Group

LONDON AND NEW YORK

First published 1996 by Routledge

2 Park Square, Milton Park, Abingdon, Oxfordshire OX14 4RN
52 Vanderbilt Avenue, New York, NY 10017

Routledge is an imprint of the Taylor & Francis Group, an informa business

First issued in paperback 2019

Copyright © 1996 by Taylor & Francis

All rights reserved. No part of this book may be reprinted or reproduced or utilised in any form or by any electronic, mechanical, or other means, now known or hereafter invented, including photocopying and recording, or in any information storage or retrieval system, without permission in writing from the publishers.

Notice:
Product or corporate names may be trademarks or registered trademarks, and are used only for identification and explanation without intent to infringe.

Typeset by Innovative Systems, West Long Branch, New Jersey

Library of Congress Cataloging-in-Publication Data

Gedo, John E.
　The languages of psychoanalysis / John E. Gedo
　　p.　cm.
　Includes bibliographical references and index.
　ISBN 0-88163-186-8
　1. Psychoanalysis—Semiotics. 2. Psychotherapist and patient.
3. Interpersonal communication.　I. Title.
RC489.S435G43 1996
616.89'17–dc20　　　　　　　　　　　　　　　　　　　　96-12827
　　　　　　　　　　　　　　　　　　　　　　　　　　　　　CIP

ISBN 13: 978-0-88163-186-9 (hbk)
ISBN 13: 978-1-138-88162-4 (pbk)

The Languages of Psychoanalysis

Acknowledgments

Although the contents of this book have, from the first, been conceived as parts of one monograph, versions of some of the material in this volume have appeared elsewhere. I am indebted to the publishers of the following books and journals for their agreement to allow publication of those items in a new context: a German version of chapter 8 appeared in *Psyche* (Gedo, 1993b); the English original appeared in *The Spectrum of Psychoanalysis*, edited by Arlene and Arnold Richards, and is reprinted here, in modified form, by permission of International Universities Press. Most of chapter 9 appeared in *The Psychoanalytic Review* (Gedo, 1993c) and is reprinted by permission of the publisher, the National Psychological Association for Psychoanalysis, Inc. An earlier version of chapter 13 was published in *The Journal of the American Psychoanalytic Association* (Gedo, 1995a); it is reprinted by permission of International Universities Press. Earlier versions of other portions of this book were published by The Analytic Press: most of chapter 7 and the Epilogue, in *Psychoanalytic Inquiry* (Gedo, 1995c,d) and of chapter 10, in *The Annual of Psychoanalysis* (Gedo, 1995e); chapter 14 appeared in *Self Analysis*, edited by James Barron (Gedo, 1993a).

I was enabled to tighten my presentation of most of this subject matter by trying out preliminary versions at various psychoanalytic venues, notably at a plenary session of the American Psychoanalytic Association (chapter 13), a Weigert Lecture of the Washington School of Psychiatry (chapter 2), the Freud Conference of Deakin University, Melbourne (chapter 5), Ferenczi Conferences in Budapest (chapter 9) and São Paulo (chapter 11), a Tufts University Symposium honoring Paul Myerson (chapter 5), the Chicago Psychoanalytic Society (chapter 1), and Institutes in Stuttgart, Ulm, Munich, and Düsseldorf (chapter 14).

In addition, I owe a great debt to Eva Sandberg for her invaluable assistance in manuscript preparation and to the entire staff of The Analytic Press for efficient and expeditious production.

Contents

Introduction ix

I: Psychoanalysis and Semiotics
Chapter 1: Psychoanalysis and Nonverbal
Communication 3
Chapter 2: Protolinguistic Phenomena in Psychoanalysis .. 13
Chapter 3: The Primitive Psyche, Communication,
and the Language of the Body 26
Chapter 4: Speech as Manipulation 37
Chapter 5: Epigenesis, Regression, and the
Problem of Consciousness 45

II: On the Analytic Dialogue
Chapter 6: Treatment as the Development of a
Shared Language 57
Chapter 7: Channels of Communication and
the Analytic Setup 68
Chapter 8: Analytic Interventions: The Question
of Form 77
Chapter 9: Empathy, New Beginnings, and
Analytic Cure 91
Chapter 10: More on the Affectivity of the Analyst 102
Chapter 11: On Countertransference and Projective
Identification, and the Question
of Intersubjectivity 114

III: Intrapsychic Communication
Chapter 12: The Self as True or False, Crazy or Sane 125
Chapter 13: Working Through as Metaphor
and Treatment Modality 134
Chapter 14: On Fastball Pitching, Astronomical
Clocks, and Self-Cognition 148

Epilogue 163

References 181

Index 193

Introduction

About 15 years ago, the Chicago Institute for Psychoanalysis organized a Supervisors' Seminar to discuss the difficulties of teaching psychoanalytic praxis. For this exercise, I volunteered to present my work with a candidate who greatly puzzled me: the supervisee was, by all the usual criteria, singularly inept, but his analysand had done extremely well—the analysis was satisfactorily concluded when the patient married and went abroad as a Fulbright scholar. The candidate's other supervisors were in complete agreement about his deficiencies, particularly the difficulty he had in communicating with teachers and patients alike. I had hoped to raise questions about our customary methods of student evaluation, but my initiative only succeeded in convincing everyone that our reliability as evaluators justified the conclusion that this student was unfit to become a psychoanalyst.

In 1980, I did not yet have the confidence to battle against such a consensus; ever since, I have been chagrined about my diffidence because we have seen our failed candidate go from success to success in the psychotherapy community. It was true that, in his mouth, even the best thought-out supervisory suggestions were transmuted into nonsense—but neither his analysand nor I ever held this against him. He was a person of charismatic *goodness*, a worthy son of fundamentalist missionaries. It was only at the Supervisors' Seminar that I learned additional relevant facts about his background: I knew that he had been the only Caucasian child at the mission and that he had spent almost all his time with people who spoke no English; I now learned that the tribal culture that became his true semiotic matrix is known for taciturnity and for the value it places on silent communion.

I recount this story not to claim that a person as inarticulate as the candidate in question would make a good *psychoanalyst*. The point I wish to make is that we have probably given undue emphasis to performing "talking cures" and have overestimated the value of verbal intelligence (as opposed to other components of the cognitive repertory). I was enormously impressed by the fact that the candidate's painful clumsiness with words (and ideas expressed in words) had hardly interfered with the progress of a very difficult patient. Moreover, I am confident that my supervision had little to do with the good result, for the candidate seldom seemed to grasp what I was attempting to teach him.

Neither do I wish to imply that my dissent from the faculty consensus about one student had an important role in persuading me that the psychoanalytic insistence on the therapeutic power of the "voice of the intellect" (Freud, 1927b) is overly one-sided. On the contrary, my experience with this supervisee merely served to crystallize my growing conviction about this issue. Starting in the late 1960s, I focused my scientific work on the elucidation of derivatives in adult life of preoedipal developmental vicissitudes, efforts that led to the formulation of a hierarchical model of psychic functioning (Gedo and Goldberg, 1973; Gedo, 1979). As a result of this conceptual framework, I began to pay more and more attention to analysands' deficits in essential psychological skills—apraxias that needed correction before other remedial measures could become effective. Among these missing functions, skills in human communication were the most significant because of their potentially deleterious effects on analytic efforts.

Over the years, I have communicated the results of my clinical observations about the rhetorical dimensions of psychoanalysis in scattered publications, including chapters in several books (Gedo, 1981a, chapter 11; 1984, chapters 8 and 9; 1986, chapters 12 and 13; 1988, chapters 6, 7, and 13), but these reports did not add up to a systematic treatment of the subject. As my thinking about the hierarchy of mental functions was gradually clarified, however, I became more and more convinced of the central importance for psychoanalytic theory and therapeutics of the communication of information.

The hierarchical model I originally formulated with Arnold Goldberg (Gedo and Goldberg, 1973) was based on correlating the developmental lines (Ferenczi, 1913; A. Freud, 1965) most frequently used in psychoanalytic discourse so as to form an ontogenetic map. I was surprised to find that the points of transition from one phase to the one succeeding it on each of the developmental lines previously elaborated by psychoanalytic theorists seemed to be temporally linked at certain nodal points in general psychological development. (This unexpected conclusion made it possible to delineate a sequence of five phases of development through childhood, each of which gives rise to a different mode of psychic functioning in adult life, albeit all five modes remain simultaneously available for the entire life span.) Because each of the developmental lines we took into account is almost entirely unaffected by the fate of the others, I eventually realized that they must enter succeeding phases in this linked manner as a result of some underlying process of biological maturation.

The foregoing insight pointed to the centrality of the maturation of neural control for a valid psychoanalytic theory of development. Another way to state this point is to acknowledge that our developmental propositions cannot be scientifically validated on the basis of psychoanalytic clinical observations alone—they must be buttressed by evidence from cognate fields, principally from brain science. Fortunately, a number of important efforts to bring the relevant data to the attention of the psychoanalytic community have become available; the one most influential for my subsequent work was Levin's (1991) *Mapping the Mind*, for which I also provided a foreword (reprinted as chapter 1 in Gedo, 1991a).

Although, at this writing, we have less evidence about the maturation of neural control through infancy than we require, the burgeoning field of infant observation is gradually demonstrating how crucial behavioral correlates of that maturation develop under various environmental conditions. The most important of these developments are those of cognition and of the infant's communicative repertory. In other words, for the time being, we have to center our developmental hypotheses on the maturational sequence of these functional capacities, which generally develop free of conflict. (To illustrate: it cannot be legitimate to postulate fantasy activity in neonates, as did Melanie Klein, 1984, because symbolic capacities do not come "on line" until later in infancy.) One prerequisite of the necessary conceptual evolution in psychoanalysis is the collection of semiotic data within the psychoanalytic situation—the recording of the continued use of relatively archaic modes of communication in adult life.

The present volume is a summary of my own clinical observations in this realm. I have organized it into four sections, although the subject matter of these often overlaps. Part One, "Psychoanalysis and Semiotics," is an effort to survey those modes of communication encountered in the psychoanalytic situation that go beyond the lexical meaning of the verbal dialogue that is the ostensible text the participants endeavor to understand. In chapter 1, I consider semiotic codes that may serve as alternatives to the verbal one, such as the music of speech or the production of wordless music—channels of communication that broaden and enrich an adult's linguistic repertory. Chapter 2 is devoted to the complementary issue of the persistence into adult life of protolinguistic phenomena—remnants from the preverbal period the communicative significance of which is no longer understood by the person who produces them. Chapter 3 takes up one category of these archaic modes of discourse, that of the "language of the body," exemplified by phenomena such as tics, hypochondriasis, or the somatic concomitants of the affects. In chapter 4, I consider the misuse of adequate verbal resources for manipulative ends. Chapter 5 is a preliminary attempt to discuss the relation of consciousness itself to the communicative function.

In Part Two, the foregoing issues are reconsidered from the vantage point of psychoanalytic technique. Chapter 6, a revised version of material that was included in my out-of-print book, *Psychoanalysis and its Discontents* (Gedo, 1984), stresses the need to attain a "shared language" between analyst and patient as the crucial prerequisite for a holding environment. In chapter 7, I survey the consequences of the customary "psychoanalytic setting," that is, the use of a couch with the analyst sitting out of sight, for the manner in which analysands are likely to encode their communications. Chapter 8 considers the converse of this issue: the consequences of the form in which the analyst chooses to make particular interventions, including both verbal and nonverbal aspects. In chapter 9, I attempt to deal with the issue of empathy, its expectable effects on therapeutic transactions and the limits of its curative influence. Chapter 10 takes up the closely related technical problem of the analyst's affectivity and the degree and manner of its communication in the treatment situation. Finally, in chapter 11, I discuss the phenomena of countertransference and projective identification from a semiotic point of view.

Part Three turns from the problems of interpersonal communication within the therapeutic dyad to those of intrapsychic communication. In chapter 12, I consider the ways in which distinct functional clusters, such as those usually called a true self and a false self, may coexist without materially influencing each other; this discussion is then extended to the closely related problem of the persistence of a "psychotic core." Chapter 13 is an effort to translate the metaphor of "working through," which refers to the elimination of isolated automatisms of the kind dealt with in the previous chapter, into operational terms, as matters of improved cognition. In chapter 14, the foregoing process is taken up in the context of self-analysis. In conclusion, an Epilogue provides a theoretical framework for the entire volume: it adheres to the characterization of psychoanalysis as a psychology of motivations, and attempts to show that the gamut of human motives can be encompassed only by a hierarchical model of psychic life based on the progressive maturation and hierarchical organization of the central nervous system. Thus, the communicative repertory of humans is a manifestation of this functional hierarchy.

I believe it is essential to provide such a biological framework for the discussion of communication in psychoanalysis. Lacking such an anchor, any emphasis on the semiotics that constitute psychoanalytic operations in their entirety is bound to give the impression that a linguistic theory, in contrast to the metapsychology proposed by Freud, can satisfy our requirements without considering our somatic substrate. I intend, instead, to stress that the function of communication, including the most sophisticated manipulations of symbols, is absolutely dependent on somatic events within the central nervous system. In other words, the appropriate study of psychoanalytic discourse does not constitute the abandonment of our biological matrix—on the contrary, it amounts to sharpening the focus of our inquiries on the biological subsystem of greatest relevance for our scientific domain.

I Psychoanalysis and Semiotics

1 Psychoanalysis and Nonverbal Communication

NONVERBAL MESSAGES

Psychoanalysts agree on the necessity of articulating psychoanalytic insights in the language of secondary process (Freud, 1911), which has the greatest likelihood of being consensually meaningful. Until recently, this consensus led most commentators on treatment technique to assume that analytic patients must be encouraged, in their turn, to *associate* in this same language. Patients' ubiquitous failure to live up to these standards of discourse was generally seen as one aspect of the resistance (Freud, 1895b, p. 269; 1916-17, Lecture XIX) that is the unavoidable concomitant of setting a psychoanalytic process in motion. Such views were so widespread that when Kohut (1957; see also Kohut and Levarie, 1959) published the now almost self-evident assertion that music is as much a secondary-process activity as is the verbal expression of rationality, this contribution had the force of true novelty. Perhaps it was the more systematic work of Noy (1968, 1969, 1972) that tipped the psychoanalytic consensus in favor of the view that nonverbal productions are not necessarily confined to using the primary process.

Four decades ago, when I was a candidate, it was not unusual to accuse patients of evasiveness if, for instance, they reported on the visual imagery that might occur to them in the psychoanalytic setting (see Warren, 1961). The first break in this solid front of misunderstanding was Hannett's (1964) fascinating report that, when her analysands became preoccupied with snatches of popular songs, it was very fruitful to ask them to reproduce these musical bits because the *lyrics* generally proved to be highly revealing about the patients' focal mental state. I was particularly impressed by this communication because, at a certain point in my own analysis with Hannett's husband, Maxwell Gitelson, I had been haunted by a currently popular melody from the Broadway hit *Pajama Game*—something about a "Hernando's Hideaway," where one could discreetly rendezvous with one's "Uncle Max." Olé!

Such a tune may come to mind as a wordless melody, so that some persistence may be required to make explicit the significance of the attached lyrics. In most instances (at least in the case of successful songs), however, the words and the music are truly congruent. Thus the melody of "Hernando's Hideaway" does, by itself, convey a triumphant aura of illicit sexuality—although it must be admitted that this is decisively underscored by the "Olé!" in which the refrain ends. Hannett did not spell out the point that her finding might be just as valid for instrumental as for vocal music, but if one kept in mind the fact that, in many instances, the words merely confirm a conclusion one can reach from the music alone, her contribution actually opened the way for the clinical exploitation of all forms of nonverbal association.

As I gradually relinquished treating such associations as "resistances," more and more of my analysands found the courage to value these productions as the equal of verbal associations— clearly, these changes were promoted by the interest I showed in these previously unwelcome channels of communication. It was not at all surprising that specific modes of communication were more frequently used by individuals who had practiced them in some other context. For example, practitioners of the visual arts tend to experience visions—a point beautifully illustrated by Gardner (1983), who happens to be an accomplished watercolorist. Similarly, musical associations are most likely to occur to trained musicians, and gestural communications are most prevalent with persons who have had training in dancing. In my experience, these correlations with specialized experience are much more significant than considerations of diagnosis, personality structure, or the nature of the prevailing transference, although (as I shall later try to show) they are not the sole determinants of such occurrences.

The analysand from whom I learned the most about this issue was not an active musician, but he was as sophisticated about music as a mere consumer is ever likely to become. He was a college professor who gave general courses in the humanities, including music history and "appreciation," but his main field of expertise was in a branch of philosophy. (I previously reported on this case in Gedo, 1981a, pp. 289–296.) Nonetheless, he often reported that particular musical passages occurred to him as part of his stream of associations, although he did so in a professorial manner: he might say, "I have just thought of the second theme of the opening movement of the Sibelius 3rd symphony." Needless to say, such statements were beyond my comprehension, and usually I remained clueless even if he agreed to hum such a theme for me. He was sometimes able, however, to give verbal associations that could illuminate the meaning of the musical one.

The clearest instance of such a sequence I can recall was the preoccupation of another patient with the slow movement of Beethoven's 7th symphony, the mood of which reminded him of his current feeling of hopelessness. Of course, there are countless musical themes with this flavor, so we looked into the meaning of his choice of the Beethoven. He was able spontaneously to come up with the interpretation that he wished he could resolve his problems as the composer concluded his symphony: the slow movement is followed by the manic joy of the most triumphant final movement in Beethoven's work.

As treatment with the first analysand proceeded, we gradually realized that our cooperative investigation of these musical meanings had significance per se as a transference enactment. The patient's mother had been a professional musician, although she had failed in her career and, starting with my analysand's preschool years, played the piano only for her private pleasure. She was young, beautiful, and overtly seductive; he was then her only child, and she was his only surviving parent. Although both mother and child were very troubled people, the most harmonious times they had together were the sessions when he sat at her knee while she played the piano. Her verbal communications were highly unreliable, for her attitude to life was that of a Pollyanna, but the child could generally gauge her true feelings by her choice of music to perform. In the analytic situation, the roles were reversed—it was the patient's inner state that had to be inferred from his choice of music.

This was not the first childhood history of this kind I had encountered. Some years previously, I had conducted an analysis for a woman whose mother had been a successful pianist who had gradually lost her hearing. The mother did not master lip-reading or learn sign language, so that one had to communicate with her mostly in writing, a procedure her daughter was too young to follow. Instead, this child also learned to read her mother's inner states from the music the latter chose to play—and even from the artist's choice of interpretation of a familiar piece. (Incidentally, this scenario is used in a surrealistic version in the recently popular motion picture *The Piano*—surreal because in the film the mother supposedly is not deaf but deliberately chooses to use only sign language—and music.) My patient was extremely alert to the nonverbal clues I gave her about my private feelings; this was an important aspect of the mother transference. In this case, however, either transference roles were seldom reversed or I was insufficiently attentive to the analysand's attempts to reenact the childhood transactions in an active mode. (Later in this chapter, I shall, however, describe one transaction in which such a reversal took place.)

Late in the analysis of the male patient, when he was reliving the frustration of his erotic longings for his mother and I felt confident that I was in touch with his emotions, I found myself conveying to him my understanding of this transaction by encoding my interpretation as wordless music. (I should mention that I feel most comfortable quoting music through whistling, and this was the medium of communication I used. Had I had a piano in my consulting room, it would have served my aim better. Recently, a senior colleague told me about a similar transaction in which he was able to use an appropriate segment of a compact disk recording to the same ends [Gunther, personal communication, 1994].) At any rate, some 25 years ago, I whistled the music he had mentioned as his mother's favorite when she was at her most seductive, the "Aragonaise" from Massenet's opera, *Le Cid*. His affective response was dramatic, and he was then able to put the whole matter into secondary-process language without further intervention on my part.

Emboldened by the success of this experiment, I began to use with a number of patients bits of musical communication, almost always widely familiar pieces and, whenever possible, passages with lyrics I could quote. I gained the impression that the affective impact of such messages was greater than that of my parallel efforts to use verbal means alone. (If I may use the analogy of opera versus drama, it is relatively easier to put on a moving performance of Verdi's *Otello* than of Shakespeare's original. Or, as R. Strauss and Hoffmansthal put it, "*Die Musik ist eine heilger Kunst.*")[1] These experiments convinced me that the then prevailing consensus that psychoanalytic "neutrality" requires that the analyst eschew dramatic behaviors was misguided.

I never tire of recounting that, about 20 years ago, in a discussion group with that great authority on analytic technique, Rudolph Loewenstein, I initiated a debate about the appropriateness of making interpretations in the medium of music (see Gedo, 1979, p. 32). Loewenstein was utterly scandalized, but (with the help of Robert Gardner) I persevered through a colloquium that lasted many hours.

---

[1] Music is a sacred art (Ariadne auf Naxos).

Loewenstein graciously ended the weekend by conceding the point. As he put it, "Jewish jokes are [permitted], but whistling is out!" In other words, skillful analysts have always tried to raise the emotional temperature of their interventions through various ingenious rhetorical devices.

In the intervening years, I have had the privilege of analyzing people skillful in various modes of nonverbal communication: artists who brought in paintings or drawings they spread on the floor and dealt with as analytic data equivalent to dreams; musicians who consciously specified how they felt by producing passages of music; often instrumental music, and even a dancer whose most revealing communications were probably postural and gestural and, alas, almost always beyond my ken. These virtuosi of the nonverbal have gradually trained me to be less reliant on words alone than publications on psychoanalytic technique recommend. From time to time, I have received support from unexpected sources; in the memoirs of one of Freud's patients, I found the following: "The professor interrupted rarely; when he did so, he mostly used metaphors and allegories. Once . . . Freud leaned over the couch to sing one or two stanzas to me from Mozart's *Don Giovanni*" (Dorsey, in Grotjahn, 1979). I have also found the partnership of Mozart and da Ponte to have much to say that an analyst may quote to patients with profit.

COMMUNICATIVE DEFICITS

Although I have invariably found it fruitful to explore the meanings of analysands' nonverbal associations—and worse than useless to label their occurrence as a "resistance"—I do think it is indispensable to assist patients to encode in words everything discovered through analysis. To put this in another way: as a symbolic system, consensual language has superior potential to correlate what needs to be symbolized (the "signified") in the broadest variety of permutations, making possible the most flexible and comprehensive employment of the information concerned. With special training, it is possible to use nonverbal symbolic systems in the same manner—witness the cognitive adequacy of the sign language of the deaf, even without translation into a text written in one of the languages of those who can hear. At any rate, spoken languages enable their users to manipulate symbols adequately, without special training, simply as a result of their acquisition. In other words, all analytic patients can be expected to master what they need to learn if they manage to encode it in words.

The other side of the same coin is that the acquisition of a consensually meaningful and syntactically correct spoken language so revolutionizes mental functioning—and, at a more fundamental level, even the functional organization of the central nervous system (Levin, 1991)—that it creates a severe disjunction between the new mode of functioning it makes hierarchically dominant (mode III in my schemata of mind, reviewed in the Epilogue, [see also Gedo, 1979, 1988]) and the more archaic modes (modes I and II) that precede it. Such a disjunction will manifest itself as an inability to correlate the experiences of the preverbal era with the verbal system.[2] This may produce one of two symptomatic clusters: either an apparent loss of early experience, with isolation of affect or alexithymia, or the periodic emergence of primitive mental states the person is unable to communicate in comprehensible words. In the unsatisfactory vocabulary we have inherited from psychiatry, we label these syndromes as "obsessional" and "borderline," respectively. It is not irrelevant to this discussion that the obsessional syndrome is distressingly prevalent among psychoanalysts; this is probably one reason for our collective refusal, for the better part of a century, to process the nonverbal material produced by our patients.

One of the reasons for the effectiveness of music in bringing to life the emotional world of the preverbal era is that it tends to bridge the verbal-nonverbal gap. Obviously, this is particularly true of vocal music, which is a veritable Rosetta Stone by virtue of the double registration of its message. Levin (1980) has made a similar point about the analyst's need to rely on metaphoric communications. When we are dealing with individuals who suffer from a major split in the mind between the verbal and nonverbal realms, however, we are likely to find that they cannot comprehend the metaphorical use either of music or of words. If you have to explain to an analysand that you are about to start whistling *Là ci darem la mano*[3] to provide an associative connection between the past and the present and not as an effort literally to seduce him or her, producing the melody is not going to have much of an affective impact. In general, patients who are severely regressed (or have suffered early arrests in development in major sectors of their personality) are very likely to

---

[2] I owe this idea to David Freedman (1982 personal communication).

[3] Don Giovanni's aria in Act II, in the scene of his attempt to seduce Zerlina. Literally, "There we shall give each other our hand."

misunderstand the analyst's resorting to metaphors or the use of irony, or any of the other rhetorical devices called tropes.

In pragmatic terms, the most difficult clinical problem is the ever-present possibility of an *unexpected* regression in the analysand's capacity to understand communications encoded as tropes. (Such a loss does not necessarily constitute a therapeutic set-back; it sometimes occurs as a result of a desirable emergence of a previously split-off nucleus of archaic mentation.[4] The most startling experience of this kind I have participated in occurred with someone who returned for one interview after terminating a difficult and lengthy analysis. I had no illusions about having succeeded in completely eliminating the patient's identification with her psychotic mother—nor had a mother transference wherein maximally difficult transactions were reexperienced ever come to the fore. Yet we had covered a great deal of ground, with appreciable benefits, and had mutually agreed that termination was appropriate.

My former analysand, who was active in the mental health field, asked me for an interview because she was indignant about the rejection of an article about a report she had submitted for publication. It turned out that she had knowingly submitted this paper to a journal whose editorial policy was unsympathetic to the viewpoint she espoused. Provocative actions of this kind had been characteristic of her childhood relations with her father. I tried tactfully to indicate that it is the better part of valor to make sure that one's submissions are congruent with the editorial policy of the journal where they are to be considered for publication.

Shortly thereafter, this person sent me a rageful letter to announce that, as a result of this interview, she was completely disillusioned with me and therefore seriously depressed as well. The letter was so abusive that I responded, also in writing, by making it clear that I was willing to absorb such transference reactions only in the context of a treatment relationship; I did not receive a reply to this communication. Many years later, I encountered this woman in a social setting, and, at my initiative, we had a brief conversation about the rupture. To my amazement, she was still enraged about what she felt was my *corruption*: she was convinced that I had urged her to falsify her views in order to be able to publish them in a prestigious journal.

---

[4] For such an occurrence in the analysis of the patient who first brought musical associations to my attention, see my account in Gedo (1981a).

Of course, this misinterpretation of my meaning most probably represented the eruption of the hitherto covert mother transference. I had probably become typecast because I had permitted myself to communicate with more irony than I had ever used with her before, and she had misheard my message as a recommendation to falsify her scientific convictions to gain editorial acceptance rather than to submit her work to journals likely to accept her viewpoint.

This worst-case scenario should not discourage us about using the full resources of rhetoric to communicate with analytic patients: in an ongoing psychoanalysis, such a regressive loss of communicative skills would be grist for the therapeutic mill. The same is true for any possible misinterpretation of our musical communications. We should keep in mind that we are much more likely to encounter patients who hear only the paraverbal—that is, musical—aspects of our speech than we are unexpectedly to face the loss of an analysand's ability to process tropes as they are intended. This means that, with patients organized in primitive modes, *all* the analyst's communications may be processed as if they were just music. If we protest that, after all, it is *vocal* music and that our listeners should pay attention to the libretto, our more archaically organized patients may well retort that they cannot help being unable to follow our English any better than most of us are able to comprehend the lyrics of an opera.

Whenever an analyst is confronted by this kind of limitation of the ability to process the lexical meaning of spoken messages, the only recourse available is to communicate by accentuating the paraverbal aspects of speech while, at the same time, minimizing the verbal component of the transaction. In other words, it is helpful in such circumstances to keep the message simple and direct and to lend it emphasis through affective coloring entirely congruent with the lexical meaning intended. Would my former analysand have misunderstood me if I had said, "You should send your work to a journal with an editorial policy in favor of your scientific views. If you disregard the need for such caution, you set up a situation in which you can once again feel as you did in childhood, 'Those goddamn sons-of-bitches are ripping me off!'"? Note that in attempting to articulate the patient's voice in this imaginary internal dialogue, it is optimal to echo the intensity of a feeling of terrible grievance, while the statement of the analyst's assessment of the situation ought, in contrast, to sound calm and thoughtful. In terms of opera, the first part should be recitative; the second part, a passionate aria. I have spelled out such rhetorical aspects of analytic work in a number of previous publications (Gedo, 1981a, chap. 11; 1984, chap. 9; 1993b).

Suffice it to say, the best we can hope for may be to convey an affective message by intensifying the emotional charge of our language. In situations that do not involve total loss of the ability to comprehend words, it is often necessary to ensure being understood by underlining one's meaning through paraverbal means congruent with the lexical message.

CLINICAL IMPLICATIONS

I trust I have supplied sufficient detail to explain the seeming paradox that communication by means of nonverbal channels is actually riskier and more difficult with individuals organized in some archaic manner than with those who function at expectable adult levels. This is no paradox, of course: successful communication is more difficult with regressed patients through verbal channels as well. With these impaired people, we decrease the risks of miscommunication by making simultaneous use of as many semiotic systems as we have at our disposal. As I spell out in chapter 7, it may be necessary to reinforce one's intended meanings by adding the language of gestures and facial expressions to our repertory; thus, with certain analysands the use of a couch may be contraindicated. In any case, the analyst should always sit in a place an analysand can easily survey visually—if the choice of looking at the analyst is clearly left to the patients, those who need visual cues to grasp the analyst's meaning will almost always avail themselves of the opportunity to gather them.

Of course, certain transference constellations demand the reenactment of some derailment of the parent-child dialogue. For example, when the analysand whose mother became deaf was reliving the frustrations of losing touch with her caretaker, this circumstance was reenacted in the analytic situation through a recurrent tendency to talk so softly that I could not understand her words. Obviously, the correlation with the past is not always that direct: another patient who engaged in the very same behavior in the analytic setting was thereby trying to provoke me to ask for an audible stream of associations, as he had tried in early childhood to provoke his mother through punitive measures to force him to produce regular bowel movements. In any case, the paraverbal qualities of patients' associations, if carefully monitored, are a rich source of information about their inner life.

If it is granted that a richer communicative repertoire on the part of the analyst is therapeutically desirable in the management of more difficult clinical problems, we may well ask whether there is any reason to adopt a more restricted manner of dealing with analysands who present fewer technical difficulties. In my experience, there are no grounds for any timidity on this score: As I outline in chapter 8, it is only in certain specific circumstances that the operatic style I now prefer may prove to be overstimulating—in that case, however, there should be no difficulty in tracing the undesirable consequences to the analyst's technical error and in altering one's subsequent mode of discourse. Minor contretemps of this kind are, once again, mere grist for the analytic mill. Other things being equal, we should make use of metaphor and allegory, music and pantomime, irony and humor—without *assuming* that our communications thereby gratify the analysand's infantile wishes. And, if they do, we have merely discovered something of real significance.

2 Protolinguistic Phenomena in Psychoanalysis

THE RHETORIC OF PSYCHOANALYSIS

For an enterprise explicitly engaged in decoding the latent meanings of human communications, psychoanalysis as a discipline has been surprisingly slow to give weight to the subtleties of speech and language. This history is doubly strange in view of the fact that Sigmund Freud, before establishing our intellectual domain, wrote a distinguished monograph about the neuropathology of language, *On Aphasia* (Freud, 1891). In much of the psychoanalytic world, through most of our century of existence and despite the Wittgensteinian revolution in philosophy, the medium of communication employed by the participants in clinical psychoanalysis has been implicitly regarded as if it were a perfectly inert solvent that facilitates chemical reactions without having any influence on them—as if analytic communication took place by way of some totally unambiguous semiotic code, analogous to the operations of a computer.

Only in the past generation have psychoanalysts become alert both to the significance and to the complexities of the *form* of human communications, over and beyond their imprecise lexical content. It must be acknowledged that much of this work originated in France, particularly in the school of Lacan, developments admirably summarized for American readers by Muller and Richardson (1982). Perhaps the most important of these contributions was the differentiation of three registers of experience: first, the unnameable and unimaginable aspect of experience, an aspect perhaps of what has been called the protolinguistic framework; second, the so-called imaginary register, which is essentially a dyadic interplay of images; and last, the later development of symbolic communications, as such (Muller, 1995).

In this country, Levin (1991) has written most cogently about the line of development of semiotic capacities. Levin based his schema on evolutionary considerations. According to this schema, the human communicative repertory first includes only the language of affects, conveyed by means of vocalization and facial expressions. It then expands with the addition of a language of gestures and postures. A third phase begins when words with consensual meaning come to be used to supplement earlier communicative skills. The next increment in these skills involves the use of syntactically organized language, and a fifth phase is reached when the child acquires the ability to construct a coherent narrative. In adults, these communicative skills are organized into an integrated assembly that makes use of various combinations of these five distinct semiotic modes.

From a clinical perspective, the earliest American contributions on the semiotics of psychoanalysis were those of Victor Rosen (1977), and the best reasoned Kleinian statements on the subject were those of Rosenfeld (1987). My own interest in semiotics was an outgrowth of attempts I had made (Gedo and Goldberg, 1973; Gedo, 1979) systematically to explore the implications of the hierarchical view of developmental psychology that was increasingly becoming the accepted standard following the conceptual work of Rapaport (1959). About 15 years ago, I committed myself to the proposition that, in response to the ever-shifting developmental levels according to which analysands' operations are organized, analysts' efforts to communicate in the treatment setting must also make use of distinctive channels and modes of discourse (Gedo, 1981a, chap. 11).

As I reviewed in the previous chapter, the crux of my argument has been that, in regressive states, analysands often become unable to process the intended meaning even of syntactically and lexically clear messages—unless those meanings are amplified by paraverbal indications of affect. For many years, in the guise of adherence to the principle of "analytic neutrality," such expressions of the analyst's affectivity were condemned as taboo: they were seen as evidence for unresolved countertransference problems. (For dissenting views, see Stone, 1961, and Greenson, 1967.) Through painful clinical experience I discovered that, whenever an "archaic transference" (Gedo, 1977) is manifest, my communications are at risk of being grossly misunderstood unless the music of my speech is congruent with the lexical meaning of my words. In this context, I concluded that, in terms of the music of speech, the lexical content of the message corresponds to melody, its timing to rhythm, its affectivity to sonic intensity, and its cognitive style to tone color. To state the implications of this conclusion in the words of an unusually discerning analysand, treatment sessions should be like the performance of an *a cappella* choir.

A dozen years ago, Tufts University organized the first American symposium on "Language and Psychoanalysis"; by then, all participants were in consensus about the importance of the nonlinguistic aspects of communication, that is, on de Saussure's differentiation between *la langue* (language) and *la parole* (speech). At this event, I proposed a conception of successful analysis as the attainment by the participants of a "shared language"—in analogy with the acquisition of the "mother tongue" in the course of felicitous development (see chapter 6). In contrast to the teaching–learning situation in childhood, in analysis it is the obligation of the analyst to master the various semiotic codes used by the analysand, no matter how eccentric they may be. (For a discussion of the rhetorical choices the analyst must confront in this process, see Gedo, 1984, chap. 9; this volume, chapter 8; and Leavy, 1980). Probably the most difficult to comprehend is the mode of dyadic dramatic enactments, the communication of meanings by way of involving all participants in a pantomime that relives an old scenario, a drama wherein any and all parts of the assembly of semiotic codes may be utilized (Gedo, 1988, chap. 9).

In chapter 1, I reviewed the nonverbal aspects of communication in the analytic situation, the analysand's frequent uses of other-than-verbal codes, such as music or gesture, albeit still in a manner characteristic of secondary process (Freud, 1911). In chapter 3, I consider primary-process codes such as the language of the body used in various types of "somatization" (see also Gedo, 1988, chap. 6). It is notable that such body language either may constitute actual symbols (this is the case in so-called conversion reactions) or may consist of concrete signals, lacking in symbolic meaning: tics, for instance, signify only whatever the given movement always denotes. In such conditions, for transmitting certain specific messages, only preverbal channels of communication are available to the individual. (For a discussion of other syndromes in which such conditions prevail, see Gedo, 1988, chap. 6, and Lichtenberg, 1983.)

PROTOLINGUISTIC PHENOMENA

In this chapter, I further explore clinical contingencies of this kind, especially those in which the loss of ability to use consensual language is more or less veiled by a continuing pattern of speech that, for the most part, consists of *seemingly* meaningful words. Clinicians familiar with the symptomatology of certain types of schizophrenia are well acquainted with paraphasic productions of this kind, which are generally referred to as "word salads." In the era of pioneering attempts to treat the psychoses by means of psychoanalytic psychotherapy, enormous effort was expended on decoding such "language," that is, on trying to translate it into secondary-process statements. Although such activities often succeed in building a communicative bridge between therapist and patient, it has seldom been possible to ascertain whether the translator has actually discerned the speaker's intended meaning.

In the great majority of cases, it is most likely that no lexical meaning is actually intended at all; world salads probably betoken regression to the earliest stage of vocalization, wherein only the articulation of a succession of phonemes is possible. In this sense, their articulation can be seen as the vomiting of words, an enactment repeating patterns of early childhood behavior. This probability does not imply that a schizophrenic's speech is completely devoid of discernible information, but the signals in question have little or no lexical significance; instead they are automatically (that is, on a neural level) correlated with a variety of affective states. In this connection, it is well to recall the work of the Franco-Hungarian linguist Fonagy (1983), who demonstrated such correlations in the speech of children speaking either French or Hungarian. (These subjects were old enough to speak in a consensually meaningful way, but the phonemic-affective correlations were nonetheless present.) It is also relevant to cite reports about the poetry produced by certain schizophrenics, such as the Swiss artist Adolf Wölfli, verse that consists of lexically unintelligible texts but succeeds *qua* music at the level of the physical properties of the speech necessary to articulate it (Morgenthaler, 1992; see also MacGregor, 1989). Gilbert Rose (1980, 1995) has convincingly argued that the power of great art to reach the human depths resides in the correlation of its formal properties (that is, its physical and hence perceptual organization) with the preverbal affectivity of its creators and consumers. The word salads of schizophrenics present the same affective universe, albeit almost always artlessly.

Until relatively recently, psychoanalysts had failed to note that (more or less) transient episodes of speech lacking all consensual meaning and constituting the enactment of early childhood events may also occur in the course of psychoanalyses, whenever the treatment induces regression to the earliest modes of psychic organization. I first reported such an event about 15 years ago (Gedo, 1981a, chap. 11) in the case of the academic I cited in the previous chapter, an analysis eventually terminated with a more than satisfactory outcome. Because the symptoms involving language were a crucial aspect of the analysis, it is worth emphasizing that, about a dozen years after termination, when he faced a dead-end in his academic career, this man began to write poetry, an activity that increasingly came to occupy a central place in his emotional economy. Poetic talent consists, in part, of the ability to monitor closely the sonic properties of utterances.

As I have previously reported (Gedo, 1981a, pp. 287-296), the analytic transference in this case relatively quickly tilted in the direction of reliving infantile rage and negativism in response to perceived "abandonment." In this context, the patient seemed to lose the ability to judge whether his communications would be comprehensible to me; when I asked for clarification, his second or third effort to convey his intended meaning was often even more confusing than the first. At the same time, not infrequently, he was also unable to comprehend my communications while I was trying to clear up the confusion. Nor could he grasp that we were talking at cross-purposes; for my part, I tended to experience his behavior as provocative. If I chose to wait out such a crisis in a passive mode, my tactic only led to escalation of the impasse, because (with some justification) the analysand would then feel that I was punishing him through deliberate neglect for his conscientious performance of the task of free association.

In time, I was able to distinguish these episodes, precipitated by negativism, from superficially similar events based on the patient's fantasy that I could magically read his mind. When this second eventuality was at issue, I usually did not feel provoked, and the analysand had much less difficulty in regaining the ability to use consensual language. In instances when he was being negativistic, the most effective way to resolve the impasse turned out to be to express my irritation with unconcealed emotion—or, if I discerned what was about to happen early enough, in tones of urgency to issue a warning about impending danger concerning our joint enterprise. This is not the place to elaborate on the technical difficulties of such analytic vicissitudes or their solutions; I wish to focus, instead, on the transference significance of these regressed behaviors.

This person had been subjected to many traumatic changes in childhood. Both parents were immature and impulsive; before the boy reached the age of two, his father killed himself in an automobile wreck by driving while intoxicated. At that juncture, the child's care was entrusted to his paternal grandparents; when his mother was about to remarry (the patient was then three), she resumed her parental role at the home of the maternal family. With the aid of unusually detailed childhood records, we were eventually able to reconstruct that, on the occasion of each of these traumatic separations, the boy had become rageful and disorganized. At the time of the earlier disruption of his life, he regressed in terms of bowel training; when his mother reclaimed him, his habitual "disobedience" was savagely punished—at times he was actually tied to his crib in a vain effort to control him.

The records contained no information about the vicissitudes of the child's mastery of language, but I think it is safe to assume that it suffered parallel deterioration. Thus, the spiteful abandonment of the communicative functions of speech in the context of an archaic transference (Gedo, 1977) seemed to constitute the repetitive reenactment of aspects of the tantrums and negativism characteristic of the analysand's early childhood, or, if you will, the unconscious repudiation of an untrustworthy world of human relatedness. By contrast, the positive aspects of his relationship to his mother were largely encoded in music, as I tried to show in chapter 1.

Lest I give the impression that regression to a preverbal state can take place only in the context of a negative transference, I should like to offer a second clinical illustration (a case I previously discussed in Gedo, 1988, pp. 153–155). The person in question began occasionally to speak in an incomprehensible manner in the third year of a lengthy analysis, after considerable improvements had taken place in his day-to-day adaptation. In his case, this pattern of communication very seldom made me feel provoked, and the analysand could always be brought out of his regressed state by an urgent warning that this strange phenomenon had to be understood through collaborative efforts. Eventually, we reached agreement that the symptom amounted to lapsing into a private language, like the babbling of an infant.

The patient emphasized that this state supervened when he felt particularly "relaxed"—but *this* word also turned out to be misleading, because it was a euphemism for a sense of depersonalization, a loss of the subjective sense of self. Eventually, he was able to recall that he had experienced similar states throughout his childhood, whenever he was not self-consciously engaged in battling his caretakers. Around the age of five, he was hospitalized for suspected poliomyelitis because of widespread muscular "paralysis" for which no somatic cause was ever found. Presumably, this was the most severe episode of total aimlessness he ever suffered. As if to confirm that his very identity depended on fighting a hostile environment, the patient's difficulty in using consensual language in the analytic situation would disappear as soon as he encountered the next crisis in his daily life.

Both of my clinical examples to some extent conform to the observations of Freud (1900, pp. 298-304, 420-426) about the occurrence of speech in dreams. It will be recalled that he cautioned the would-be dream interpreter not to accept the overt lexical meaning of these "utterances" at face value. Freud pointed out, however, that these sonic manifest contents are associated with unconscious latent thoughts in an associative manner: if they form sentences, they turn out to be quotations and thus merely serve as tags that locate an experience to which the latent thoughts refer. Of course, in the illustrations I have used, it was not possible to extract any meaning from the manifest utterances, nor did my efforts to discern some latent meaning ever bear fruit. I mention Freud's discovery nonetheless because it does parallel my conclusion about regression to a preverbal state in the sense that neither dreams nor the kinds of association I have highlighted are organized in accord with secondary-process mentation.

The foregoing considerations should alert us to the possibility that certain syntactically and lexically comprehensible communications may also be devoid of authentic significance. I am trying to focus on instances of language that might be characterized as "blathering." (In the dictionary, blather is defined as talk that is both voluble and empty—close to "babble," which denotes not only the meaningless sounds made by infants but also "meaningless chatter.") Although blather may occasionally betray some hidden significance, it is generally intended to cover over an *absence* of meaning. In this sense, its function is analogous to that of "secondary revision" in dreaming (Freud, 1900, pp. 488-508)—to lend a pseudorational façade to overt senselessness. The ability to blather *effectively* depends on the individual's linguistic talent in the verbal arena; in my clinical work, the best blatherer I ever encountered was a successful television personality, well known for his mellifluous language.

Although the therapeutic results we achieved were respectable, my attempt to conduct a *psychoanalysis* with this person was utterly defeated by his inability to convey authentically his inner experience in words. (For further details of this treatment, see Gedo, 1981a, pp. 68-77, or 1991a, pp. 72-78.) The patient correctly predicted that analysis would not prove to be feasible for him because, as soon as he tried to articulate what he was experiencing, he knew that it became falsified by virtue of having been translated into his sophisticated adult language. In other words, he had self-awareness concerning his blathering, and he was distressed about being saddled with this handicap. I have the impression that such insight into the condition is relatively rare.

I do not wish to imply, however, that the appearance of blathering fails to convey any meaning—on the contrary, such an event is a highly significant analytic finding. It is merely the lexical content of such communications that is lacking in importance; the phenomenon as a whole is an "iconic enactment" (Muller, 1995) that betrays an urgent need to screen threatening inner developments, usually in the affectomotor realm. Blathering might well be described as a smoke-screen of relatively insignificant verbiage. I have not encountered the phenomenon in a sufficient number of cases to permit me to form any hypothesis about what makes it possible for certain people to ward off threatened traumatization by the mere distraction of such "whistling in the dark."

SILENCE

In certain analysands with regressive propensities, analogous threats lead not to such "white noise" but to silence. Interruptions of the stream of associations were formerly routinely classified as manifestations of "resistance," and in some instances, on further investigation, that is what they turn out to be. (From a technical viewpoint, it is prudent to ask on every such occasion, "What made you stop talking?") In other cases, silence betokens a return to a preverbal universe, often one of inchoate feeling states, "involuntary" motor acts, or both. The single most dramatic incident of this kind I have witnessed in my consulting room was an episode of Charcot's *grande hystérie*, complete with opisthotonos, convulsions, and the clouding of consciousness. Spontaneous orgasm without prior sexual arousal, the loss of bladder control, and the onset of vomiting or diarrhea are further examples of iconic enactments that usually supervene in silence. Muller (1995, quoting Petitto and Marentette, 1991) has called attention to the equivalence of such phenomena to the vocalization of infants; consequently, they have been referred to as "sign-babbling." But, even without the occurrence of such motoric phenomena, the appearance of a "blank space" in inner experience is as profoundly significant as is the temporary cessation of sound in the middle of a musical composition. And it is well to remember that the emergence of such primitive phenomena in the analytic situation usually means that something of great importance from the past is being relived in the present—hence it is seldom to be understood as an untoward development.

In this connection, I should like to remind you that intervals of silence frequently supervene during the terminal phase of successful analyses. In instances of that kind, I have usually felt completely comfortable in joining my analysands in "sessions of sweet, silent thought," to quote Shakespeare—although the only thoughts either of us could capture in these circumstances were retrospective self-observations about having felt comfortable, without "thinking" anything that could be put into words. I experienced such intervals in the last stages of my own analysis; the probability that they represented the repetition of feeling states from the first year of life was suggested by a unique sensation that several times "joined in the conversation" (Freud, 1895b, p. 296): I experienced pronounced aching of the gums, presumably a somatic recollection of the first emergence of teeth and the onset of weaning. For me, it was a dramatic introduction to protolinguistic phenomena in psychoanalysis.

Of course, lapses into silence more frequently occur in circumstances that repeat childhood vicissitudes of pathogenic import. I have the impression that, whenever it is such an event that is being reenacted, the lapse into silence tends to make both participants more or less uncomfortable. Analysands who undergo such regressive episodes often appear stunned; upon recovery, they generally describe having felt bewildered or "empty." The most memorable incident of this kind I have witnessed proved to be so contagious that I found my own capacity for reflection to be temporarily almost as impaired as was the analysand's. In my own bewilderment, the only associations I had were snatches of discordant music. In time, these coalesced into a recognizable melody—part of the great quartet from the last act of Verdi's *Rigoletto*. It then occurred to me that my analysand was reliving the trauma she had experienced when, as a four-year-old, she witnessed an atrocity—as does the audience at the climax of the Verdi opera. To be specific, the child was present when her mother literally mangled her own infant daughter by running her limbs through a machine for pressing laundry.

Of course, I had for some time known about these historical data, and I had always assumed that in all probability the incident had been traumatic. What the mutual regression into a preverbal universe taught me was not a fresh bit of childhood history but something about the depth of the child's regression when the tragedy occurred. It was my inability to "think" (in the sense of "thought" as the processing of abstract symbols) that convinced me that my analysand was suffering from a homologous loss of functional capacity—as a dyad, we were temporarily in a state of complete attunement through the mechanism Kleinians call "projective identification" (see Muller, 1995).

Note that my musical associations were at first devoid of symbolic meaning and, when their significance finally emerged, it was not as symbol but as a concrete sign, a mere *index* to an act of murder (see Muller, 1995). You will recall that, in the opera, Rigoletto hires an assassin, who double-crosses him by killing the protagonist's own daughter. In exact conformity with Freud's claims about the occurrence of speeches in dreams, in quoting music that accompanies certain actions in an opera, I was merely tagging the time and the place where answers to my bewilderment could be found, without as yet having in any way arrived at those answers. To follow this clue and thus to gain the insights I am now able to articulate was a lengthy and tortuous process, but I did ultimately figure out that my analysand felt that she was the true murderer, like Rigoletto. In her view, responsibility was primarily not the mother's, who was a mere hireling. At bottom, the "accident" proved to be severely traumatic because it confirmed the child's fantasy of her own omnipotence.

SHIFTS IN LEVELS OF FUNCTIONING

I do not doubt that the foregoing survey of the protolinguistic phenomena I have encountered in analytic practice leaves many analogous behaviors out of account. Instead of trying for comprehensiveness in the absence of first-hand exposure to a sufficiently broad sample, let me discuss some conceptual implications of the material I have presented thus far. To begin with, I wish to consider how to explain the emergence of such behaviors in either analyst or analysand, individuals whose everyday linguistic repertory outside the analytic situation continues to meet expectable adult standards. In the case of the analyst, I assume that the ability temporarily to identify with a patient's regression to a preverbal state is one of the requirements of the effective and conflict-free use of empathy in analytic work—the kind of refinement of so-called primitive functional capacities that Kris (1952) long ago called "regression in the service of the ego." The analysand's regression is, in favorable instances, in the service of the therapeutic enterprise, and it is both confined within the analytic setting and (as several of my illustrative accounts suggest) circumscribed to certain specific functions.

The occurrence of regressions limited in extent and duration suggests that, prior to their emergence, the relevant sector of the personality was split off and unable to organize overall behavior. In other words, the safety of the analytic holding environment must account for a relaxation of the defensive operations that otherwise conceal these nuclei of personality organization (Gedo and Goldberg, 1973). Hence the therapeutic mobilization of these behavioral potentialities allows them, for the first time, to become integrated with the generally prevalent aspects of self-organization. (For a more detailed discussion, see Gedo, 1988, chap. 4.)

The possibility of abrupt shifts back and forth between relatively archaic and relatively more mature modes of functioning (also demonstrated in most of my clinical examples) shows that patterns of behavior are never completely lost; in the hierarchical arrangement of behavior regulation I use, it is assumed that the whole repertory of previous patterns indefinitely coexists, ready for use whenever they are most advantageous from an adaptive viewpoint. From this perspective, we may infer that protolinguistic phenomena are not necessarily entirely confined to sectors split off from the prevalent self-organization—they may remain readily accessible when needed, as in the case of an analyst-at-work. This conclusion, in turn, should alert us to the fact that the paraverbal aspect of everyday speech must of necessity consist of the very elements that, when they emerge in pure culture, are seen as preverbal forms of communication.

Let me briefly illustrate this point through the simplest of examples, that of the tempo of the analysand's speech production. It is generally accepted that this may undergo drastic changes without discernible alteration of any other aspect of the linguistic code, and there is also wide consensus about the correlation of marked acceleration of one's typical spoken tempo with certain affective states, especially hypomania or extreme anxiety, and of its marked slowing with other affective conditions, mostly depression. These correlations with basic moods are already evident in the vocal patterns of young children, and, of course, they are congruent with the fact that the emotional tone of music depends on tempo, from lento to prestissimo.

I shall offer only one additional example, that of iconic gestural communication that overrides the significance of verbal discourse, although the latter goes on more or less without interruption. In my clinical work, I most frequently observed this state of affairs during the analysis of the young woman I have already mentioned, who had been trained as a ballet dancer. Even without leaving the couch, she was able to convey certain fundamental matters by way of her posture—for instance, by turning her head to the wall when she unconsciously desired to "turn her back on me." (When she was aware of such a wish, she generally stopped talking; she might then literally turn her trunk away from me or even leave the room for several minutes.) Note that the patient's change of posture had no symbolic significance and that she, because of her training, was more than ordinarily prone to encode meanings in the language of gestures. She turned her head as a signal most people would have verbalized by way of an expletive like, "Fuck off!" But she was able to do this, like the ladies described by T. S. Eliot, while she continued politely to talk "of Michelangelo."

Let us now turn from describing various protolinguistic phenomena encountered in the psychoanalytic situation to the therapeutic significance of careful attention to their emergence. I have already noted that, at a minimum, the initial appearance of such primitive modes of communication signifies that a therapeutic regression to an archaic state of self-organization has taken place (see Gedo and Goldberg, 1973); giving due weight to such an observation should alert the analyst to shift focus to the most regressive aspects of the analytic transaction and to be particularly careful to avoid miscommunicating by overestimating the analysand's current ability to process complex messages. If only the paraverbal aspects of speech are affected, while its lexical and syntactic aspects remain unaltered, calling attention to these specific changes and inquiry into their meaning and genesis usually leads to fruitful results in elucidating the analysand's affective state.

Beyond these generalities, we should note that the specific protolinguistic phenomenon that emerges in the context of the analytic transference is likely to be a reasonable duplicate of an early childhood state of pathogenic import. As all the clinical illustrations I have provided here exemplify, such a repetition of aspects of the past that have no symbolic encoding in memory is always an optimal entrée—and sometimes the only one available—through which the past may be recaptured.

Until relatively recently, psychoanalysis could offer only arbitrary interpretive schemata, based on unsubstantiated developmental hypotheses, as therapeutic tools to deal with preverbal material. Because these matters are experienced wordlessly (as they were experienced in infancy), secure inferences about them must perforce follow not from the lexical content of the analysand's associations but from their *form*. Hence protolinguistic phenomena constitute our Rosetta Stone for deciphering these "prehistoric" events.

3 The Primitive Psyche, Communication, and the Language of the Body

THE MYSTERIOUS LEAP

Toward the end of the 19th century, students of human behavior, led by French psychiatrists such as Charcot and Bernheim, rediscovered that the Cartesian boundary between body and mind is far from being impermeable. As their disciple, Sigmund Freud, was later to put the matter, certain ideas tend, in specific contexts, to make a "mysterious leap" from mind to body. It is widely understood that psychoanalysis developed in a medical (and, in particular, a neurological) setting because the initial target of Freud's investigations (see Breuer and Freud, 1895) was hysteria, which was then viewed as a somatic syndrome: In *Studies on Hysteria*, Breuer reported his great discovery of 1881 that hysterical symptoms could be influenced through a "talking cure," a finding that compelled the logical conclusion that such somatic symptoms represent a "conversion" of mental processes to the bodily realm.

As Freud's clinical procedures gradually evolved into the psychoanalytic method, it soon became evident that somatization can be observed *in statu nascendi* in the psychoanalytic setting itself. Ferenczi (1912) was the first to enunciate explicitly the concept that such temporary symptoms in the course of analysis amount to communications from patient to analyst; as Freud (1895c) had already stated, the symptoms may "join in the conversation" (p. 269). Incidentally, the waxing and waning of such symptoms in response to the vicissitudes of transference is the most dramatic and persuasive evidence for the validity of the basic hypotheses of the Freudian enterprise—an experience one hopes every candidate will encounter during his or her training analysis.

I can think of no better illustration of the significance of an episode of conversion hysteria in the course of treatment than my own encounter with such a syndrome at the height of a transference neurosis. I emphasize the timing of this occurrence somewhat late in the analysis because it is important to note that somatization is a relatively archaic mechanism; individuals who characteristically function in more mature modes (see Gedo and Goldberg, 1973) are unlikely to resort to such primitive behaviors unless a regressive process has first been set in motion within the analytic situation. I shall return later in this chapter to the question of the level of maturity of "transitory symptoms" that involve the body in the course of analysis (once again to use the vocabulary of Ferenczi about these matters). At this point, I need to provide a more detailed clinical illustration.

In latency, I developed a mildly obsessional character structure that proved to be very useful for certain adaptive purposes, especially in scholarly or theoretical enterprises. I felt the need for a personal analysis because this "character armor" (see Reich, 1930) also inhibited my affectivity and confined my relationships within certain uncomfortable limits. The first 18 months of my analysis were marked by vigorous defensive efforts to maintain this adaptation, efforts that gradually eroded with the emergence of a variety of hostile transferences. I do not think it would be relevant to enumerate the (reasonably conventional) infantile determinants of these attitudes; for the point to be made now, the crux of the matter was the repetition of an unconscious and archaic fear of retaliation. Be it noted that, on the conscious level, I was firmly convinced that the analyst was a benign figure, and I was highly ashamed about having developed irrationally hostile attitudes toward him.

During a few analytic sessions covering a very brief period of time, I experienced several episodes of violent muscular spasms of the back—to my knowledge, symptoms unprecedented in my past and never to be repeated after their significance was elucidated in the analysis. It was the analyst who articulated the meaning of these strange gestures as representations of unconscious attempts to evade various kinds of physical attack from the rear; in response to this interpretation, I recovered a number of childhood memories of physical experiences I had regarded as punishments at the hands of both of my parents. No better example is conceivable of the power of the past to cast a shadow over the present.

At the height of the enthusiasm for "psychosomatic medicine," some 46 years ago, Alexander (1950) suggested that conversion hysteria, wherein a bodily event symbolizes an idea in a concrete manner, can be differentiated from other kinds of somatization by virtue of the fact that instances of conversion either make use of the musculature that is under voluntary control or involve the sensory apparatus. The clinical illustration I have just presented certainly conforms to the rule Alexander enunciated. It is also true that many bodily symptoms mediated via the autonomic nervous system or through endocrine mechanisms (or through both) do not appear to have any discernible symbolic referent and are therefore never classified as hysterical. Nonetheless, my clinical experience has, I believe, invalidated the sharp distinction Alexander proposed.

To describe only the simplest of instances that did not conform to Alexander's dichotomy, I have had the opportunity to analyze a young woman who had all her life suffered from bronchial asthma, which she regarded as unconnected to the psychological problems for which she sought help. She was justified in her opinion, insofar as the asthma most frequently occurred in conjunction with seasonal allergies and was also triggered by upper respiratory infections of any kind. After several years of analytic work, when an erotic transference to an older brother came into focus, she experienced several asthmatic attacks in the analytic setting. These turned out to represent the repetition of highly charged physical encounters in latency, in the course of which her brother literally smothered her as the climax of these covertly sexual battles. When the symptom was interpreted as symbolic fulfillment of a wish to experience similar tussles with me, these *hysterical* episodes came to their end.

I also had the impression (obviously impossible to prove) that the severity of the patient's asthmatic syndrome as a whole was thenceforth mitigated, although occasional attacks caused by allergic and infectious agents did persist. (I am quite certain that she began to use medication more effectively, thereby aborting the potential asthmatic episodes that had both gratified these unconscious wishes and punished her for them.) Of course, it is also impossible to demonstrate that the instances of hysterical asthma she had suffered were physiologically homologous with her other attacks: all I can assert is that in my presence the patient had difficulty in breathing *out* and was audibly wheezing, as asthmatics characteristically do. Thus the example is offered not as a datum that should by itself invalidate Alexander's generalization—only as a highly suggestive illustration of the caution advisable in reaching conclusions about these murky problems. At any rate, the phenomena of biofeedback have called into question the idea that humans lack all voluntary control over the "autonomic" system.

At the same time, I have had the opportunity to make similar observations in the course of other analyses, involving a wide variety of bodily symptoms generally not considered to have symbolic significance. In some of these cases, the symptom constituted the recurrence in the analytic setting of an existing syndrome; in others, it was a novel phenomenon—and sometimes one that was never to be repeated. It is hardly surprising that a syndrome such as a sudden attack of diarrhea can on occasion have a symbolic meaning (let us say, in the context of a mother transference focused on the events of bowel training, that of an ambivalent *gift*). What is most notable about such an event is that this symbolic meaning is expressed by means of visceral reactions and is mediated through the autonomic nervous system.

Emphasizing the fact that certain visceral symptoms may have a hysterical structure does not call into question the widely held belief that, in most instances, the same symptoms are lacking in symbolic significance and may simply represent nonspecific stress reactions, which are expressed in this manner as a consequence of some constitutional vulnerability. Thus, the recurrent diarrhea of a patient with mucous colitis is *not* a symbolic presentation of "being scared shitless"—on the contrary, it is this metaphor concerning the concrete effects of chronic terror that is the symbol growing out of countless observations about the expectable physiology of wide segments of the population. (I assume that this is the kind of thing Lacanians call "the real.") Mucous colitis probably constitutes a pathological variant of this expectable propensity. In my clinical experience, the syndrome is capable of being relieved *only* if the chronic stress under which the patient has been living is brought to an end. My attempts to deal with such a condition by making interpretations of putative symbolic meaning(s) have invariably been unavailing.

The same differentiation between specific symbolic instances and nonspecific, stress-related ones may be made for a variety of syndromes, such as migraine, epilepsy, nausea, vomiting, amenorrhea, pseudocyesis, spontaneous orgasm, constipation, urinary urgency, and nasal discharge, as well as bronchial spasm and diarrhea. One of the more common specific meanings I have encountered clinically is the use of such a symptom to express an identification with someone who frequently suffers from it. Note, for instance, the occurrence of pseudocyetic developments in males strongly identified with their pregnant wives. In the process of doing analysis, one may discover a counteridentification with an analysand through the sudden occurrence of such a somatic event, in a relatively mild version, it is to be hoped, such as nausea, borborygmus, headache, rhinorrhea, or the like.

Thus far, I have focused on two possibilities in considering how the soma may join the analytic dialogue: first, that bodily functions may communicate symbolic meanings, in which case they are capable of being translated into discursive language; second, that they may occur as incidental, albeit dramatic, concomitants of some persistent affective state. (Anxiety, the instance of affectivity already illustrated as implicated in the case of colitis, is by no means the only one that may operate in this way: in clinical practice, grief, depression, or both are almost as frequently involved; rage, shame, and guilt may be causative in a similar manner.) In this second possibility, communication takes place through the music of affectivity itself, and the accompanying somatic by-products are of secondary import. In addition to these two distinct modes in which "conversation" of somatic symptoms may take place, there are, however, some transitional possibilities.

Let us, in the first place, consider the instance of hypochondriasis, a condition in which the physician finds neither physiological alteration nor symbolic significance, but the patient confuses a psychological state with a somatic alteration. In this sense, hypochondriasis achieves somatization by sheer *fiat* (much as this occurs in conversion hysteria), but in this syndrome (in contrast to cases of conversion) the only message communicated is a concrete one, that of sensing an abnormality. As a sentient adult, the patient misconstrues what he or she feels as a sign of somatic pathology. As I have stated elsewhere (Gedo, 1979, pp. 180–184), this amounts to the recurrence of mentation at a presymbolic level: instead of the idea that something is amiss being encoded in words, this notion is experienced bodily (usually in an organ system or body part that was implicated in a similar manner in early childhood).

To illustrate these points, I can cite the case of an aborted trial of analysis with a man who became depressed after giving up a masochistic perversion. He had made this difficult decision because of his concern about the risks involved in dealing with the prostitutes willing to follow his rigid and unusual requirements. When, after some months of analysis, he realized that I would *not* be generally willing to comply with his demands (particularly to manipulate my schedule), he decided during my summer vacation to discontinue working with me. The night before my scheduled return, when he planned to finalize this resolution, he experienced chest pains that led him to rush to an emergency room with the conviction that he was having a heart attack. He was told that there was no evidence for any physical illness; I infer that the notion of a sudden cardiac emergency, concretized in physical sensations conforming to his concept of such an experience, reflected his understanding that vital aspects of his existence were coming to an end. The hypochondriacal symptom was the equivalent of the idea of dying. Note, however, that it is such an *idea* that involves symbolization, whereas the bodily sensation is merely a concrete *signal* that may be associated with impending death.

As another example of somatization of a transitional kind, let me offer the instance of tics—symptoms as conspicuous as the back spasms I discussed to illustrate a conversion reaction, but ones utterly devoid of symbolic meaning: the tic does not represent something else. The tiqueur "suffers" from unconsciously motivated gestures or postures (perhaps facial expressions) that mean only whatever they convey directly to the viewer. The tic is a *Ding an sich*, a thing (or action) that stands for itself. Hence its occurrence constitutes a different form of presymbolic mentation from that of hypochondriasis; a tic is a primitive communication by means of gesture (or facial expression) alone. Note that, to the tiqueur, his wink (let us say) does not signify anything that can be expressed in words; it is merely an inexplicable and passively endured event. Further examples of bodily events of this kind have been described by Lichtenberg (1983, pp. 200-201).

A DEVELOPMENTAL LINE

Instead of trying to develop a full list of syndromes in which the language of the body takes some transitional form, beyond affectivity but short of using actual symbols, let me proceed by noting that we are now in a position to describe a developmental line concerning somatization, one based on the underlying capacities for increasingly complex intrapsychic and interpersonal communication. Obviously, in proposing to outline such a developmental sequence, I am bringing this contribution into conformity with my past theoretical work, including the hierarchical model of mind Goldberg and I articulated in 1973 and I later revised (see Gedo, 1979, 1988; for illustrations and detailed explanations, see Epilogue, this volume). I have always found it useful to attempt to correlate more and more developmental lines with the five modes of mental functioning described in that hierarchical schema. I shall now make this attempt for that of somatization.

I assume that somatizations that merely form one facet of affective expression are characteristic of mode I; this inference is buttressed by the consideration that the very fact of being stress induced approximates these phenomena to those of trauma. I classify various kinds of "transitional" behaviors in mode II, and I believe it is justifiable to do this with regard to somatizations that constitute concrete communications, without symbolic referents. Both syndromes I have cited to illustrate such conditions, hypochondriasis and tics, overtly display the coexistence of significant splitoff realms of mentation; it is this lack of self-cohesion that I look upon as the most salient characteristic of mode II. In terms of communicative capabilities, this mode adds the language of gestures and facial expressions to that of affectivity (see Levin, 1991), and this system of signals is the predominant carrier of messages in these syndromes.

Communication by means of symbols, observable in conversion reactions, betokens the attainment of mode III. In this mode, there is stable self-cohesion; as we can easily observe, there is no threat to this in cases of conversion. Although in conversion hysteria intrapsychic conflicts are generally present, note the outstanding feature of the clinical material I have presented: the predominant danger situation was punishment in the interpersonal sphere. This feature, as well as the relatively concrete quality of the symbols used point to mode III, rather than mode IV, as the one implicated. In mode IV, we are more likely to encounter symbols of a more abstract sort, which obviate the need for somatization; issues that produce conversion reactions in mode III would, in mode IV, be most likely to lead to anxiety hysteria, that is, to an infantile neurosis. Hence mode IV is the realm of purely "psychological" phenomenology; it is "beyond somatization." Mode V is, by definition, the condition in which symptom formation of any kind is unnecessary.

Although it is relatively easy to classify the phenomena I have thus far discussed in terms of their communicative functions and the modes of psychic organization to which the latter belong, it remains to be seen whether the entire range of psychosomatic occurrences does, in fact, possess significance as communication. I myself have in the past published case material (Gedo, 1988, pp. 18–25) in which the recurrence of a psychosomatic condition in the course of psychoanalysis "joined in the conversation" only because I insisted on eavesdropping on what seemed to be an essentially private experience.

The pathological state in question was an ectopic dermatitis that had flared up many times throughout the patient's life; the problem started in his infancy in the form of severe eczema. In the second year of analysis, there was an exacerbation set off by an episode of shingles. The cycle of itching, scratching, and (temporary) relief now assumed an autoerotic function that, for this analysand, warded off the frustrations inherent in the analytic transference as well as in other potential love relationships. Consequently, he was strangely reluctant to seek effective dermatological assistance—an attitude analogous to the *belle indifférence* of the classical hysteric. The symptom waxed and waned during analytic sessions in accord with vicissitudes of the transference, and I was well placed to discern its significance as an indicator of the patient's withdrawal from an object relationship in favor of self-preoccupation. These conclusions, however, did not result from my having understood a *message*; whether they were right or wrong, they were the more or less objective inferences of a natural scientist working in an ethological mode.

At the same time, in this case it is possible to conceive of the skin pathology as the concomitant of a sequence of affective states, in analogy to the terror I postulated as the emotional background in my cases of mucous colitis. In one sense, the dermatitis constituted an aversive reaction in a situation of relative helplessness; in such circumstances, it is reasonable to assume that the affected person may be experiencing disgust. In another sense, the skin changes also constituted an overstimulated state, resulting from continuing reactions of joyful excitement. The affective reactions in their most primitive form, however, can become carriers of information only if the caretakers lend emotional meaning to what is, from the infant's point of view, a purely physiological event. I believe that, in this analysis, discerning the transference meaning of the symptom constituted just such a transaction. In this sense, we may think of instances of this kind as examples of the initiation of human communication, that is, as representative of conditions at the very beginning of the first phase of development (and of mode I).

Perhaps even more remarkable was the case (also reported in Gedo, 1988, pp. 86-89) of a man who regularly lapsed, whenever he was alone for more than a few hours, into a state of withdrawal, somnolence, and depersonalization. This condition was accompanied by a cluster of somatic symptoms similar to the syndrome called "neurasthenia" in the late 19th century. These symptoms were all manifestations of vasomotor instability, for which no cause could be found through medical examinations. The fact that the complaints were not hypochondriacal was documented by objective findings, such as extremities that turned cold and blue, or severe rhinorrhea. I call the case remarkable not because the syndrome is relatively rare, although it is (in my clinical experience of over 40 years, I have never seen another one like it). I do so because of its most unusual feature, which was that, after the patient learned to avoid prolonged solitude and its consequences, the syndrome would acutely supervene within the analytic situation whenever my behavior caused the patient to prefer to keep his distance from me. Such episodes were marked not only through changes in the flow of verbal associations but also by visible blanching of the analysand's fingers and, in time, by their turning blue. It was truly astonishing to see, if I succeeded in intervening in a manner that reestablished the patient's trust, a sudden reversal of this ominous vascular symptomatology.

As in the case of the patient with dermatitis, so in that of the man with this Raynaud's syndrome; an expert observer should be in a position to use the physical evidence to initiate the symbolically encoded exchange of information about the putative emotionality that gave rise to these phenomena. And in this case, detection of the physiological changes that accompanied the primitive aversive behavior often made it possible to alter the dyadic transaction (as far as I was able to determine, mostly through linguistic channels), thus establishing a system of communicative feedback with the power to transcend the need to resort to this archaic mode of functioning.

SOMATIZATION AS COMMUNICATIVE APRAXIA

As these examples suggest, even where somatization seems to possess no primary communicative function, the clinical situation may take advantage of observations about the relevant phenomena to establish an exchange of (verbally encoded) information about the patient's organismic state. Thus it probably is useful to conceptualize all psychosomatic processes in terms of their (intended or potential) functions as communications. As I have stated elsewhere (Gedo, 1988, chap. 6), from this viewpoint it becomes relevant to ask what in certain circumstances disposes a person verbally competent about certain matters to fall back on such presymbolic modes of communication.

I can do no better than to restate my conclusion from that 1988 monograph:

> Bodily symptoms caused by psychic activities will occur in the context of otherwise intact adult functioning only if the cohesiveness of the self-organization was imperfectly established in early childhood. Under such circumstances, certain nuclei of function remain isolated [either as a consequence of defensive splitting or because of a developmental failure of integration] and do not undergo symbolic

encoding. Consequently, these discrete functions may, in regressive situations, manifest themselves in their primitive guise. Without this kind of "vertical split" in the personality, the need to regress to such archaic levels [would] produce [a traumatic state characterized by] alteration of the normal state of consciousness [pp. 93-94].

The issue of states of altered consciousness is discussed in greater detail in chapter 5.

At any rate, it seems that what we have hitherto agreed to call "somatization" always amounts to a resort to potential communications that are encoded in relatively primitive ways. From this perspective, the very term somatization is seriously misleading, implying as it does that a message is encrypted in the relatively poorly understood language of the body, presumably for defensive reasons. It is true that, in early childhood, a need for defense may be one of the determinants of a focal arrest in development that will not permit the symbolic encoding of certain matters;[1] however, this does not mean that something "psychical" has been "somatized," either in childhood or later. On the contrary, we should understand the occurrence of somatic symptoms as a failure in achieving full-fledged psychic elaboration in the sense of symbolic thought (see Krystal, 1974). Such conditions are therefore basically apraxic (Gedo, 1988, see esp. chap. 13); when, in the clinical situation, we succeed in attaching verbal symbols to what was previously confined to concrete bodily processes, we have filled in a deficit through direct, remedial instruction.

Whenever treatment succeeds in promoting the preferential use of consensual verbal codes about issues that were previously processed only through the language of the body substrate, analysands are enabled to begin to reflect consciously about those matters, to delay action, and to formulate optimal adaptive strategies. To describe the analytic process in these terms (analogous to substituting rational thinking for mentation via the primary process, as we do in much of our interpretive work) is to clarify that the communications that must concern us are, in the first instance, those required to make self-reflection possible. As we know, this kind of reflexive self-awareness normally develops with the acquisition of the mother tongue, generally starting in the second half of the second year of life.

---

[1] In all likelihood, this is the process that Freud (1911) called "primary repression."

If we focus our consideration of the archaic psyche on issues of communication, as I have attempted to do in this chapter, we are able to grasp that Freud's puzzlement, 100 years ago, about a "mysterious leap" from mind to body was the mischievous consequence of entrapment by a schema employing fictive entities. There is no mystery about the progressive development of an ever-expanding assembly of channels of communication—affective, gestural, verbal, syntactic. Obviously, verbally encoded thoughts are just as much products of somatic processes as are motor activities or affects. There is no boundary between "mind" and "body" to leap over: these words refer to entities that do not belong to the same realm of discourse. The abandonment of terms like somatization, which are based on Descartes's discredited dualism, is long overdue.

4 Speech as Manipulation

THE ABUSE OF FREE ASSOCIATION

Since before the outbreak of World War I, free association has constituted the bedrock of psychoanalytic technique. The idea of putting into words everything that comes to mind, without censorship or selectivity, is a deceptively simple one, for many thoughts lend themselves to more or less accurate verbalization in more than one manner. Hence the specific form in which each association is encoded can make a considerable difference in clarifying an analysand's state of mind. For instance, the same mental contents might be put very differently by persons with differing characterological dispositions: thus mistrust of the analyst might be articulated by a guilt-ridden neurotic through a screen of profound apologies about putative ingratitude or impudence; someone with characterological attitudes of ruthlessness and entitlement might express the same idea without reservation.

Until relatively recently, of course, analysis-qua-treatment was allegedly reserved for individuals of "good character." Such people could be expected to say only things they could endorse as authentic convictions; if "ego-alien" thoughts came into their awareness, these patients could be counted on to indicate that they rejected those ideas. As the scope of psychoanalysis has expanded to attempt treating *disorders* of character, we have found ourselves' processing verbalizations that under the guise of free associations, did not accurately reflect the analysand's overall mentality. Not only might the analysand's statements fail to include some aspect of a complex state of mind—let us say as a consequence either of splitting or a primary lack of integration that prevents simultaneous consideration of more than one uncoordinated nucleus of mental activity—in certain cases, we face even more misleading situations: some people cannot resist trying to manipulate the analyst by saying things they do not actually believe, either because they do not hesitate to lie or because they are (temporarily or permanently) unable to determine what their true convictions are. In conditions of that kind, what passes for free association actually consists of the hysterical enactment of a role, as if the person were taking part in a piece of theater.

A particularly cogent example of such a pattern was recently presented to me in a clinical seminar. The analysand was a depressed young woman, financially dependent on capricious parents unconvinced about the necessity for the treatment. The relatively inexperienced analyst was reduced to making ineffectual attempts to contradict the patient's continual stream of self-depreciation, in spite of the fact that he realized that his patient was echoing, almost literally, the diatribes her abusive father was in the habit of directing at her. It took persistent inquiry on my part to elucidate that, in his turn, the analyst felt abused by the analysand's barrage of apparent self-criticism, which, on a deeper level, expressed contempt for the analytic effort. Because he had failed to ascertain whether the patient had any reservations about the validity of her assertions, the analyst was unable to determine whether the analysand knew that her self-accusations were generally invalid. Nor did the analyst realize that the repetition of a stereotypical litany of statements, whatever their subject matter may be, does not qualify as free association. (For a parallel instance in my own practice, see Gedo and Gehrie, 1993, chap. 2, esp. pp. 23–25, 50, 58.)

Transactions of this kind constitute disorders of communication, albeit they do not involve any impairment in the capacity to use language per se. Rather, they are based on illusions (or delusions) about the consequences of misusing language for delinquent purposes—false beliefs that reflect a profound impairment of judgment. After all, efforts to manipulate the analyst to make particular responses amount to a refusal to use the only treatment method available in an analytic setting; this is exactly analogous to a covert refusal by psychotic patients to take the medication their caretakers believe them to be using. To be sure, such enactments are almost always expressions of archaic transference reactions, but their intent to mislead the analyst generally makes it extremely difficult (if not impossible) to use them interpretively, unless the analyst realizes he or she is being manipulated. If and when this is understood, very often on the basis of the analyst's affective responses to the clinical situation as a whole, the meaning of the enactment can be investigated. This is best done by starting with a statement of the nature of the feelings provoked in the analyst by the patient's violation of the agreement to be completely truthful—to offer total candor in exchange for total discretion, to repeat a familiar summary of the analytic compact.

SPEECH AS ASSAULT OR CONCEALMENT

In my experience, by far the most common among the manipulative misuses of the absolute freedom of speech taken for granted in the analytic situation is the use of speech directly to assault the analyst. Judging from my participation in numerous case presentations, I suspect that many colleagues do not look upon such behavior as an abuse of the privilege of free association. Such laissez-faire views are, however, based on a misunderstanding: free association does not imply that hostile feelings and thoughts can legitimately be translated into hostile acts, not even hostile speech acts. It must be kept in mind that such feelings and thoughts can be *reported* in many forms and need not be encoded in statements addressed directly to the analyst-as-adversary. There is all the difference in the world between assaulting someone by shouting, venomously, "Drop dead, you goddamned bastard," and telling that person, "I am very angry at you and feel like telling you to drop dead."

Of course, there are many ways of putting such matters that make it difficult to decide whether they constitute free association or unwarranted abuse. These intermediate forms present the same quandary raised by so-called hate speech for those who would attempt to regulate civil discourse in various institutional settings. Do analysts have to tolerate, in a passive manner, direct expressions of hate, such as mockery of their age, appearance, or health status, or derogatory comments about their sex, religion, or ethnic origin? In my judgment, such assaults cannot and must not be licensed, for they will, sooner or later, inevitably undermine the working alliance by provoking uncontrolled hate in the countertransference. (For further discussion of countertransference issues, see chapter 11.)

The appropriate response to any direct outburst of hatred is to clarify that the thoughts and feelings that it expresses can be communicated in other ways that neither hurt the analyst nor, secondarily, cause harm to the analysand. (In this regard, I have found that the parable of the scorpion that in midstream bites the frog whom it begged to ferry it across a river has never failed to make this point clear to my patients, and I have never dealt with anyone who prefers mutual destruction to the acceptance of workable ground rules for analytic discourse. Nor have I found that instructing analysands that their inner world, including its affectivity, can be shared without their indulging in assaultiveness has prevented them from experiencing their hostile transference attitudes with full intensity.)

In a certain sense, almost all patients seeking psychological assistance understand these self-evident propositions without having to be reminded of them. The occasional exceptions are persons whose past experience has led them to believe that need-satisfying objects can be coerced into compliance by intimidation. In other words, assaultiveness through speech is a form of manipulation that is, at the same time, a manifestation of transference, one that has generally congealed into a characterological attribute. Hence it is not sufficient as early as possible to stop any abuse of the analyst; from a technical standpoint, it is important to challenge assaultive patients to investigate how they acquired the illusion that they can gain something by such behavior. In some instances, the answer turns out to be that it is not secondary gain (Freud, 1916–17, Lecture XXIV) they are looking for but the primary one of satisfying their sadistic (or masochistic) proclivities. I trust it is clear that passive tolerance for such enactments constitutes inadvertent collusion with such a subversion (if the analysand experiences sexual arousal, even perversion!) of the analytic procedure.

Although they probably constitute the most prevalent form of manipulative speech in analysis, direct assaults on the analyst are actually relatively easy to cope with, largely because they are so blatantly contrary to the dictates of common sense—so unsophisticated, if you will. Skillful manipulators generally cover their tracks, so that it may be very difficult to recognize what they are doing. The most insidious form of such behavior may well be the propensity of certain patients to agree uncritically with any analytic intervention, in the manner of Polonius trying to humor Hamlet (Act III, Scene 2) in order to gull him into cooperation with his enemies. With my analysands, any intention to pull the wool over my eyes was almost always unconscious and generally turned out to have some specific transference significance.

The most dramatic example of the foregoing constellation I have encountered supervened in the analysis of a middle-aged professional man whose characterological attitude to external demands was somewhat negativistic, so that I was completely unprepared when this pattern was reversed into equally automatic compliance with my interventions. I only realized that his seeming acceptance of my interpretations was empty because I felt increasingly irritated by the lack of fruitful associations following the patient's agreement with my statements. When I told him about my dissatisfaction, the patient was hurt and bewildered. Eventually, however, he realized that he was unconcerned about the validity of my conjectures—he was focused on maintaining "harmony" between us. Further investigation revealed that this had been his way of keeping the peace with his mother, a chronically schizophrenic woman who was dangerously assaultive when she encountered opposition. My analysand was the youngest of her children and the only one capable of obeying her automatically, without affective reservations. His characterological negativism was a later reaction formation that defended him against this dangerous surrender of autonomous volition.

SPEECH AS IMPOSTURE

Occasionally, one encounters other personality types whose verbal communications are scarcely less misleading. People may grow up to look upon glibness as the greatest of virtues, so much so that they will continually sacrifice the goal of making themselves understood at the altar of verbal pyrotechnics—a syndrome rather akin to imposture. Some of these con artists are more or less aware of what they are doing but will nevertheless disregard the necessity to face the truth in their analysis. (A more ingenuous form of this insistence on avoiding anything that may provoke shame is the outright refusal of some patients to discuss certain topics or to disclose particular mental contents.)

Perhaps the clearest instance of this syndrome I have observed was that of a young woman who had—by no means coincidentally!—training as an actress. (For a fuller account, see Gedo, 1984, pp. 116-118.) Among the many fictive roles she attempted to enact, generally to avoid acknowledging her actual status because this was so embarrassing, the most fraudulent was her impersonation of a person of wide cultural interests, like those of her sophisticated older sisters. Although this pretense led her to try to mislead me, she was actually desperately lying to herself: she turned out to be far less intelligent than most other members of her family, probably as a result of severe understimulation during infancy. I can perhaps characterize her confusing communications by quoting one of Dostoievsky's personages, Katerina Ivanovna, about her motives for bearing false witness against Dmitry Karamazov: "I went and told slanderous lies. . . . on purpose, in order to wound [his brother Ivan] again. . . . It was all of it, all caused by my fury"—in that scenario, rage about feeling depreciated. My analysand's envy of her sisters was equally murderous. In both instances, the misrepresentations were convincing because, when they were made, the impostor fully believed them. The impairment of judgment that deters such a personality from using analysis to seek for truth is part of a wider syndrome that includes some difficulty in testing reality.

As Kris (1956b) was the first to note, living in accord with a "personal myth" is not at all uncommon; the personalities on whom I wish to focus are unusual in their inability to distinguish their myth from the actualities. This kind of confusion is only one step removed from outright delusion, the condition in which the reality of the myth is asserted with certitude. Isolated delusions (or, if you prefer, a small psychotic core) may actually occur within personalities otherwise reasonably well integrated. For example, I have completed an analysis, with an otherwise satisfactory outcome, without shaking the patient's conviction in the reality of a screen memory that, around the age of five, she entered and safely left the cage of a lion at the circus. Other patients might vacillate between such a belief and the acknowledgment that the experience must have been a (day)dream. And such a veil of doubt makes it easier to articulate fictions for manipulative ends.

Perhaps the most frequent fiction I have encountered in practice is that of the analysand as victim. Patients often convince themselves that they are tragic, vulnerable figures; one form of this illusion is that of giving uncritical credence to thoughts of suicide. (In the case where I dealt with the most persistent occurrence of such idle threats, they echoed the masochistic blackmail the patient's mother had used with consummate skill.) Ehrenberg (1992, pp. 7-8) has published a particularly clear illustration of such a transaction: she responded to her analysand's suicidal threat with the indignant statement that she did not like being threatened—whereupon the patient sheepishly confessed that she knew that she did not really mean what she had said. (Incidentally, this fine vignette also demonstrates the value of intervening in an affectively charged manner, a topic I discuss in greater detail in chapter 10.)

SPEECH AS PROVOCATION

Manipulative communications are often much subtler than the crude blackmail of empty threats of suicide. To judge by my experience as a supervisor and consultant, analysts seem to have the greatest difficulty dealing with covert attempts to excite them sexually, but provocations to evoke their anger often defeat them as well. The motives for such manipulations are many and varied, so that I have to omit detailed consideration of that issue. Rather, I shall focus on the fact that many analysands who engage in either of these forms of provocation are well aware of what they are attempting to do but avoid "confessing" their intentions. For example, one colleague who consulted me described a seductive analysand who often succeeded in arousing him sexually, largely through her erotically charged narratives and vocabulary. We later realized that she was thereby taking revenge on him for the fact that she reacted with overstimulated states, including sexual excitement, to his repeated demonstrations of insight and empathy. The analyst's ability to stop this enactment was paralyzed by his counteridentification with his analysand's vulnerability on this score.

In my experience, the fastest way to interfere with such enactments is to confront these patients with the fact that they have, for the time being, stopped adhering to the method of free association—I generally remind them that, alas!, it is the only method I am able to use therapeutically. If necessary, I spell out that, instead of *staging* a scene the outcome of which is a particular response on my part, free association calls on them *to state* that they desire such a response and are tempted to provoke it in such and such a manner. (Note that this intervention is essentially identical with the one I recommend to stop direct assaults on the analyst.) This is an instruction to substitute a verbal code for one in which (misleading) words screen the true purport of a communication primarily encoded as a dramatic scenario.

Any failure to detect that an analysand's verbal communications have been misleading is likely ultimately to have deleterious consequences on the analytic collaboration. To illustrate: Shortly after I qualified as an analyst, I accepted, without asking for details, a prosperous patient's claim that she needed a reduced fee because her husband had recently sustained heavy financial losses. When, many months later, she revealed that this alleged loss actually consisted of a missed opportunity to make a good investment, I felt outraged about having been gulled. The analysand, in turn, felt unjustly criticized, for she had merely echoed her husband's customary way of referring to the story of his investments, and she had not intended to cheat me. It took some time to overcome the mutual mistrust that resulted—arguably, we never entirely forgave each other. Had I been sufficiently alert to question her original assertion more closely, not only could we have reached agreement on an equitable fee, but it should have led us directly to one of the principal issues of this analysis, the propensity of this woman masochistically to abandon her own point of view to echo those of people whom she feared. In other words, this was an instance in which the analysand's manipulative language merely constituted an identification with an aggressor.

The foregoing case shows that the occurrence of manipulative communications should not lead one to jump to the conclusion that this signifies, ipso facto, that the patient is characterologically unreliable and delinquent, although such defects of character may well be the most frequent among the dynamics behind such behaviors. In the instance cited, the main issue was an identification with the delinquent traits of an intimidating spouse, but the actual possibilities are, in principle, endless. Hence each occurrence of this kind has to be investigated with an open mind, without preconceptions.

5 Epigenesis, Regression, and the Problem of Consciousness

COMMUNICATION, THE HIERARCHICAL MODEL, AND NEUROSCIENCE

The conclusion drawn from the first century of psychoanalytic work that may be of greatest relevance for a theory of behavior regulation is the realization that predictable regulatory modes succeed each other in the course of ontogenesis (see Gedo and Goldberg, 1973; Gedo, 1979). These modes of behavioral regulation constitute an epigenetic sequence; each mode persists as a potentiality throughout the life cycle and may be called upon whenever it offers the opportunity for optimal adaptation. The various modes have a hierarchical relation to each other; under most circumstances, the ones consolidated later in the course of development tend to supersede those of earlier origin (see Wilson and Gedo, 1993). The term psychological regression refers to conditions in which predominance of one of the more "archaic" modes of self-regulation is observable. This model of behavior regulation is fully congruent with the hierarchical organization of brain functions first proposed by Hughlings Jackson (1884).

The clinical method of psychoanalysis provides an unparalleled observational setting wherein the kaleidoscopic shifts from mode to mode of behavior regulation are made evident, both over long spans of time and even within the same session. Not only do analysands who profit from the procedure tend ultimately to make less frequent use of primitive modes and to maintain organization within the more mature ones, but also, at any particular juncture, analysands are seen to function in a more regressed manner within the analytic situation proper than they do on the stage of everyday life. For obvious reasons, psychoanalysts tend to describe the relevant modes of organization in behavioral terms, focused on mental operations. The psychological skills that are assessed in every mode to be described, when they are listed in the sequence of their initial acquisition, are often termed lines of development. (This term originated with Ferenczi, 1913, and gained wide currency when espoused by A. Freud, 1965.) In my own past efforts to delineate the crucial modes of psychic organization, I focused on such developmental lines as typical situations of danger, typical defensive operations, characteristic manner of object relations, and so on. For purposes of validation, however, it is preferable to define the modes in terms of developmental lines more easily studied outside the treatment situation. Hence I have also considered lines such as cognitive development, and it would be highly desirable to include that of an individual's communicative repertory, as I have outlined in chapter 3, as well.

It must be noted that such hierarchical models of behavior regulation were originally developed solely on the basis of clinical evidence obtained in the observational setting of the psychoanalytic situation, almost exclusively in the treatment of adults. In other words, they were constructed by making use of those lines of development that are most cogent in assessing *maladaptation*. Thus, despite their clinical usefulness (which has been fully substantiated in more than one formal psychological research program [see Grand, Feiner, and Reisner, 1993; Wilson and Passik, 1993]), from an epistemological viewpoint such schemata cannot be properly validated by means of clinical data alone: the fact that psychoanalytic and other clinical observations are invariably congruent with a schema is not sufficient to demonstrate that it reflects the actual maturational sequence of the central nervous system, as it should do. Only evidence from the realm of neuroscience can settle this issue once and for all.

To be sure, attempts have been made to validate a psychoanalytic schema of human behavioral development by recourse to psychological data obtained in settings other than that of clinical psychoanalysis, mostly through the direct observation of children (see Demos, 1992; Lichtenberg, 1983; Stern, 1985). However, conclusions about the mental operations of infants before they acquire the ability to communicate through syntactically encoded messages are difficult to reach and even harder to substantiate. For the time being, therefore, there is as much uncertainty about early stages in the line of development of cognition as there is about those traditionally highlighted in psychoanalytic discourse. It was Levin (1991) who suggested another potential solution for the methodological quandary inherent in studying the mental operations of preverbal infants. Levin was the first to focus attention on a line of development equally accessible for study through the methods of neuroscience, cognitive psychology, semiotics, and psychoanalysis—the progressive acquisition of the ever more sophisticated tools of human communication.

Let me once again list the major phases of this line of development, about which, fortunately, there is broad consensus (see Levin, 1991, esp. chap. 7). The neonate begins to communicate through affects alone; soon, however, a language of ready-made gestures is added, including the motor component of the affective repertory. This mode of discourse is gradually supplemented through the addition of a capacity to send (and to receive) concrete signals that possess the same meaning for all the participants. It does not take too long before the infant learns that a reliable caretaker's mere appearance in response to its cries of distress signals the predictable satisfaction of its needs. The third phase in the development of communication is the gradual predominance of verbal language, that is, of the ability to make use of presentational symbols. This is the first of our communicative tools that is uniquely human. Once it is acquired, instead of sending relatively undifferentiated signals of distress, the baby is able to indicate in a more specific way the nature of its need—"water," for example, or "bottle." A fourth stage has supervened when verbal communication becomes syntactically encoded, enabling the child for the first time to deal with some level of abstraction. The next stage, which is the last I wish to consider in this sequence, is characterized by the ability to construct a narrative. Together, these five functional modes constitute an integrated hierarchical assembly of communicative skills.

I believe that the functional skills I have borrowed from Levin's account constitute an unbroken line of development and that few would dispute that they are here arranged in the proper temporal order of their genesis. It must be admitted, however, that the five steps of this hierarchy are, at the same time, arbitrary, for each stage could easily be subdivided into two or more subphases. Take the ability to construct a narrative: there is an almost infinite variety of skills between a three-year-old's account of having visited the zoo and the tapestry woven by a major novelist to present a sample of the human condition. Similarly, the archaic language of gestures is used with increasing skill as the infant matures—nor does its elaboration stop when verbalization becomes available. The artistic skills of mimes, dancers, singers, and actors constitute the most sophisticated form of this mode of communication.

Why, then, have I chosen to construct a five-stage line of development? I could say that I did so for sheer convenience: five steps are neither too difficult to remember nor too few to provide significant distinctions. Although this happens to be true, I must acknowledge that I made this choice simply because it has been conventional in psychoanalysis since the early 1920s, when the line of development of the libido was codified (Abraham, 1924). Whenever efforts have been made to elaborate a more complex schema, they have been defeated by the refusal of the majority of users to consider more than five stages: oral, anal, phallic, oedipal, and postoedipal. Consequently, most psychoanalytic schemata of epigenesis have employed a five-phase sequence (see Wilson and Gedo, 1993) without testing whether all the lines of development they include enter succeeding phases at nodal points that precisely coincide with each other. Thus far, we have simply assumed that, when a number of relevant skills have been acquired, behavior regulation potentially entered a new era governed by principles different from those that prevailed previously. (The earliest statement of such a sea change was Freud's, 1911, differentiation of behaviors governed by the pleasure principle from those regulated by the reality principle).

Only findings from neurophysiology and neurochemistry can help us to understand when and how such decisive shifts in behavior regulation will occur: how procedural skills are acquired, whether they are genetically preprogrammed (like the maturation of cognition and communication) or learned in transaction with the milieu once the neural structures required to sustain them become functional. To illustrate this point, let me cite the simultaneous independent conclusions of Basch (1983) and Levin (1991, pp. 17–42) that (in right-handed persons) the defense mechanisms of disavowal and repression involve blocking the input of the right and left cerebral hemispheres, respectively. This implies that repression and disavowal can begin to take place only after the establishment of close connections between the hemispheres through the maturation of the corpus callosum, around the age of three and a half. In my judgment, this conclusion, based on neuroscience, should resolve the hitherto intractable controversy in psychoanalysis about the timing of the onset of intrapsychic (as opposed to interpersonal) conflicts. Developmental theories which assume that intrapsychic conflicts operate from birth (or shortly thereafter) are biologically unsound. It also seems that one of the crucial nodal points in behavior regulation is the establishment of true bicamerality in brain function.

To put my argument in another way: if we accept that brain and mind are isomorphic, so that psychology and neuroscience are merely studying the same phenomena from different observational vantage points, it is essential to base all psychological conclusions within a context that does not clash with secure knowledge about their biological substrate. Unfortunately, despite all the progress in understanding the central nervous system in recent years, the developmental map of the progressive organization of the brain seems far from complete (but see Edelman, 1987). As I have stated, from the perspective of psychoanalysis, the hierarchy of modes of behavior regulation inferred on the basis of clinical data should reflect the underlying hierarchic organization of cerebral functions, so that we must look to neuroscience for ultimate validation of these developmental propositions. Psychoanalysis must at all costs resist the temptation to lapse into an antiscientific, "mentalist" position.

Apropos, it should also be noted that from the opposite perspective, that of brain science, psychoanalysis can potentially become a fruitful source of relevant input. It is now well established that the process of organizing the central nervous system is decisively influenced by early environmental transactions, about which no other discipline has accumulated as much evidence as has psychoanalysis. Hence, if neuroscientists were to alert them to specific questions about early patterns of experience, psychoanalysts would be in a position to devise research programs using the psychoanalytic method that could answer many such questions.

THE PROBLEM OF CONSCIOUSNESS

Among the questions that can best be answered through collaboration between students of brain and mind, the problem of consciousness may be the most important. Neuroscience has so far failed to find any fruitful avenue of approach to its investigation, nor has the psychological laboratory yielded better results.[1] I would now like to discuss what psychoanalytic experience reveals about the problem. Because consciousness as a phenomenon is entirely subjective, it is extremely difficult to monitor in early childhood, and it must necessarily be studied largely in terms of its vicissitudes in those adults who are capable of describing these subjective conditions in consensually meaningful terms.

The great difficulty in drawing conclusions about development on the basis of adult pathology is that of differentiating regressions to earlier states that were originally expectable aspects of developmental

---

[1] As the book goes to press, Hadley (personal communication) conjectures that the "adult" form of consciousness may come "on line" with the functional development of the amygdala, at approximately three months of age.

progress from those regressions that bring back childhood conditions that, when they first occurred, already constituted derailments of development, that is, pathology rather than immaturity. In other words, it is not legitimate to assume that any altered state of consciousness in the course of psychological regression in an adult represents a return to some early but "normal" mode of consciousness. Yet the psychoanalytic situation regularly brings about a regressive movement; in most properly managed cases, this therapeutic regression will eventually reproduce early childhood conditions referable to each of the modes of behavior regulation I have discussed.

It is true, at the same time, that many psychological functions, once they have been solidly established, acquire a "quasi-stationary" status, as David Rapaport (1967) put it. This means that a particular skill, such as the ability to communicate by means of consensual language using syntax, could well be retained even when in other respects a person regresses to a mode of organization characteristic of the phases that precede the original acquisition of that skill. It is entirely possible that, with regard to consciousness, the conditions expectable in adults may be retained in the same fashion, even in profound regressive states, although those stable conditions of consciousness actually supervene relatively late in development. On the other hand, most adults who experience temporary regressions involving altered states of consciousness retain the communicative skills that subsequently (or even in the midst of the event) permit us to learn about their inner state.

Let me now report on my psychoanalytic observation of 62 consecutive cases—a total of well over 50,000 analytic sessions. Psychological regression to early modes of behavior regulation was observable in almost every instance, often bringing to the fore modes of organization characteristic of the second or third year of life (modes II or III in my own hierarchical schema). The emergence of altered states of consciousness *in the analytic setting proper* was, however, observed extremely rarely; it did not even occur in most regressions that led to temporary loss of the ability for comprehensible verbal communication. I am therefore of the opinion that consciousness as it is experienced by adults supervenes relatively early and that, once it is established, it is extraordinarily impervious to regressive psychological vicissitudes. It is even conceivable that consciousness is already available in its ultimate form at birth or shortly thereafter.

As a matter of fact, all instances of altered consciousness I had the opportunity to observe in my series took place with only three of these 62 analysands, always in states of regression that brought to the fore the very earliest of the modes of behavioral organization (mode I), referable to the first year of life. From a clinical vantage point, these three patients were the only ones in my analytic practice who actually fell into a traumatic state *during their analytic sessions*. (In each case, such an apparent emergency occurred repeatedly and clearly represented a lifelong vulnerability.) From a psychoanalytic clinical viewpoint, all three analyses were of unusual historical interest, because they demonstrated syndromes often described in the 1890s (see Breuer and Freud, 1895) that, in the intervening century, have dropped out of the literature—conditions originally called "hypnoid states" and "neurasthenia."

Although my sample is clearly too small to permit any definitive conclusions, I think it is highly suggestive that all three of the cases in which I observed altered states of consciousness during analytic sessions shared one specific feature in their early history: each of these patients experienced, during the first year of life, living conditions that alternated in an incomprehensible way between two radically different environments. I do not mean that the infant simply had to adjust to one abrupt change in its milieu; the changes occurred with great frequency and over a considerable period of time.

The most dramatic instance was that of a brilliant graduate student who entered treatment because she was unable to sustain human relationships. Shortly after starting analysis, whenever I failed to respond as she expected, she would withdraw into an inaccessible state; when our communications were reestablished, she described her consciousness at these times through metaphors such as "lost in a fog." After lengthy efforts, we uncovered an early history of bewildering variations in her experiences. When she was an infant, her father was working on the construction of the Boulder Dam, on a different eight-hour shift every week. He absolutely insisted that his wife conform to his schedule, and she reluctantly complied. The baby was, however, unable to accommodate to the required shifts in biological rhythms; much of the time she was awake while her parents were trying to sleep. Her mother was forced not to respond to the baby's crying. Eventually, the infant would lapse into a quiescent state. Subsequently, the patient fell into such states whenever she was unable to master a challenge, and our difficulties in establishing a working relationship constituted the current version of these regressive conditions.

The other two patients had similar symptoms and roughly analogous early experiences. A young mental health professional thought of herself as a "borderline" personality because of her tendency to "flip out," often in evidence in our sessions, even more frequently when she felt gratified than when she was unduly frustrated. She soon began to experience such altered states of consciousness mostly on weekends. These episodes led her to recall that her early childhood had also been characterized by difficult weekends because of the absence of her live-in nursemaid. The patient's mother was mostly involved in successful professional enterprises and did not even pretend to be interested in the care of her small child. In contrast, the nursemaid was tender and devoted. Adding to the difficulty of bridging the disjunction between their styles of child rearing, the nursemaid communicated with the baby in a foreign language, while the mother conducted her life in English. These conditions finally came to an end when the patient was about two and a half, when the nursemaid had to leave town—a devastating loss, after which the child was "beside herself" for a considerable period.

The third of my patients (whom I have already described in chapter 3) had episodes of clouded consciousness accompanied by easily observable circulatory changes involving blanching of the extremities; as I have mentioned, these dramatic symptoms could be abruptly relieved if I found exactly the right thing to say, in the optimal tone of voice. This man had also had two early caretakers with widely differing modes of relating to a baby: his mother, who suffered a postpartum psychosis, and an adolescent half-sister, who was doting and ebullient. Not long after the patient's birth, the mother was hospitalized for some months. Upon her return, there ensued a fierce competition for the infant between her and her stepdaughter. At that point, the mother was not so much ungiving or frustrating, but the baby reacted to her with stranger anxiety, and this enraged her. The tug of war for the child finally came to an end when the younger woman left home to get married.

These histories suggest that children in the age range of six to thirty months have a propensity to respond to overwhelming adaptive challenge by falling into states of altered consciousness—awake but "clouded over." I am unable to judge whether these are the conditions described in the French analytic literature through the metaphor of *l'espace blanc*—blank space. Nor does my clinical experience permit a decision on the question whether or not this "mental fog" is a return to the expectable state of earliest infancy, before the myelinization of the neocortical areas most probably implicated in normal consciousness (see Schore, 1994).[2]

In other words, the sum total of my experience with such conditions is insufficient to formulate a conclusion favoring either a hypothesis that certain "altered" states of consciousness are expectable in infancy or one proposing that they constitute a pathological state whenever they occur. It does, however, seem very likely that the disorganization we call "trauma" always involves some clouding of consciousness, and I suspect that such a "clouded" state will turn out to be an expectable concomitant of the absence of most, perhaps all, cortical control. This is a question for which answers cannot be provided through the methods of psychoanalysis. If my analytic observations turn out to be reliable, however, they will demonstrate that, beyond the first several months of life, at any rate, altered states of consciousness always represent sequelae to some other pathological process.

It should be added that a propensity to lapse into such clouded-over states almost always results in further pathological sequelae because the occurrence of such conditions precludes the processing of relevant information through reflection, that is, the use of abstract thinking and the secondary process. As I have already mentioned, Freud (1915a) referred to events of this kind as the operation of "primary repression." I address issues of intrapsychic communication in Part Three of this volume.

---

[2] Hadley (1992) has proposed the hypothesis that memories of affective phenomena, attributable to activity in the amygdala, are available earlier than those of ideational content, which depend on activation of mechanisms in the temporal neocortex (hippocampus). This would imply that altered states of consciousness can supervene only with the acquisition of control over thalamocortical information flow. Thus the capacity for dissociation is probably acquired toward the end of the first year of life, providing a first line of defense against affective storms that would otherwise cause potentially lethal biochemical changes. If Hadley's conjectures prove to be valid, the neurophysiological data would be congruent with the conclusions I propose in this chapter.

II On the Analytic Dialogue

6 Treatment as the Development of a Shared Language

ON TALKING CURES

We have reached the centenary of the publication of the case of Anna O (Breuer, 1895), which recounted the invention of the "talking cure" by that excellent pair of Viennese wordsmiths, Joseph Breuer and his patient, Bertha Pappenheim. Recall that one of the symptoms of Fräulein P's acute illness was mutism and that Breuer succeeded, in a most ingenious manner, in circumventing her inability to communicate: he adapted the hypnotic techniques of contemporary psychiatry for the novel purpose of psychological investigation. For her part, Bertha P complied with these coercive measures with an exquisitely subtle rebelliousness: she engaged Breuer in conversation, but, for some time, she avoided the use of German in favor of English. This prototypical therapeutic encounter already exemplified the need for the development of a private language by means of which the participants may optimally communicate.

According to Freud's later account (E. Freud, 1960, pp. 412-413; see also Jones, 1953, pp. 224-226), Fräulein Pappenheim's English proved to be insufficient for the communication of some of the most vital concerns that preoccupied her during the treatment, matters encoded through the language of the body in the form of a pseudocyesis. Some historians have cast doubt on the accuracy of Freud's recollection (see Muller, 1995, chap. 10)—but whether Freud's version of the sequel to Anna O is valid or not, there can be no doubt that forbidden impulses are often manifested only through such nonverbal codes.

In a wonderfully hysteroid way, Bertha Pappenheim gave her "talking cure" a second name: she called it "chimney sweeping." For my point here, it is not the seductive and menacing allusion to dammed up love and hate implicit in this metaphor that is significant; I wish to stress, instead, Bertha's conception of treatment in terms of a wordless struggle to repair a defective mechanism. On one level, the term talking cure accurately portrays the therapist's hopes and intentions for any psychological treatment effort; to put the matter in the conceptual framework of psychoanalysis, it is the patient's view of her therapy formulated in the language of secondary process. In these terms, but on a different level, the metaphor of chimney sweeping employs the primary process to convey an alternative—dare one say more profound?—perception on the part of this brilliant woman.

Implicit in this communication is a view of treatment as passively endured and therefore devoid of responsibility on the part of the patient, who has never been granted the human prerogative of freely choosing her destiny. Bertha P was letting Breuer know that hypnosis is equivalent to rape—anal rape, at that. (Of course, still other interpretations of her choice of words come equally readily to mind.) I offer that of rape merely to illustrate the self-evident point that the transactions between patients and therapists are communicated through a multiplicity of codes and channels. Even if we focus on consensual meanings, the aspects of treatment properly designated as a talking cure, we must simultaneously monitor the primary-process elements woven into the fabric of verbal discourse, usually present even when that communication makes coherent sense in terms of secondary process.

In the foregoing discussion, I have betrayed my dissatisfaction with a concept of treatment based on a model of exchanging written messages. How could such a conception accommodate any form of somatization (see chapter 3)? The shared language that must evolve between patient and therapist must clearly include protolinguistic phenomena (reviewed in chapter 2), including the kind of complex dramatic enactments Freud described as the climax of Breuer's treatment of Anna O. The crux of their communication must be the affective interchange, which, in the traditional psychoanalytic situation, is predominantly (but not exclusively) conveyed by the music of the participants' vocalization.

It is hardly necessary to point out that, in the presence of unequivocal affective cues, we tend to discount the lexical meaning of messages that seem incongruous in the light of those cues. A patient may, in all sincerity, agree with a series of the therapist's interpretations in a tone of voice so laden with doubt, irony, or sarcasm that this "assent" must be taken as weighty evidence of the inaccuracy or the irrelevance of the interpretations. These matters are well known to every clinician. As Pascal said, "The heart has its reasons that reason knows not." It is the language of the heart therapists must both speak and learn to understand.

When a shared language is attained within a therapeutic dyad, those conditions have supervened that are often called a "therapeutic alliance" (Zetzel, 1965) or, in the language of Winnicott (1960), a "holding environment" (see also Modell, 1976). It is impossible to list the precise interventions that will fulfill this prerequisite of a workable treatment situation. Clearly, the therapist's messages must be encoded in one or more of the systems of communication also available to the patient; it follows that an optimal therapeutic ambiance (often called "empathic" [Wolf, 1976]) is forged through increasing refinement of the participants' communicative transactions. It has been a commonplace in discussing treatment outcomes to look upon prospective patients' verbal skills as one of the crucial factors that promise a good prognosis in any type of psychological treatment. Conversely, wide cultural differences between patient and therapist create great obstacles to a successful outcome because they increase the difficulties of precise communication. It has not been sufficiently emphasized, however, that therapeutic talent consists in large measure in an ability to use the widest variety of communicative modes in a flexible manner.

In treatment, the danger of misunderstandings, particularly by way of apparent agreement masking real differences, is always present—even in the absence of obvious disparities in sociocultural background. One of the most mischievous sources of semantic problems is our tendency to lapse into professional jargon, to use terms that have passed into the public domain at the cost of losing their precise meaning. How often do patient and therapist truly understand each other when either talks about such psychological traits as passivity, narcissism, identity, or fragmentation? How certain can they be that they use such words as shame or guilt, depression, or emptiness in ways that convey consensual meaning?

To forge a "shared language," both participants in treatment must take care to help each other as much as possible to grasp the intended meaning of their communications. They must listen to each other with as much empathy as possible for the probable intentions of the speaker, including those conveyed by the paraverbal aspects of speech and the accompanying body language. Latent meanings encoded within primary-process elements, veiled by the lexical meaning of utterances, as well as protolinguistic modes of communication become particularly crucial in analyses that succeed in bringing to the surface increasingly archaic elements of a patient's mental functioning. The more primitive the roots of these mental dispositions are, the less likely they are to be encoded in the form of secondary-process statements.

Let me illustrate this point by means of a brief clinical vignette. A young analysand with a history of unusually slow speech development showed the first signs of an archaic transference when he had an olfactory hallucination of fecal odors in my consulting room. Careful investigation of this occurrence eventually revealed that it constituted the repetition of a situation from the middle of the second year of his life, when his entire vocabulary consisted of two words: "Mamma" and "out." Through much of his life as a toddler, this person suffered from severe and foul-smelling diarrhea; because sprue was suspected, he was put on a diet of bananas. In the analysis, the patient now recovered memories of his tearful mother's vainly trying to force him to eat them. Clearly, his refusal could be summed up in the phrase, "Mamma out!" It was this early experience that was relived in the transference, with the roles reversed. It was now the analysand who could have said (echoing his mother), "You stink; I cry in rage; we struggle." At the climax of the repetition, unable to conceptualize the enactment as a recollection, he was as negativistic about my explanation of our transactions as he had been about his mother's intrusive efforts to help him as a toddler. To be sure, the patient did not regress to a vocabulary consisting of two words in the process; we were able to persevere with the analytic task because we were able to use consensual language to discuss every aspect of the essentially wordless enactment that was simultaneously taking place.

It was precisely the crux of the matter that the patient had been unable to express in the sophisticated adult language he customarily employed. Only when "stink" became concretized as a foul smell and the patient's intractability had provoked me into worry almost as acute as his mother's had been when she thought he had sprue were we communicating in a manner that reproduced the affective transactions of the relevant phase of his childhood. (For a discussion of the issues of countertransference and projective identification illustrated by this incident, see chapter 11). Once these issues were understood both in terms of current transference dynamics and in their childhood guise, translating them into the language of secondary process served to dispel their long-term psychological consequences, such as the grandiose illusions through which in childhood this person had tried to disavow his sense of basic defectiveness.

This incident from the middle of a long and complex analysis shows how the development of a shared private language within a particular therapist—patient dyad can be facilitated. After the events I have summarized, this analysand and I understood at all times that, whenever he began to be preoccupied with my stinking performance, he was letting me know that his chronic humiliation about his various limitations was, once again, causing him more distress than he could tolerate. With the aid of this insight, I could address myself directly to his need to blunt this pain by focusing on actual or imminent disappointments in others. Before we had formulated the insight in clear and abstract terms, any such intervention on my part only led to deeper suspicions about my putative need to disclaim responsibility for my own imperfections. Even more important than the content of my communication—by then quite familiar to the patient in any case—was the progressive change in the tone of our dialogue.

The agonizing flavor of the analysand's earlier accusations against me and the strained sobriety of my responses (carefully avoiding both defensiveness and retaliation) could gradually give way: on the patient's part, the accusatory tone was gradually supplanted by matter-of-fact reports about his quasi-paranoid ideation, even detached curiosity about the reasons for its occurrence; on my side, pessimistic concern about these seemingly untoward developments was generally replaced by an attitude tinged with humor about the inevitable discomforts of our respective roles. In the vocabulary introduced by Stern (1985), we had become affectively "attuned" to each other.

I trust that the foregoing clinical example also suffices to show that the paraverbal aspects of communication in the psychoanalytic situation lead, if only we can grasp their significance, to the elucidation of vital aspects of early transactions between the patient and the childhood caretakers. One great advantage of psychoanalysis proper over other types of psychotherapy is the opportunity provided by the daily use of free association to make detailed observations about these formal parameters of the analysand's communicative style. (In my clinical experience, two or even three treatment sessions per week will not generally allow the focus of the associative material to shift away from a topical mode of organization, usually concentrated on ongoing vicissitudes of everyday life.)

Be that as it may, whenever the process of free association does in fact lead to the production of material organized primarily in terms of transferential vicissitudes, minor derailments in the formal aspects of the therapeutic dialogue constitute a crucial source of information about the nature of early infant-caretaker transactions for that particular analysand. Insofar as these departures from the patient's more customary modes of communication involve paraverbal or mimetic channels, these therapeutic incidents lead us directly to certain aspects of the preverbal period of the analysand's past. That subsequent developmental phases will have altered these behavioral patterns in various ways must, however, always be taken into account: we can never assume that transference reenactments provide us with actual homologues of an analysand's early childhood.

As I have tried to demonstrate through the illustrative case, every time we succeed in identifying a source of miscommunication within the analytic situation, both participants subsequently have a better chance of avoiding that source of misunderstanding. An accumulation of such incidents can, in the course of time, lead to the evolution of a new and unique set of communicative tools, a shared language characteristic to that particular therapeutic dyad. Obviously, in this regard, as in all others, perfection is unattainable; some core of each person's subjectivity is destined to remain incommunicable, perhaps even in identical twins. As the French say, *il faut vivre sa vie dans sa peau*—we live life sewn inside our own skin. Nonetheless, a successful analytic experience may achieve a degree of mutual understanding probably unattainable in any other situation in adult life.

A SHARED LANGUAGE AS A NEW BEGINNING

The attainment of a state of harmony in communication is an extremely gratifying experience. From the analyst's vantage point, it is probably the most precious among the legitimate satisfactions clinical work may provide. From that of the analysand, it may well turn out to be almost unprecedented and never to be duplicated as a "holding environment." It will be recalled that Alexander (Alexander and French, 1946; Alexander, 1956) founded a school of psychotherapy on the assumption that such benign therapeutic occurrences have the power to undo the damaging results of childhood deprivations and traumata. Many other voices within psychoanalysis have seconded such views: recently, Alexander's concept of "corrective emotional experience" has been echoed in a more sophisticated form by those self psychologists who rely on the healing power of empathy (see Wolf, 1976, 1992).[1]

Although I also believe that the provision of an empathic ambiance in treatment (that is, the attainment of a shared language)

---

[1] From a historical perspective, these modern developments in psychoanalysis follow a tradition initiated by Ferenczi in the last several years of his life (see Dupont, 1988). The clearest statement of Ferenczi's views was made by his student Michael Bálint (1932). For a more detailed account, see chapter 9, this volume.

may initiate a "new beginning" (Bálint, 1932) of emotional integration—an issue I discuss in detail in chapter 9—I think the beneficial aspects of such a transaction are nonspecific. In other words, the attainment of a shared language in psychoanalysis is merely a preliminary step toward the full therapeutic goal of structural reorganization. To be sure, the establishment of a holding environment may produce real improvements in the analysand's capacity to cope with the adaptive problems of everyday life—as long as the source of external assistance remains available.[2] Although even a temporary period of peace and prosperity, however it was reached, generally has further desirable consequences that may yield long-term benefits, adaptive changes of this kind are not to be confused with genuine personality change.

In other words, I do not look upon the attainment of harmonious therapeutic dialogue as a therapeutic agent in its own right; I believe it makes better sense to view it as an indication that a change has taken place in the patient's capacity to make constructive use of a human relationship for whatever else the therapist may be able to offer. In psychoanalysis proper, the analyst is generally in a position to offer interpretations of hitherto unconscious mental contents as well as various explanations, "beyond interpretation" (see Gedo, 1979), about the analysand's psychobiological functioning, including that of communication. Thus the establishment of a holding environment paves the way for the more specifically "curative" aspects of the analytic task.

We must never forget, however, that the course of true love never does run smoothly—persons in need of psychological assistance are seldom able to maintain lasting collaborative relationships. Generally, they are compelled to repeat in treatment the difficulties that have characterized most of their human interactions throughout life. It follows that the analyst's best efforts to listen empathically and to respond with clarity, tact, and relevance are at first more likely to arouse "resistances" and "negative therapeutic reactions" than to produce concord and enlightenment. To arrive at that stage of *entente cordiale* we term a therapeutic alliance, further preliminary work usually has to be done.

What can we do to overcome an analysand's inability to tolerate being so well understood that the voice of the analyst may actually

---

[2] I have dealt with the issue of what patients actually need to learn in treatment at greatest length in chapter 12 and the Epilogue of The *Mind in Disorder* [Gedo, 1988]. See also chapter 13, this volume.

articulate part of what the patient thinks and feels? To pose the question in this way makes evident that we seek to outline a method for achieving the optimal conditions in which interpretive work may be performed. One global way to answer the question is to state that, in order to tackle the intrapsychic conflicts that originate in the era of symbolic communication, we must first overcome the archaic problems that cause miscommunication, many of which are apraxic in nature, that is, due to a lack of certain psychological skills. This therapeutic prescription is difficult to carry out because the effort is likely to arouse considerable resistance. The problem may defeat us, for our attempts to deal with these resistances, that is, to overcome miscommunication, may themselves run into formidable barriers of miscommunication. Many psychotherapies disintegrate into an infinite regress of such misunderstandings.

It should go without saying that a comprehensive discussion of these problems would have to examine the analyst's contribution to any failure of communication as carefully as it pinpoints that of the patient. Problems of countertransference and counteridentification are more or less ubiquitous (see chapter 11), certainly expectable at the very least. We now know that identifying and mastering such reactions probably yields more fruitful insights than we can expect from periods of "untroubled" analytic work. When the problem involves disorders of communication, the analyst's tendency toward counteridentification is likely to manifest itself in episodes of miscommunication echoing or complementing those of the analysand.

COMPLICATIONS

Let me turn to the major issues that make patients unable to bear the longed-for intimacy of communicative harmony with their therapists. The acquisition of consensual language, usually syntactically organized by the second half of the second year of life, vastly expands the toddler's capacity to process information. This expansion may be particularly dramatic for children whose caretakers have had unusual difficulties in comprehending the protolinguistic signals of infancy. Whatever the specific quality of early childhood experience in communicating, whenever treatment gets off to a good start, the novel understanding of the patient's communications that results inevitably echoes the mastery of consensual language in early childhood. Unfortunately, with the maturation that makes symbolic thinking possible, the small child enters an era of particular vulnerability because of the concomitant reorganization of the control of behavior—a major nodal point in development.

Newly self-aware as a person, the toddler will have fewer or more difficulties in maintaining a sense of autonomous volition. The outward manifestations of this unavoidable challenge have been described by Mahler (Mahler, Pine, and Bergman, 1975) as the "crisis of rapprochement." In the throes of this crisis, the child may experience on numerous occasions urgent needs to keep "mamma out," if I may allude once again to the earliest words of my negativistic analysand. This need is often frustrated, however: as Shakespeare reminds us, the devil can assume a pleasing shape—most of all, he can seduce us through language. Caretakers who invade the child's private space through the use of words (in contrast to those who do so by actions such as force-feeding or the administration of enemas) create conflicts for that individual that center around the very process of communication, especially in the form of verbal dialogue.

Hence, it is precisely those patients who are most uneasy about the consequences of intimacy for their sense of separateness and autonomy—who have, if you will, the greatest anxiety about symbiotic experiences—who will prove to be the most resistant to the establishment of harmonious and untroubled communication with their therapists. Another variant of this therapeutic dilemma is not intolerance of harmonious intimacy but perceiving it as strange and emotionally flat. This flatness occurs with persons who have learned to define meaningful relationships in terms of pain, tension, and discord. Insofar as verbal communication plays its role in producing such conditions, these patients use it to promote misunderstanding. On investigation, one usually discovers that the caretakers of these analysands often misused verbal discourse for the purpose of obfuscation. Such patients, in other words, do not actually *resist* mutual understanding by means of therapeutic dialogue; to be more precise, they are addicted to creating false accord and its predictably painful consequences.

When we are confronted with negativism, we can be reasonably certain that the analysand's behavior represents a derivative of early childhood transactions from the phase of separation-individuation, to use Mahler's vocabulary. In contrast, the reenactment of painful episodes of miscommunication cannot be referred back with the same kind of specificity to any particular phase of early development. Traumatic vicissitudes at various ages may draw verbal communication into the area of conflict in a manner that leads to compulsive repetition in adult life. This is particularly likely to be true in instances of loss of the original caretaker whenever the painful misuse of consensual language takes place in the relationship with those who replace her. Despite these exceptions, most cases in which patients are addicted to miscommunication ultimately point to a pattern of relatedness that antedates primary reliance on a spoken language—such a pattern constitutes a regression to the preverbal uses of speech (see chapter 2).

My discussion thus far has focused only on those circumstances in early childhood that lead to a pattern of disharmony largely because the caretakers behaved in ways that had deleterious consequences. The majority of persons in my practice who had such problems had experiences of this kind; however, it should not be assumed a priori that psychopathology invariably derives from failures on the part of caretakers: The rights of infants, after all, do not include parental perfection! Even in the case I have used to illustrate this chapter, it may well have been the child's atypical language development (among other constitutional anomalies), rather than the mother's limitations, that contributed most heavily to the derailment of their dialogue. Despite her characterological intrusiveness, this mother was reasonably successful in raising a number of other children without provoking their negativism. The ease with which a coherent self-organization is established (guaranteeing the child's sense of autonomy) and, conversely, its vulnerability to disruption in the event of unfortunate transactions with the caretakers, may well be maturational givens, largely under the influence of constitutional variables. At any rate, in the present state of our ignorance about the genesis of such archaic psychological dispositions, we must at all cost avoid dogmatism.

To recapitulate: If we acknowledge that psychological treatment must of necessity consist of an exchange of messages encoded in a variety of "languages," it follows that its success is absolutely dependent on the ability of the participants to learn communicating in several "shared languages." The therapist's ability to adjust his or her communications in accord with the patient's assets and limitations in information processing, along with the analyst's aptitude for learning the patient's various languages, may well constitute two of the most essential aspects of native endowment for successful psychotherapeutic work.

Although the achievement of shared languages is a prerequisite for analytically mutative interventions, this precondition for further remedial work has, as I have tried to show, only nonspecific beneficial effects. Close scrutiny of difficulties in communication does, however, provide unparalleled opportunities for the reconstruction of crucial infant-caretaker transactions occurring as early as the second year of life. These transactions often include certain vicissitudes that preceded the child's mastery of consensual language. Psychoanalysis provides matchless conditions for detailed study of such matters and thus is the optimal arena for understanding and treating archaic personality disorders.

7 Channels of Communication and the Analytic Setup

THE USE OF THE COUCH: PRO AND CON

There is much to be said in favor of performing tasks of daunting complexity, including the conduct of psychoanalyses, within a reliable framework—a set of conventions that may be taken for granted, in order to reduce to a relatively manageable number the variables that the practitioner has to monitor. Winnicott (1954), referring to the conventions generally accepted by large sections of our community, called the almost banal results produced by these traditions—our liturgy, if you will—the "psychoanalytic situation." Unlike the rituals of religion, however, no aspect of these conventions of ours is actually sacred. In America, we do not shake hands before and after each session, we do not provide analysands with warm coverlets—for that matter, we do not demand that they pay us in cash; yet these are routine aspects of the psychoanalytic situation in certain milieux abroad.

Perhaps no component of the psychoanalytic situation is as widely practiced as is the use of the couch. Although this convention was originally dictated by the requirements of Freud's preanalytic "pressure technique," wherein he strove to overcome the obstacles to the recollection of repressed mental contents by taking hold of the patient's head, it was retained when he changed the technique of treatment to that of relying first on directed and later on free associations. Freud apparently rationalized his perpetuation of the arrangement on the ground that he disliked being looked at hour after hour, but this subjective factor doubtless screened the considerable pragmatic gain that resulted from this serendipitous arrangement. Yet we know that when Ferenczi served in the army in World War I, he did not hesitate to analyze his commanding officer while they went horseback riding together, and in contemporary conditions analyses by long-distance telephone are not all that rare. In other words, the use of the couch has never achieved the status of a defining characteristic of psychoanalysis; more often, it has been misused by pretend-analysts eager to borrow the prestige of our discipline. All cartoon therapists in *The New Yorker* possess couches.

In stressing the subjective dimension of his preference for seating himself out of his patients' view, Freud actually overlooked an important consideration, one called to my attention by Therese Benedek when she supervised my work (ca. 1957): being shielded from having his or her facial expression continuously observed allows the analyst to respond to the material without constraint and thus to become more readily aware of the affective aspects of that response. In doing face-to-face psychotherapy, it is incumbent upon us to be more guarded about our facial expressions, and in the process, we lose some of our emotional responsiveness. It *has* been widely understood, however, that monitoring the analyst's facial expressions by a patient may seriously interfere with the opportunity to focus attention on the patient's own internal world. The traditional recumbent posture of analysands greatly restricts the range of visual stimuli they perceive, and thereby also promotes the desirable focus of attention inward.

Another often mentioned pragmatic advantage of using the couch is that this arrangement tends to favor verbal communication (with a consequent tilt in the direction of more precise and explicit secondary processes). This tendency is brought about because the recumbent posture interferes, to a greater or lesser extent depending on individual factors, with the language of gestures most people employ to complement their speech. Obviously, lying on a couch does not preclude the use of the hands to accompany one's words, and the specific posture the analysand assumes during sessions may also speak volumes; but most patients do not do much wriggling while in analysis, and many fail to use gestures to communicate with someone they do not see.

However, by far the most important effect of using the couch—while the analyst is sitting more or less erect—is to place the analysand in a setting most individuals experience as infantile. In adult life, such conditions are generally encountered only when one becomes a patient; nonpsychoanalytic medical contexts also possess archaic connotations and therefore promote the development of transference reactions of a regressive nature. As long as analysis was recommended only for persons who suffered (for the most part, at any rate) from "transference neuroses" (Freud, 1914a), the regressive pull of the patient's recumbent posture had the primary effect of aiding the development of intrapsychic conditions wherein archaic material tends to rise toward consciousness and the customary operations of the defensive apparatus may become insufficient to ward off this potential threat. In other words, whenever narrow criteria of analyzability are in use, the traditional reliance on the analysand's position on the couch, with the analyst more or less out of sight, has a solid theoretical rationale.

Those of us who have attempted to widen the "scope" of psychoanalysis as treatment (see Stone, 1954) frequently encounter clinical contingencies in which the traditional setting of couch and analyst's chair fails to facilitate the analytic process or may even become a seeming obstacle to the continuance of therapeutic collaboration. The most dramatic example of such a crisis I can cite from my practice is that of a middle-aged professional man who sought assistance as his marriage was falling apart. After providing enough support by means of brief psychotherapy to stabilize the situation, I recommended that the patient seek analysis in another city where he was soon scheduled to move. To my surprise, this man changed his mind about accepting his new position and requested that I take responsibility for his analysis in Chicago. Despite some misgivings about the transference implications of this abrupt shift, I felt obliged to assent to the request, because the decision to stay in town had become irreversible.

For about a year, the analysis outwardly conformed to traditional procedures, although the patient was implicitly demanding a magical solution to his problems. Because I consistently disclaimed the power to provide this, he angrily turned for guidance to more charismatic figures. His adaptive equilibrium nonetheless continued to be preserved by steady attendance at his five weekly sessions, and he experienced intensification of his subjective sense of depending on the analysis. Shortly before my summer vacation at the end of our first year of work, the patient had a nightmare in which he was supine while floating in the air and was helplessly pulled along, head first, as if by suction. He arrived for his next session in great agitation and announced, as if in association to this dream, that he could not bear to lie on the couch: I simply had to put up with his walking about my consulting room to work off his restlessness. I never concurred in his decision to refuse to lie on the couch: but neither did I succeed in overcoming his negativism in this regard, although we continued to work together for several years and I made many vain attempts to interpret the meaning of his behavior.

Of course, there is no way to know whether some variation of this traditional approach to initiating an analysis would have been more successful in leading into a workable analytic process, and it would be even less legitimate to assert that the use of the couch was one of the crucial variables in determining the outcome, despite the reference to a horizontal posture in the manifest content of the patient's pivotal dream. It is notable, however, that, both before and after this incident, the patient repeatedly complained that, when he tried to put his inner life into words, whatever he was able to say appeared to falsify the actualities. (I have already mentioned this person as the most accomplished "blatherer" I have ever encountered.) In this connection, it is highly relevant that in other respects he was unusually articulate: being articulate was one of the primary requirements of his profession as a television performer. In parallel with this complaint, the analysand found that my verbal communications failed to address his emotional concerns—a problem I have very seldom encountered with analytic patients, with whom I generally do manage to find a shared language. In view of these difficulties, the very rationale for the physical setup of classical psychoanalysis, that of ensuring that the exchange of information should as much as possible take place by means of verbally encoded messages, increased the patient's frustration and his ultimate decision to dictate his own ground rules in treatment.

Another way to put these matters is that the analysis began with the patient already in a regressive state, probably one of primitive idealization, leading to his irrational decision to sacrifice an excellent professional opportunity for the sake of continuing contact with me. The psychoanalytic situation began to exert a further regressive pull that he experienced as the imminent onset of helpless passivity; against this felt danger, he instituted the emergency defense of negativism. Nor was the patient's fear of further regression unjustified, as I was to learn during the summer vacation at the end of the second year of treatment, when my absence happened to coincide with that of everyone else he could depend on: In those circumstances, he developed a severe, agitated depression (see also Gedo, 1981a, case 9; 1991a, chap. 6, case 2). I now believe it might have been more prudent to adopt a therapeutic strategy that did not promote regression, including a physical setup without the disadvantage of the infantile connotations of using the couch or that of discouraging nonverbal channels of communication.

At the same time, it should never be overlooked that in some cases reluctance to lie on the couch is merely a symptomatic act, the meaning of which is both interpretable and crucially relevant for continued analytic progress. Perhaps the clearest instance of this kind to have come to my attention was shared with me by a colleague who sought consultation because of this very dilemma: he felt that he was unable to "get the patient into analysis." The analysand in question neither agreed to come more than three times a week nor would consent to lie on the couch. With the participants sitting face-to-face, at this frequency of sessions, a therapeutic impasse lasting for several years supervened.

What I learned in the course of a series of consultations was that, for this patient, "being in analysis" had the significance of being prematurely made responsible for herself, thereby letting her socially and professionally ambitious mother off the hook of parental obligations. The adult analysand's overt insistence on an infantile tie to her parents constituted a transference repetition of circumstances that first occurred when she was about nine or ten, when her psychoanalytically sophisticated mother decided to deal with the child's evident unhappiness by sending her to a child analyst. Although this coercive effort was maintained for several years, the preadolescent girl managed to make it a travesty by resolutely refusing to speak to the analyst. Ultimately, the adults had to acknowledge that they could not "get her into analysis" against her wishes.

Needless to say, these transactions in late latency already had meaningful precedents earlier in the patient's life. This wealthy family employed a nursemaid, officially to assist the mother with the care of her children, but in actuality to be the primary caretaker who freed the parents of the responsibilities of child-rearing. Perhaps because she was the only girl, the patient was the nursemaid's favorite, so that she became sufficiently attached to this woman to wound the narcissistically vulnerable mother. There ensued a vicious circle of mutual rejection that left the child with the impression that her mother simply wanted no part of her. The resultant dysphoria came to a head at the time of the referral to the child analyst, which once again confirmed the patient in her grievance.

When, in adulthood, the analyst of this woman was able to put the "resistance" to "getting into analysis" into its proper context as still another repetition of this childhood pattern—a reenactment made more exact because once again it was the mother who urged the choice of an analysis when this young woman acknowledged that she was unhappy enough to want help—the patient realized that it was now futile to seek anything from her parents, that the analyst was (like the childhood nursemaid) a reliable ally, and that "getting into analysis" might enable her to overcome her childhood disappointments. The couch therefore lost its primary connotation as a place of exile.

To summarize the thesis I have presented thus far: In certain cases, the use of the couch may have severe disadvantages, but one should not decide that it is contraindicated simply because of an analysand's subjective reluctance to comply with this analytic routine. Such a resistance should be carefully investigated, for it may prove either to be the legitimate expression of a special need or to have crucial psychological significance, insight into which will promote the analytic process.

ANALYSIS AND THE LANGUAGE OF GESTURES

Despite occasional experiences with would-be analysands who were unable to tolerate the use of the couch, I have continued to stick to the traditional physical setup of psychoanalysis, so that I cannot report on successful analyses conducted in settings of another kind. When one of my patients could not abide my routine set-up, I went along with that limitation, but in those rare instances I never obtained an *analytic* result. In each of these cases, I ultimately came to the conclusion that I had bitten off more than I could chew and would have done better to recommend a less ambitious program of treatment, or perhaps a different analyst, one less reliant on verbal channels of communication.

The opposite side of this coin is the importance I attach to the opportunity to read the cues provided by the analysand's changing facial expressions. To facilitate these observations, I have always positioned my chair so that I might look at the analysand's face more or less from the side, rather than having a view of the top of the patient's head or glimpsing a face upside down. I have always insisted on supplementing the analysand's associations with information I could collect through direct visual observation. One consequence of the resultant arrangement is that it also made it relatively easy for analysands to look at me; at most, it required turning their head in my direction—persons with a wide angle of vision had only to move their eyes to perceive me. Consequently, I interfered with nonverbal communication to a lesser extent than do analysts who sit directly behind their patients. It is conceivable that this circumstance may somewhat have broadened the range of analyzable conditions within the setting I provided.

Obviously, nonverbal communication does not depend on visual cues alone, and, with respect to the other sensory channels, using the couch makes no difference at all: for practical purposes, we simply cannot avail ourselves of taste, smell, and touch; with regard to auditory cues, the physical setup of the consulting room is almost irrelevant. I have tried to stress the importance of paying close analytic attention to the paraverbal aspects of speech (see chapter 1; see also Gedo, 1984, chaps. 8 and 9; 1993b); here it may suffice to reiterate that these aspects of linguistic communication are particularly important as carriers of meaning with regard to psychological materials referable to the earliest phases of development, those preceding the establishment of the primacy of words meanings (and, even more emphatically, of meanings conveyed through syntax).

From this viewpoint, it is essential to recall that the nonverbal realm is characterized not only by the music of vocalizations that lack consensual meanings with regard to the phonemes they employ; as I reviewed in chapter 5, a language consisting of understandable words or even of sound-signals is preceded by one of gestures, including postures and facial expressions (see Levin, 1991, chap. 7). These communications forever remain a vital part of the individual's repertory in conveying meanings. To be reminded that nonverbal methods of transmission are a regular feature of normal information exchange we need only observe how often a person's communications, easily understood when delivered in person, become unintelligible when transcribed as a written message. When we are dealing with archaic mental contents, often already permanently split off from the predominant personality organization in early childhood, encoding in words may never have taken place. In such cases, these legacies of early experience are communicable mostly through nonverbal signs, be they sonic, protolinguistic, or gestural; the traditional setting of psychoanalysis does not provide the optimal venue for the transmission of messages through these nonverbal media.

Clearly, I do not mean that analysands' gestures and facial expressions necessarily go unobserved as the patients lie on the couch, although our tendency to focus on the syntactical meanings of the stream of associations may interfere with our ability to perceive the analysands' signals visually. What I do have in mind is that the recumbent posture may inhibit patients so that they will not "talk with their hands" (or with other parts of their body) to the same extent as they do when they are free to choose their own posture. In my experience, it is rare for analytic patients to turn to the wall (or, if you will, to turn their back on me), to mention only the simplest of examples of a gestural communication of obvious significance—yet we know from observing babies that such gestures of withdrawal are the most common signs of their having been intruded on. Analysands may well be unable to articulate such feelings in words; for patients in this predicament, an analytic setting that functions like the stage of a ballet or a pantomime might prove to be optimal. To use a simile somewhat closer to home, these analysands might do best in a setting like that of the child analyst's playroom.

As I have already mentioned, the analysand who, in my experience, showed the greatest degree of freedom to use my entire office as analytic space was—not at all coincidentally, I believe!—the one person I have worked with to have had serious childhood training in ballet. I have previously reported (Gedo, 1988, chap. 13) that this person became interested in dancing because her caretakers had subverted the meaning of words so that she could not rely on speech to convey reliable information about human transactions: only the language of gestures remained available to communicate about her inner world. This is the patient who did turn to the wall whenever she felt emotionally crowded; she went into the opisthotonos of *grande hystérie* in reaction to overstimulation; she would abruptly sit up in protest against ill-judged interventions on my part that required straightening out by way of giving me instructions about what made them inadvisable; her gait to and from the door, the position of her arms and legs on the couch, always seemed to express meanings I was generally too imperceptive to decipher without the aid of verbal associations.

What is particularly worthy of note, however, was not just her behavior *on* the couch but her enactments involving walking about my office or even flights into the public corridor outside it. Such excursions took place on many occasions, especially in the middle phases of the analysis; like a prima ballerina, however, the protagonist of these dramatic scenes invariably returned for the dénouement. In other words, by leaving the couch she was not running away from the analytic task; her departures and reentries constituted symbolic actions expressing an implicit narrative—ultimately referable to the early experience of having had a primary caretaker who regularly disappeared on Friday afternoons only to return on Monday morning. In my judgment, these experiences had never become encoded in words; hence they were accessible as memories only in terms of reproduction in action.[1]

---

[1] It may be relevant to add in this connection that even some animals have the capacity to reproduce traumatic experiences in this manner. I have witnessed a dog reenacting the sequence of being hit by a vehicle and falling into a ditch, complete with expressive vocalization.

I am indebted to Fred Levin (personal communication) for analogous clinical accounts about the recovery of memories from early childhood, before they could have been organized in terms of syntactic language, through "priming" by means of reproducing a sequence of physical activities (see also Levin, 1991). In one dramatic instance, Levin reports that an analysand had to wedge himself into a narrow space behind a piece of furniture and crouch to the floor before recapturing imagery suggestive of significant, hitherto unconscious, experiences in early life.

In view of clinical encounters in which the expansion of the analytic stage onto the consulting room as a whole and even beyond it appears to have deepened the analytic process and promoted its progress, it has become appropriate to question the uniform routine we have imposed on our procedures in terms of their physical setup. Do we insist on this routine because, on balance, it is still the most reliable framework for the majority of analysands? Or are we indulging our own preference for whatever is familiar by adhering to a formula that has lost credibility? Be it noted that even if we continue a particular arrangement for our own sake, such a choice is by no means illegitimate: analysis can work only if the situation meets the analyst's minimum requirements, and these undoubtedly include psychological matters as much as financial considerations.

Having performed analyses within the traditional setup for close to four decades, I was certainly too much wedded to old habits to conduct the technical experiments needed to answer the foregoing questions on the basis of empirical evidence. For the moment, we have to be content with the realization that we can no longer look upon the appropriate answers as self-evident.

8 Analytic Interventions
The Question of Form

THE ANALYST AS THE VOICE OF THE PATIENT

In his book on the mode of action of psychoanalysis-as-therapy, Arnold Modell (1990) makes the cogent observation that, when treatment is proceeding in an optimal manner, it is virtually impossible to discern whether a specific insight originated with the analyst or the analysand. Although Modell's hypothesis does not cover every contingency that may arise in the course of psychoanalysis, I do agree that in those portions of treatment that, in a paraphrase of Kris's (1956a) "good hour" concept, have been called "good analytic segments" (P. Gedo, 1991), the functions producing insight are shared between analyst and patient.

Some years ago, I tried to express this idea, from a slightly different perspective (Gedo 1984, chapter 9). I stated that, once the participants in an analysis have achieved a "shared language," it becomes possible for the analyst's communications to be experienced by the analysand as one of the voices in an *internal* dialogue within his or her mind. In Modell's (1990) vocabulary, this amounts to the attainment of a "shared reality" within the frame of the psychoanalytic setting. My way of putting this matter highlights the implication that optimal therapeutic work takes place when the analyst's separateness scarcely impinges on the patient, so that his interventions are not experienced as the intrusion of an Other into the process of "self inquiry" (Gardner, 1983). If we conceive of psychoanalysis, in Freud's terms, as a *Nacherziehung* (a reeducation), we must acknowledge that optimally instruction merely evokes the learner's developmental potential (see Wilson and Weinstein, 1992a and b).

Of course, it is by no means easy to achieve the kind of therapeutic harmony wherein the roles of the collaborators become difficult to differentiate. In the first place, the analyst cannot always avoid betraying a lack of understanding of the patient's current emotional position and/or motivations. These are the circumstances Kohut (1971) designated as "breaks in empathy"—which, it will be recalled, he believed to be especially troublesome in the context of a "merger transference," that is, when the analysand has been experiencing the analyst as an aspect of his own subjectivity.[1] Beyond these instances of disharmony, caused by the analyst's limitations, in numerous circumstances it is the analysand who needs to preserve separateness or distance from the Other—either for defensive reasons or as one aspect of some specific transference constellation. At any rate, analytic segments wherein the voices of the participants blend, as they do in a performance of an *a cappella* choir (once again to quote a former analysand of mine on this matter), may be relatively brief, as well as relatively infrequent.

As I stated in a previous attempt to address the rhetorical dimensions of psychoanalytic technique (Gedo, 1984, chap. 9), it is very important to encode analytic communications in a manner specifically appropriate to the interpersonal situation prevalent within the therapeutic dyad at a given time. The analyst's usual communicative repertory ranges from the vocalization of affects without the use of words (by means of expressive signals such as laughing or growling), through exclamations and expletives, to the subtleties of the consensual use of language. With regard to the latter, it is essential to note again that the paraverbal aspects are at least as important as is the lexical meaning of words. To put this differently, psychoanalysis must never be confused with an *explication du texte* (as the French put it); it comes much closer to the task of apprehending an operatic performance: the main carrier of meaning is the music, with which the words of the libretto may or may not be congruent (see Gedo, 1986, chap. 13).

Because of the decisive significance of the music of the analyst's communications, the widespread practice of equating analytic neutrality with a colorless, low-keyed, self-effacing, or unemotional manner of speaking is decidedly ill conceived. There may be times when it is best for the analyst to sound that way—for example, whenever an analysand is likely to experience almost any intervention as an unwelcome intrusion that must be resisted—but, *in principle*, such a choice has nothing to do with neutrality or

---

[1] *En passant*, I should like to note that it is entirely possible that what Kohut interpreted as regression to an archaic state of "merger" is often nothing more than (a constructive) readiness on the part of the analysand for optimal collaboration. In this context, the analyst's inability to participate on the proper basis is, indeed, unempathic and may require the kind of acknowledgment of responsibility for therapeutic derailments that self psychologists advocate.

equidistance from the agencies of the mind (as portrayed in Freud's tripartite model); it is a response to the requirements dictated by the status of the analytic relationship.

If the analyst wishes to assume the role of an internal voice within the analysand's mental universe, however, it becomes necessary to speak in a manner that echoes the latter's language—syntactically, in the choice of words, as well as in the crucial paraverbal aspects of conveying affect. Internal dialogue will lead to clearer insight insofar as one of the voices, often the one assumed by the analyst, conveys a more precise portrait of the affective situation than was previously available. Of course, this aim might well be achieved simply by *naming* the affective state in question, but doing so involves adding something to the analysand's fund of information in an *objective* mode and thus tends to remind him that he is in the presence of another person. By contrast, the *embodiment* of such an affective state by means of a tone of voice emphatically impregnated with recognizable emotion may achieve the same clarification without disrupting the illusion of internal dialogue.

Obviously, the impact of the paraverbal communication will be greatly enhanced if vocabulary and syntax are calculated to be congruent with the emotional message. I believe I can best explain what I have in mind by means of a concrete example; for the sake of clarity, I shall risk being somewhat schematic by leaving out of consideration many subtleties of this clinical transaction:

A middle-aged professional man in the fourth year of a productive analysis was coming to grips with his tendency to accept without complaint ill treatment that would eventually lead him to burst into intense and seemingly disproportionate rage. In one fruitful session, I was able to point out that the guilt he always felt after his outbursts was, in itself, part of the pattern of self-restriction and self-blame that led to his seemingly masochistic behavior in failing to make known his minimum requirements. The session that followed this successful correlation of phenomena he had not understood to be connected contained a rare lengthy segment wherein he allowed me to represent one of his internal voices.

He began this hour in a reflective way, reminding himself that his efforts to be accommodating with a variety of people were in accord with the moral ideals of his adolescence and thus also served to enhance his self-esteem. After some (relatively mild) self-flagellation about his ubiquitous narcissism, he went on to wonder why he continued to withhold his feelings of dissatisfaction not only at work, where this policy may have been prudent, but also in situations that called for candor, like his relationship with his lover. During this monologue, I had permitted myself several interjections that merely echoed what he said, with some degree of added emphasis. He now elaborated the fantasy that he might ruin his love affair by revealing his selfishness; after all, his lady friend did not have to accept a person with such characteristics.

It was at this point that I made the intervention on which I want to focus in this case example. Be it noted that this patient was of French-Canadian origin and occasionally lapsed into his native language in the course of associating, secure in the knowledge that I would understand him. I now chose to address him in French (i.e., in his *mother* tongue), adapting some phrases he had used in the past, "Elle va s'enfuir, pour parcourir le monde!" [She will run away, to wander the world.] I said this in a tone conveying a threat, frustrated anger, and a great deal of certitude, but very much like an actor delivering a line. Without noting what this paraphrase referred to, the patient immediately began to cogitate about the ways in which his relationship to his lover were impregnated with his childhood attitudes toward his mother.

I trust it is evident that it had been the patient's mother who had long ago used the angry, dramatic threat to run away and become a wanderer, to terrify him into compliance with her demands. Thus, by adopting her words to characterize the present (and to refer to transactions encoded in a different language), I was certainly providing an associative link between then and now—but it was left to the analysand to arrive at the insight that his behavior constituted a transference. In other words, the analysand's understanding was achieved by means of self-inquiry, without requiring interpretation. I believe Modell's (1990) statement about the joint responsibility of the participants for analytic insights refers to transactions of this nature.

The foregoing illustration is intended to show not only that the analyst's communications can, if they convey relevant affects, reverberate with the analysand's current inner experience; it also demonstrates the facilitating power of using a "shared language" (Gedo, 1984, chap. 8) in promoting what Gardner (1983) has called "assisted self-inquiry." In this particular instance, the language shared was a combination of English and French, and specifically the phraseology that was part of a set of significant early memories. I should add that this form of bilingualism truly constituted a bond of shared past experience between my analysand and me, for we had both learned these two languages more or less concurrently—albeit our personal attitudes about having done so did not entirely coincide. Nonetheless, resorting to "franglais" brought to the fore our tendency to represent for each other aspects of a remote past and to experience our discourse as an immersion in private recollection.

It is also worth noting that my contribution to the dialogue within this "good segment" of analysis took the form of a line from a piece of theater—its syntax was that of addressing the patient directly. By contrast, most interpretations are encoded in a manner characteristic for a scientific observation, suitable for a general audience, with some effort to be "objective," indications that the statement is conjectural, and so forth. Had I wished to make my presence felt in that manner, I might have said, "It seems to me that you are afraid to make your wishes known to your lover, as if she were likely to threaten you with abandonment, as your mother used to do when you were little." I have every reason to believe that such an interpretation would have led, as usual, to lengthy intellectualizations about the differences between past and present. It was difficult for this man to accept the accomplishments of others; signs of therapeutic ambition on my part aroused his competitive hostility.

I do not mean to imply that diverting the course of the analysis from an episode of smooth collaboration to one of transference resistance would have constituted a technical error. On the contrary, it is imperative *not* to circumvent the emergence of that form of transference through some consistent policy of appeasement (such as the recommendation of certain authors [e.g., Schwaber, 1981] always to espouse the analysand's subjective point of view). As Freud (1915c) clearly indicated in his earliest works on technique, it is precisely the experience of endopsychic resistance, when it emerges in the transference arena, that leads to the most fruitful insights about the genesis of psychopathology. In the case from which my clinical example is drawn, it was certainly crucially important sooner or later to focus on his angry competitiveness, with its attendant envy and malice—at least as important as it was to gain insight into his passivity vis-à-vis women. (Of course, at bottom these issues were interconnected and could be transcended only after both were thoroughly analyzed.)

Hence my choice in favor of promoting further partnership was dictated by tactical considerations, matters such as my feeling that the analysand was in urgent need of assistance with his interpersonal problem concerning the love affair—my calculation that, if this acute difficulty could be overcome by means of analytic work, this achievement would both solidify the patient's commitment to the treatment *and* bring his tendency to sabotage the collaboration into sharper focus. At a different stage of the analysis, a very different approach would probably be preferable.

I should perhaps add that there are, indeed, analytic patients who *do* require the espousal of their subjectivity, as Schwaber (1981) recommends; these are the analysands who develop an *archaic* transference (Gedo, 1977) of the kind Kohut (1971) characterized as a "merger." If one attempts to make interpretations to patients in that state in the form of "objective," scientific exposition, they are very likely to be traumatized. One such person was able ultimately to tell me that when I thought I was being dispassionately accurate, she felt that I was treating her as a pathological specimen in a laboratory. This, too, proved to be transference repetition, to be sure, but the repetition of infantile traumata is hardly ever desirable for promoting an analytic process.

THE ANALYST AS DISPASSIONATE TECHNICIAN

Is it *ever* desirable to encode analytic interventions in the language of a scientific observer dispassionately reporting his data and the conclusions one might draw from them? In my experience, this mode of discourse seldom turns out to be the most productive among the choices available, although (to be sure) it is generally safe and prudent enough. Yet there are special circumstances wherein the rhetoric of scientific expository reportage is truly the optimal choice, or even the only means of communication that has a chance of success. In general terms, one might characterize these contingencies as moments of intense transference, laden with strong affect (especially on the part of the analysand)—episodes that threaten to assume the proportions of a crisis because the participants' capacity to differentiate the repetition of something from the past from an unmanageable reality in the present is stretched to its outer limits. I should like to illustrate a transaction of this kind with a brief example from the early stages of a lengthy analysis, eventually carried to a successful termination with a felicitous result, but punctuated by frequent crises of volcanic intensity:

Within a few weeks of starting analysis, an attractive young woman who believed herself to be suffering from a "sickness unto death" (if I may use this religious category in lieu of her self-description) announced with threatening emphasis that the only chance the treatment had of saving her life was to initiate a sexual affair between us. I was initially stunned by her statement, for I had neither anticipated such an alarming transference development nor observed earlier signs of the formation of an emotional bond with me. Because our consultations prior to the beginning of the analysis proper had yielded few anamnestic details to which any great significance could be attached, I was completely mystified and quite at a loss for a response.

The moment was charged with tension and suspense, so much so that I needed time to recover my composure. But this patient could not tolerate my silence: She began urgently to demand some answer to her "life and death" inquiry. It took all the self-control I could muster to articulate my response in a relatively matter-of-fact, albeit serious, tone of voice, one that I hoped would not communicate the full extent of my anxiety. As I recall, I started out by stating my conviction that she meant what she said literally and that her sense of my importance to her was, at the same time, doing me great honor by offering me what I already knew she looked upon as her greatest assets, her youth and her feminine appeal. I went on to say that I was also certain that she knew that complying with her suggestion was completely impermissible and that our task was to discern why she regarded an unacceptable course of action as absolutely necessary at the same time. The patient accepted this answer, on a provisional basis, and the acute crisis was over.

Many years later, I asked this analysand how she would have reacted if I had agreed to "save her" through the magic of personal contact, and she unhesitatingly replied that she would have concluded that I was crazy and would have transferred to another analyst. Yet I do not believe that she was primarily *testing* me; on the contrary, it was because she had come to trust my reliability that she felt safe enough to articulate her fantasy (see Sandler, 1989). Hence the content of my response, about which I felt very uncertain, turned out to have been reasonably accurate. Of course, the only part of my statement that amounted to an interpretation was the conjecture that what manifestly sounded like a demand had a latent meaning as a *gift*. For this aspect of the response, I had no overt evidence at all—I was proceeding exclusively on the basis of empathy. As it later turned out, this empathy had not misled us: we discovered that, as a child, the patient had been sexually involved with an adolescent boy, but this seeming exploitation had been a highly prized experience, a gift that patched over a period of "disorder and early sorrow."

I mention these details because it needs to be acknowledged that my intervention was effective in part because the content of the verbal message was both clear and generally valid. Yet I do not think that this was the crux of the transaction I have described. First of all, we had countless subsequent experiences wherein my interventions failed, although the message was both correct and understandable; I believe I have never worked with a patient who was as sensitive about the *form* of my communications as was this analysand. Beyond this consideration, I am convinced that the most important aspect of this therapeutic crisis was the effect of the patient's announcement on me—that I came close to panic (in the face of an implicit threat of suicide). This was the first sign, effected by means of projective identification, of the emergence of the patient's chronic traumatic state, the legacy of sexual overstimulation in childhood. From this perspective, the demonstration-in-action that I was able to contain my reaction to her seeming assault and to respond in a reasonable manner was also the first step in leading her in the direction of mastering her anxiety states.

It will be recalled that Freud (1915c) once compared the appropriate attitude of the psychoanalyst vis-à-vis the transference to that of a surgeon in the operating room. I must say that his statement implies some idealization of surgeons, whose emotions are not always under optimal control. Be that as it may, it is now generally understood that Freud was not recommending the kind of dehumanization of the patient that is almost mandatory if the surgeon is to work effectively at the level of tissues and organs. Nonetheless, the conviction is still widespread that optimally the analyst had best communicate in a maximally "objective" manner. This viewpoint overlooks the fact that Freud's recommendation deals only with the problem of how best to respond to an overtly erotic (or hostile) transference. As the second case illustrates, when transference demands are out in the open, it may indeed be most expedient to emulate the emotionally uninvolved technician; this formula should not, however, be applied in an unthinking manner to other circumstances.

AFFECT-LADEN INTERVENTIONS

Some years ago I stated that, in order to communicate with archaic aspects of the analysand's personality, the analyst's language must be penetrating, concrete, simple, affect-laden, and dramatic (Gedo, 1984, chap. 9). In agreement with this viewpoint, Levin (1980) has pointed out, on both clinical and neurophysiological grounds, that the best chance of affecting, through verbal channels, mental dispositions formed in early childhood is the employment of metaphors. I would add that tropes in general (i.e., metonymy, synecdoche, and irony, as well as metaphor) possess precisely the qualities I listed as desirable in 1984. Obviously, I do not propose this manner of intervention as a general formula to be applied in all contingencies—as I have just discussed at some length, there are situations in which it works best to communicate in a more "objective" or literal manner, further removed from primary process mentation.

The issue of choice of language (or rhetoric, if you will) should not be conflated with that of striving to represent one voice in the analysand's internal world, the issue with which I began this chapter. Whatever the analyst's rhetorical strategies may be, they will not suffice by themselves to overcome the patient's realistic experience that communication with another person is taking place; in this regard, the proper choice of language is necessary but not sufficient. As I have tried to indicate, the most decisive factor influencing the analysand's experience about the presence of an Other is the current status of the transference, something that may undergo several changes within a single analytic session. I should like to give an illustration of a transference constellation that began in an adversarial fashion but was decisively shifted by means of repeated, forceful, affect-laden analytic interventions:

In the fifth year of a lengthy analysis, a middle-aged bureaucrat had sufficiently relaxed his schizoid avoidance of meaningful relationships to have become a valued member of a group of local politicians and a confidant of the leader of this circle. For a considerable period of time, his analytic sessions were devoted to his anxious concerns about these relationships, particularly his fear that he would be rejected because he would be seen as an unscrupulous exploiter of his new "friends." It may be superfluous to note that, in part, this represented a displacement from the analytic transference; as I knew from previous vicissitudes in the treatment, the patient was very likely to lapse into a paranoid alternative to this attitude, in which he felt boundless rage about being exploited in his turn. Whenever these issues had come up in acute form within the analytic relationship, I had not succeeded in making constructive use of these developments, so that I was now content to work with them in their displaced guise.

In this mode, the patient actively used me as an arbiter of his reality testing, one who would give him advance warning whenever he might come too close to any abuse of his friends. In the meantime, it gradually became clearer that, with his political "boss," he was reexperiencing an intensely ambivalent brother transference. Although the analysand had made several allusions to the political circle as a band of brothers and to its patron as a revenant of the sibling to whom he had been closest as a small child, this knowledge did not prevent him from suddenly feeling enormously hurt and enraged because of alleged slights by his cronies. Although it was reasonably certain that this was a transference reaction, I did not then have information about any specific childhood circumstance with which it could be correlated.[2] Moreover, the patient was too wrought up by his paranoia to allow any shift of focus away from his immediate grievances.

In this emergency, which threatened not only the most important relationships the patient had formed as an adult but also his livelihood, I tried to continue my role of supplying an important assessment of the actualities. Insofar as my judgment disagreed with his paranoid distortions, however, the patient now began to mock my naïveté. Thus I had not succeeded in sidestepping an archaic transference altogether; although I did not realize this at the time, I was being assigned the role of the analysand's childhood self, too trusting and guileless to defend himself against the forces of evil. The analytic dialogue was gradually assuming the form of a heated argument.

I cannot exactly reproduce the details of this confrontation, nor would they be particularly relevant; suffice it to say that I felt increasingly irritated by the patient's insistence that the burden of proof was on me, and even that his most absurd suspicions were worthy of credence unless disproved. I began to respond in an angry tone of voice, comparing him to his crazy mother, whom I called "Lady Asshole," as some neighbors used to do when the patient was in his latency. Finally I burst into a string of curses and expletives, called him a "shithead" so wedded to obstinacy that he would not allow anyone to save his life. I ended by yelling, "Okay, it's none of my business, so drown!"

There was a brief silence. The patient then sat up, shaking; he started to sob. When he regained control, he said that he would never be able to reciprocate for what I had just offered him. He realized that he had been arguing with me out of sheer sadism,

---

[2] Later in the treatment, I learned about the sadistic manner in which his favorite sibling had undermined the patient's reality testing by deliberately confusing him and laughing at his distress. I believe he was reexperiencing such transactions in the brother transference, displaced onto the political leader.

thereby enacting precisely the scenario he was always afraid of staging with his friends. He added that he well knew that it would have been much easier to avoid the struggle to correct his distortions and that, by allowing myself to get angry to defend the truth, I had gone beyond the strict boundaries of analytic duty. In other words, the analysand himself gained insight into the displacement of the transference, as well as the projective distortion about who was abusing whom. The acute crisis had come to an end.

I had, indeed, crossed the customary boundaries of therapeutic duty, not to mention decorum; however, I trust it is evident that I was not simply indulging in a temper tantrum—I would scarcely dare to report these events if that had been the case. My emotions were genuine enough, but they were not particularly intense until I decided to allow myself to be swept along by the unfolding transaction, as in a psychodrama. Elsewhere, I have named this manner of discourse a "dyadic enactment" (Gedo, 1988, chap. 9). It is a form of communication more basic—primitive, if you prefer—than is the text of a dialogue within a piece of theater: it involves an actual *mise-en-scène* on the analytic stage, and, through much of it, words do not carry the principal import of the interchange. In those intervals, communication is in the form of pantomime; insofar as words are used at all, they do not represent the speaker's full meaning. This was just as true of the patient's unreasonable arguments as of my curses and imprecations.

It should be noted that several years of effort to conduct this analysis along more conventional lines had preceded these events. Before they occurred, I had already had a number of experiences with this analysand of promoting insight by means of entering into such a dyadic enactment, so that I had some confidence in the method. Moreover, the patient knew perfectly well that what I might say and do in certain analytic contingencies should not be understood literally—that many of my communications were metonymic. Thus, when I called him "shithead," he did not feel insulted (although, in other circumstances, he was extremely thin-skinned!). He also knew that I always chose my words with great care, so that *this* trope was also intended to convey a precise meaning—to form an associative link with his anal sadism.[3]

---

[3] Some years later, it became evident that his obstinate withholding (of rationality) had its earliest precedents in analogous provocativeness as a small child, which was intended to force his caretaker (usually his father) to give him an enema. In telling him, at the climax of the enactment, that his conduct was none of my business, I stopped just short of repeating the childhood pattern in its entirety.

Chapter 8

CONFUSION OF TONGUES IN THE ANALYTIC SITUATION

Whenever, in small discussion groups, I have presented excerpts from my analytic work similar to the last clinical example, some colleagues have wondered how I could get away with such behavior—are patients not likely to be hurt or insulted, seduced or overstimulated, or covertly encouraged to discharge their sadism? The answer to such inquiries is that occasionally undesirable reactions of that kind do occur, just as they will occur on occasion in response to analytic interventions of any other type. The incidence of such complications in my practice has not increased since I have begun to allow myself greater freedom to employ all the resources of rhetoric in clinical work. If we recall how many analysands find the minimalist technique that often passes for psychoanalytic classicism unbearable, it is entirely likely that *skillful* use of communications employing tropes and laden with affects actually leads to fewer misadventures. There is no denying, of course, that it is much more difficult to be skillful in using a complex technique than a simpler one.

One indispensable component of the requisite skill is gradually to accustom patients to the fact that we do not intend everything we say to be taken literally, that we are likely to quote statements from the past without prior indication of their source, and—most difficult of all!—that we may communicate in a manner conveying emotion without being affectively aroused at the time. Naturally, success is also contingent on being free of unrecognized countertransference or counteridentification problems that could masquerade under the guise of this technique, or any other, for that matter.

Since I gained some experience with these methods and some skill in applying them, I have seldom had misadventures as a result of their use. I do not mean to say that misunderstandings have never occurred; what I do mean is that an analysand's inability to hear such communications as they are intended to be understood is a clinical finding of great significance. Depending on whether the miscarriage of communication is a result of a (temporary) regression or is a permanent defect—what I have elsewhere proposed to call an "apraxia" (Gedo, 1988, see esp. chaps. 12 and 13)—different remedial measures are called for. When the problem is regressive, it is usually necessary to address the etiology of the regression; if one is dealing with an apraxia, it is generally desirable to assist the patient in acquiring the missing psychological skills (see Gedo, 1988, Epilogue).

As one example of a communicative apraxia, let me cite the not infrequent defect called the lack of a sense of humor. Not only will persons who suffer from this fail to grasp the purport of jokes and witty remarks (for instance, reacting with hurt feelings when the analyst is less than fully "serious" in their presence); they will also miss any *irony* in the analyst's communications, either taking them quite literally (for an illustration, see chapter 1) or, if that does not yield any sensible meaning, confusing them with the use of sarcasm. Obviously, when one becomes aware of defect of this kind, it is incumbent on the analyst to accommodate to the analysand's limitations; any other policy would be equivalent to trying to communicate in a language unfamiliar to the patient.

In my judgment, the complication caused by the miscarriage of one's initial efforts to use a particular rhetorical device is likely to be trivial; it should not be too difficult to reach agreement that the problem is a consequence of a handicap suffered by the patient. If we then avoid stepping on these painful corns, it becomes possible to study the genesis of the psychological defect—a matter often intimately related to other aspects of the person's maladaptation. The problem is much more likely to get out of hand in those instances where certain rhetorical forms have become customary but an undetected regressive movement has occurred so that the analysand is temporarily unable to make use of his full repertory of communicative skills. Far from being internal dialogue within the mind of the analysand, such contingencies amount to a confusion of tongues.

Yet, even such an untoward event is merely grist for the analytic mill: once the acute episode of misunderstanding has been identified, it can be transcended if it is employed as an indicator of the regressive process and the focus of attention is shifted to the genesis of the latter. Subsequently, it should be feasible to correlate the shift from a more mature mode of functioning to one that is more primitive or archaic (see chapter 15) with childhood precedents. I should like to conclude this chapter by offering a highly condensed illustration of an analytic sequence of this kind (for a different account, see Gedo, 1984, pp. 133-135; for an example in which the miscommunication could not be corrected, see chapter 1, pp. xx-44).

After several years of analysis that employed affect-laden interventions on my part, a young professional man of rebellious character (already described in part in chapter 1, this volume) was reliving a father transference stemming from the oedipal period. The transference took the form of allying himself with a hostile woman who chose to depreciate him by attacking the analysis; the patient joined her in this campaign, thereby preserving the illusion that she held him in high esteem. Laboring under the misapprehension that the foregoing understanding of the situation was still valid, I responded to one flagrant instance of analytic subversion by echoing his childhood father, in a tone of exasperation, to the effect that someone was turning him against me.

To my astonishment, the patient interpreted my intervention as an utter loss of self-control on my part, developed the conviction that I was psychotic, was unable to make constructive use of the remainder of the session, and was too panicky to return the next day. He called me on the telephone, instead, and was quickly calmed by hearing my customary tone of voice. In our subsequent work, we discovered that this episode was an abrupt shift of focus to an archaic mother transference, specifically referable to a crisis in the mother–child relationship late in the second year of life. As mentioned in chapter 6, the patient at that time suffered from a lengthy bout of foul-smelling diarrhea that overtaxed the mother's resources and caused her severe exasperation. (Note that in the transference the roles were reversed: it was he who rejected me, and I articulated his childhood bewilderment about such a betrayal. His reaction, in turn, echoed his mother's propensity to be self-righteous even if that attitude could be maintained only by the construction of delusional convictions.)

The principal therapeutic gain resulting from this transaction was not the identification of a mother transference—a temporary phenomenon at this stage of a lengthy analysis. It was, rather, the revelation of the potential of alarming regressive developments, involving a loss of the consensual meaning of words and almost exclusive reliance on communication by means of the affective tones of speech. Focus on these issues proved to be essential in correcting the most severe aspect of this person's maladaptation, the almost complete dissociation between conceptual thought and affectivity. Further discussion of these fascinating matters falls outside the scope of this chapter; suffice it to say here that the "complication" created by an ill-timed intervention not intended to be understood in a literal sense actually turned out to spotlight the genesis of an important aspect of the psychopathology.

In conclusion, I wish to reiterate that our theory of technique will have to answer in greater detail the question of the optimal form of analytic intervention in various therapeutic contingencies. These considerations have until recently been relegated to that catch-all category, "the art of psychoanalysis." We need to lend them scientific status by validating their role as therapeutic tools within the learning process that we wish to create in the psychoanalytic situation.

9 Empathy, New Beginnings, and Analytic Cure

DEVELOPMENTAL ARREST AND A NEW BEGINNING

In contrast to Adler or Jung, who both created therapeutic schools that seceded from psychoanalysis, Sándor Ferenczi was the first psychoanalytic dissident, the lifelong leader of a loyal opposition (see Gedo, 1986, esp. chaps. 3 and 9). Contemporary enthusiasts for his work (e.g., Haynal, 1989) go so far as to claim that most subsequent dissidents, such as Kohut or the English "middle group" for instance, are in actuality perpetuating Ferenczi's ideas or procedures. Although any position of loyal opposition within psychoanalysis does belong in the tradition initiated by Ferenczi, in my opinion some contributors have espoused dissident positions without being directly influenced by him. His true intellectual heirs might be called the "Budapest school," although the tragic recent history of Hungary has driven many of them into exile.

By far the most prominent of these exiles was Michael Bálint, whose activities in England did have some influence on the London middle group, as Haynal recounts. Bálint never ceased his advocacy of Ferenczi's valuable contributions, particularly with regard to analytic technique. He summarized the most important of Ferenczi's emphases as follows:

> the immense therapeutic value of regression in the analytic situation, provided it is properly handled; [the] overriding importance of transference interpretations as compared with anything else that the analyst may do; the influence of the analyst's "professional hypocrisy" in the developing transference relationship and, with it, the need for absolute sincerity to the extent of the use of what is nowadays called countertransference interpretations; the dangers of driving the patient by consistently adhering to. . . objective passivity into a repetition of the original pathogenic trauma . . . [Bálint, 1967, p. 148].

In his *Clinical Diary* (Dupont, 1988), Ferenczi noted that in 1932 Bálint articulated their shared conviction that, in cases where character problems resulted from early childhood traumata, "the patient must be taken back to the blissful time before the trauma and to the corresponding period of sexual development . . ." (p. 190). In other words, Bálint's (1932) pivotal paper on "Character Analysis and New Beginning" (which was not to appear in English until 1952!) was a product of a close intellectual collaboration with Ferenczi.

As Haynal's (1989) review of the Budapest dissension made clear, Ferenczi's differences with Freud centered on a controversy about therapeutic methods. Bálint's (1967) résumé of these technical differences is entirely accurate, but it modestly leaves out of account that Ferenczi advocated his particular methods because of the conviction that reliving early traumata in an empathic setting—as he thought of it, one of forbearance, kindness, and even some indulgence—enables the analysand to resume psychological development in a healthy direction, to take advantage of a "new beginning." This is what was meant by the "proper handling" of the analytic situation.

As I have stated on several occasions (Gedo, 1967a, 1986; Bacon and Gedo, 1993), there can be no doubt that Ferenczi's technical recommendations are uniquely effective in a certain range of cases, although they appear to be superfluous in others and insufficient in still another group. On this occasion, I cannot consider the type of problem in which the techniques advocated by the "Freudian mainstream" of psychoanalysts prove to be sufficient or even optimal (but see Gedo and Goldberg, 1973; Gedo, 1993b; and Gedo and Gehrie, 1993, for discussions of this issue). I wish to focus, instead, on differentiating analysands who, after reliving early traumata in the therapeutic context, do experience a fruitful new beginning in a seemingly automatic manner from those who require additional technical measures to be able to leave behind the repetition of their unsatisfactory past.

As an excellent illustration of the efficacy of Ferenczi's technical approach, let me cite a case published by another exile from Budapest, E. Ludowyk-Gyömröi (1963). The late adolescent she analyzed had been rescued from the concentration camp at Auschwitz around the age of four. The child was then raised in England in a children's home devoted to the care of such young survivors. She requested treatment at the age of 17 because she realized that she did not have a stable identity but was successively impersonating a series of other people. Observers at the children's home confirmed that she tended to shift abruptly from identification with one person to identification with another. She clung tenaciously to the woman in charge of the home and to a year-older sister who had been with her through all her experiences.

When, in 1964, Ludowyk-Gyömröi presented this case in Chicago, she made clear something left out of her written account: that she had used, in an intuitive and innovative manner, whatever intervention she thought would be helpful, (see also Gedo, 1967b). As she put it in her paper, she tried to "adapt analytic technique to the task of treating a person whose object relations did not proceed beyond the identifications of early infancy." She assumed that the patient had been separated from her mother during the second year of her life and that this trauma had reactivated a need for symbiosis that could not be transcended until these issues were replicated in analysis. Gradually, intervals between analytic sessions took on the significance of traumatic object loss—without recovery of memories of separation from the mother or those of the subsequent horrors of the camp. Nonetheless, the patient experienced a new beginning in learning to readjust from the realities of Auschwitz to those of England in peacetime. The analyst's ways were gradually "internalized, and slowly [the patient] started to behave in the way she thought was demanded of her even when she was unobserved." The analysis was terminated when she was able to form an age-appropriate love relationship.

In my judgment, Ludowyk-Gyömröi's case was one of massive but essentially uncomplicated developmental arrest, caused primarily by object loss. The only structuralization that had to be undone through analytic work was the patient's acceptance of the attitudes of the concentration camp guards who had kept her alive as an infrahuman pet. Her consequent self-contempt and idealization of her oppressors were overcome through acceptance of the analyst's humane attitudes.

Because the foregoing report summarizes a relatively simple case, it resembles accounts of the psychotherapy of children. Even Anna Freud (1965) conceded that in certain child analyses, on the basis of a "new and different emotional experience," there may be developmental progress to age-appropriate levels; she, however, was unwilling to grant that developmental arrests can be corrected after a lapse of time beyond some "critical period." Winnicott (1965b) also stressed that "unhitching a developmental catch" is effective in the therapy of children because "environmental influences [then] resume their function of facilitating the process of maturation" (p. 81).

My own clinical experience has led me to conclude that we may count on the resumption of maturation as a result of a new beginning much more frequently in children and adolescents than in persons who have reached adulthood; but that, as Ludowyk-Gyömröi's case report demonstrates, Anna Freud was incorrect in assuming that, after the passage of a critical period, arrested development cannot be started up by favorable experiences. Spontaneous improvements in adaptation in persons who have not engaged in any therapy (in a formal sense) are probably attributable to the undoing of developmental arrests by such fortunate life experiences (see also Gedo, 1981a, chap. 2). Hartmann and Loewenstein (1962) made this point when they wrote, "Powerful identifications as they sometimes are made even by adult persons can produce . . . [significant] changes in individuals whose...superego has remained more open to change than is commonly the case" (p. 177).

Insofar as a "new beginning" is feasible because the overall problem is one of developmental arrest, not only is the traditional technique of psychoanalysis unsuitable to initiate the resumption of progress, frequently; if the therapeutic atmosphere advocated by Ferenczi is established, it is not even necessary to use the external parameters of an analytic situation. To illustrate the relative ease of promoting maturation in such cases, I can cite the treatment of a 30-year-old college professor who originally consulted me because of marital problems and some vocational inhibition. Because of his uncertain motivation for treatment, this man started psychotherapy on a once-a-week basis; later, he attended twice a week. For about a year, he talked about his wife's difficulties, and he absorbed my comments about how I might go about living with a spouse who was so impaired. Gradually, he realized that he had been unnecessarily indulgent with his wife because, in other circumstances, it was he who felt a need to be indulged.

As a result of this insight, the patient changed his behavior at home; because his wife was enraged by this change, he later decided that he had to get a divorce. With profound emotion, he realized that he had been denying his own emotional needs, both at home and in the therapy with me—that he had been enacting a fantasy of invulnerability and grandiose power. These attitudes had supervened when his beloved nursemaid left him when he was six years old, to get married. He had managed to deny that her choice had been a matter of preference and attributed it instead to his parents' decision to leave their native land to escape racial persecution.

As these matters unfolded in treatment, the patient overcame his scholarly inhibition: he no longer needed to feel like an indulged *Wunderkind*, and he soon proceeded to terminate his stultifying marriage. He experienced feelings of loss and sadness in giving up the therapeutic relationship, a repetition of the loneliness he had felt as a child after losing the nursemaid and opting for premature independence. This time, he did not have to cope with these feelings through disavowal. In subsequent years, I occasionally heard from him—about his remarriage and his considerable vocational success.

CHARACTEROLOGICAL PROBLEMS AND REPETITION

In contrast to the ease with which psychotherapeutic success was achieved in the foregoing case of developmental arrest, whenever analysands present themselves with disturbances of character, therapeutic regression and the reliving of early traumata seldom eventuate in a fresh start of this happy sort. In most instances, what we encounter instead is repetition within the transference of the characterological difficulties within which the traumatic experiences were embedded. To provide a schematic example: A young woman who presented herself for analysis with a syndrome generally described as "borderline" soon showed herself to be suffering from a chronic traumatic neurosis, with frequent episodes during her sessions of dissociation, panic attacks, and even *grande hystérie*. It took more than a year of analytic work to clarify that these were sequelae of long-lasting sexual molestation in childhood, starting between the ages of four and five. The "holding environment" of analysis (Winnicott, 1960) was experienced as the continuation of the childhood seduction, which she had never experienced as abusive despite its traumatic consequences. (The reader will recognize that I have already given excerpts from this analytic encounter in previous chapters.)

As the analytic work proceeded, the patient gradually mastered her vulnerability to pleasurable stimuli, but her overall clinical state was, if anything, less satisfactory than before: the consequences of further therapeutic regression revealed that her life before the sexual traumatization had been far from blissful. Although this aspect of her experience had been covered over by a façade of competence (or temporarily rendered irrelevant by seeking stimulation despite the risk of traumatization), her basic mood was one of loneliness and desperation. For a considerable period there appeared to be a real risk of suicide. (This was the person I have already described who threatened suicide unless I agreed to have an affair with her.) We did discover that this state originally supervened when she was about two and a half years old, after the departure of a benign and competent *Kinderfrau* who had been her primary caretaker. Both parents were busy professional people, and the little girl was left with various baby-sitters, including older siblings, one of whom was extremely hostile and occasionally abusive.

One might say, of course, that Ferenczi's prescription calls for the recovery of the happy state before the analysand's loss of her original holding environment. However, analytic work around her reactions to interruptions of our schedule and resumptions of regular sessions provided numerous opportunities for her to reexperience the emotional ambience of her early childhood, before the departure of her nursemaid. The problem of being unable to transcend object loss without lapsing into suicidal despair could not be overcome by means of reconstruction of its precedents in the past. Each time she made a new beginning, she ran into the same problem that had defeated her as a child: when the primary caretaker became unavailable, she felt utterly worthless. Systematic interpretation of the transference significance of this reaction, in terms of her mother's preference for a career over devoting herself to her child, did not suffice to mitigate the problem. In the vocabulary suggested by Kohut (1971), a "merger transference" had supervened and persisted despite the analysand's clear understanding of its significance.

In my experience, this kind of therapeutic impasse frequently follows a chance for a new beginning. To overcome the stalemate, further interventions are required, but there are no clear guidelines in the literature indicating how to proceed in such circumstances. I believe the not infrequent occurrence of seemingly interminable analyses that maintain patients in some kind of adaptive equilibrium is accounted for, at least in some measure, by the insufficiency of relying, as Ferenczi did, on the maturational impetus inherent in human biology. In this connection, it is worth noting that Kohut (1984), in his last statements about the matter of analytic cures, took the position that permanent reliance on the availability of need-satisfying caretakers (what he called selfobjects) is not, in itself, an indication of maladaptation. In my judgment, this was an attempt to overcome stalemate by arbitrarily proclaiming victory. Renik (1992), by contrast, calls contingencies of this kind the employment of the analyst as a fetish. His suggested remedy, that of an enforced time limit for termination, is a counsel of despair and, in terms of the traditional theory of technique, an abandonment of analytic methods.

Now that Ferenczi's *Clinical Diary* (Dupont, 1988) is available, we can see that the new beginnings he catalyzed in his analysands often did not proceed to happy endings either. At this juncture, Ferenczi appears to have developed the ambition to become a model of therapeutic goodness, so that he tried to explain his analytic stalemates on the ground of his own shortcomings as an analyst, accusing himself of sadistic (and, implicitly, narcissistic) abuse of his patients. His experiments with "mutual analysis" were efforts to overcome such putative countertransference problems through humility. As I read these accounts, Ferenczi was actually trapped in "counteridentification" with a number of patients who made unreasonable demands on him. (From my vantage point, this is one of the principal pitfalls of the analytic technique recommended by most present-day self psychologists as well.)

Experienced clinicians, however, are unlikely suddenly to develop such a problem without first having accepted certain technical constraints dictated by their theoretical assumptions. Ferenczi (and many self psychologists) assumed that empathy is sufficient by itself to initiate a new beginning that will achieve satisfactory developmental progress, provided the analyst does not repeat the pathogenic behaviors of the original caretakers. (This concept was later codified as "corrective emotional experience" by Alexander [Alexander and French, 1946]–although before his emigration from Berlin Alexander had been an opponent of Ferenczi.) On this basis, if progress does not occur, one can only conclude that the analyst's countertransference is to blame.

I do not mean to imply that analysts can afford to ignore their countertransference potentials. These possibilities are particularly significant when we are struggling with problems of deep regression, when analysands' boundaries between subject and object are uncertain. These are the circumstances that Melanie Klein (1952) succeeded in clarifying through her concept of "projective identification." (For further discussion of these issues, see chapter 11, this volume.) Had he understood this issue, Ferenczi would have been able to formulate transference interpretations on the basis of the self-accusations his analysands provoked in him. In my experience, however, in many instances even our ability to illuminate early childhood by interpreting that analysands try to make us feel as their caretakers made them feel in the past has not proved to be sufficient to promote emotional growth: the obstacle that must be overcome often does not lie in the realm of object relations.

Chapter 9

INTRACTABLE PATHOLOGY AND PROBLEMS OF COMMUNICATION

In my own practice, I have most frequently found the cause of such an inability to grow to be covert adherence (often in a split-off nucleus of mental function) to magical thinking. This circumstance is most likely to occur if the person was raised in a milieu that unquestioningly believed that such a cognitive schema is applicable to matters of daily life. In such cases, magical thinking is not a matter of regression to the primary process; it is characteristic of the person's secondary-process mentation (see Rapaport, 1951). In Western societies, children are rarely allowed to live undisturbed in such a magic-filled world; this is why their continued adherence to these exciting and wish-fulfilling beliefs is likely to be disavowed or repressed or both. The persistence of covert magical thinking will, by itself, make it impossible to master later developmental challenges such as the relinquishment of grandiose illusions or the renunciation of oedipal wishes.

Clinical contingencies of this kind are extraordinarily difficult to overcome. In one instance, already discussed in chapter 1, I had failed to alter such a state of affairs after ten years of analysis—over 2,000 sessions!—and I was by no means the first analyst to treat this person. She was the child of a mother who displayed overtly delusional thinking and a father who seldom contradicted his tyrannical spouse. When she was three, her mother gave birth to twins, a circumstance that filled the little girl with murderous jealousy. Shortly thereafter, one of the babies was horribly injured through the mother's negligence; the patient was an eyewitness to this drama. No later experience, including her countless years of analysis, could shake her conviction about the destructive power of her wishes—or about her ability to use magic in other ways. Her conscious attitudes could not have been more reasonable, and interpretation of the defenses whereby she fended off her delusional ideas did not have any effect. After a decade of discouraging effort, this persistent "psychotic core" (Winnicott, 1952) remained unaltered. It was enacted in the transference through continuing disregard of the ground rules of an analytic procedure. When I began to express pessimism about my ability to help her to change, this woman made a heroic effort to alter her behavior on the stage of everyday life and set a termination date for her analysis.

That the improvement of her day-to-day adaptation was caused by a reinforcement of her defenses against her irrationalities was revealed a couple of years after termination, when (as I have already recounted) I received a letter from her filled with rageful accusations based on a paranoid misconstruction of certain past statements of mine. She reported feeling disorganized and disillusioned in what she now characterized as her former belief in *my* magical powers. And I had worked so hard to demonstrate that I did not have any! As I have reported elsewhere (Gedo, 1981a, chap. 3; see also 1984, chap. 7; 1991a, chap. 10), most of my analytic failures have involved attempts to work with people who were similarly unable to abandon delusional thinking. (The foregoing case is again discussed, at greater length, in chapter 11.)

At the same time, it should be emphasized that cognitive impairment of this kind is by no means the sole determinant of analytic impasse within a merger transference. To illustrate just one additional possibility, let me return to the case of the analysand behind whose chronic traumatic neurosis we found an inability to transcend a need for symbiosis without lapsing into suicidal despair. Her failure to master this problem turned out to be a function of a defective sense of reality about her subjectivity. There was no defect in this person's capacity to test reality; it was a pervasive doubt about the legitimacy or' appropriateness of her own reactions to interpersonal transactions that made it impossible for her to master disappointments without a collapse in self-esteem. *This* cognitive defect came about, in part, because her family of origin did not use a consensually reliable, shared language, so that the child was unable to connect her own emotions with any system of symbols through which she could have thought *about* them. (For details about this essential capacity, see Bucci, 1993.) A second determinant of the defect was the effort of the child's older sister to force her to share the latter's psychotic perceptions of various interpersonal situations. In this sense, the "blissful" time before severe traumata were inflicted on this person was an era when she did not have enough linguistic capacity to consolidate a sense of confidence about her own emotions.

In this instance, we succeeded in the course of some 1,200 analytic sessions in establishing a "shared language" (see chapter 6) about human subjectivity, and this enabled the analysand to experience conscious rage about mistreatment, instead of falling into bewildered desperation. Thus the repair of a deficiency in psychological skills was the prerequisite for transcending her need for a symbiotic adaptation. In order to teach this woman correctly to identify her emotions—and to trust them as appropriate signals of what was impinging on her—it was not sufficient to name her affects, although this was frequently done and was certainly one essential component of success. It was also necessary to allow her to exercise the power to provoke various emotions in me and, on my part, candidly to name them. It is in this sense, of being *moved* by the patient, that I understand Ferenczi's injunction to abandon the customary "professional hypocrisy" of the analyst who pretends to be an uninvolved technician. Those of us who truly remain uninvolved should not attempt to work with patients with communicative deficits.

We have barely begun to examine the kinds of deficits in psychological skills—conditions I have proposed to call "apraxic" (Gedo, 1988, chap. 12)—that cause archaic transference repetitions *not* to lead to developmental progress, even following accurate interpretation. In my experience, they may involve tension regulation, planning, organizing priorities, communication skills, and cognitive issues of the kind I have illustrated in this chapter, and so on. This list cannot pretend to be exhaustive, nor is this the place to attempt to extend it. It may be more useful to end this discussion by considering what makes particular deficits irreparable in certain instances although the very same apraxia may be overcome through relatively simple measures in seemingly comparable cases.

I believe the answer to this conundrum is to be found in the realm Freud (1920) conceptualized under the rubric of the "repetition compulsion." As I have discussed elsewhere (most recently in Gedo, 1991a, b), the phenomena contained within this category stem from the earliest patterns of subjective experience (mostly sensory and affective) that constitute the bedrock of the individual's primary identity—what I call "self-organization." These patterns cannot be abandoned without severe disorganization (as an illustration, witness the testimony of the analysand who became disillusioned following termination, after having reorganized herself around the delusion of my magical powers). Whether or not any bit of maladaptive behavior can be given up depends on how closely it is tied to the core of the individual's identity.[1]

---

[1] The most dramatic illustration of such repetitive phenomena was provided by Valenstein (1973), that of an "attachment to painful feelings." As he made clear, what analysts have classified as "negative therapeutic reactions" are best understood as compulsive repetitions of the foregoing kind. If the person is not in treatment, such phenomena are usually explained as manifestations of masochism. In my judgment, any inability to alter maladaptive behavior patterns must be caused by the compulsion to

From this perspective, the essential disagreement between Freud and Ferenczi—and their respective heirs and followers—is not merely one of clinical methods, as Haynal (1989) believes. Behind these procedural choices are fundamental differences in assumptions about human plasticity. Although it would be an exaggeration to call Freud an outright pessimist, he certainly maintained great reserve about the possibility of therapeutic change. Ferenczi, on the other hand, expressed his boundless optimism through the promise of the "new beginning."

---

repeat established activities, whatever their consequences may be. (Moraitis [1988, 1991] has made the same point from a different perspective by explaining avoidances on the basis of fears of novelty—what he calls "the unknown.") In chapter 12, I summarize an analysis in the course of which a pattern of negativism became manifest in the transference; when I interfered with this enactment by refusing to play a complementary role, a serious decompensation supervened.

10 More on the Affectivity of the Analyst

THE PRAGMATICS OF EMPATHY

For a generation at the very least, there has been no disagreement within psychoanalysis about the essential role of empathy in making possible the accomplishment of the clinical goals of its procedures (see Kohut, 1959; Stone, 1961, 1981; Schwaber, 1981; Gedo, 1981a, chap. 6; Gehrie, 1993). We also have consensus about defining empathy as a mode of observation based on a trial identification with the person observed, an attempt predicated on the common human characteristics of the participants. It is not uncommon, however, to encounter statements in the literature equating empathy with the acceptance, without demurral, of the subjective viewpoint of the analysand (see Kohut, 1984, p. 174; also Schwaber, 1983); self psychologists, in particular, tend to look upon any analytic intervention that causes the analysand pain or humiliation as "unempathic." Hence, it is by no means obvious how, in practice, analysts should conduct themselves "empathically." Is it sufficient to devise interventions informed by the results of empathic observation? Should the analyst, in addition, affirm the legitimacy of the analysand's subjectivity or strive to avoid injuries to the latter's self-esteem? Is it desirable, by communicating one's empathy, to make certain that the analysand feels the "healing power" so often attributed to its operation?

In my clinical experience, most analysands regard the ordinary routines of psychoanalysis as empathic to a degree unprecedented in their past: the nonjudgmental effort to discern their motivations is generally appreciated as true acceptance. Whenever this is an analysand's reaction to treatment, any doubts we may express about the rationality, wisdom, or accuracy of his or her subjectivity is easily accommodated as helpful and potentially illuminating. These are the conditions Zetzel (1965) called a therapeutic alliance, Winnicott (1954) and later Modell (1976) named a "holding environment," and

Kohut (1977) regarded as the establishment of a "selfobject transference" of the idealizing kind (see also Gedo, 1975).[1]

The questions I have posed about how to be effectively empathic become relevant with those analysands who develop an archaic transference (Gedo, 1977; Gedo and Gehrie, 1993; Gehrie, 1993; Gunther, 1984) wherein the analyst is experienced as the reincarnation of a traumatically unempathic caretaker of early childhood. In such circumstances, our attempts to make (even accurate) transference interpretations are likely to be misconstrued as denials of responsibility that only prove our guilt, and any assertion that the patient is distorting reality will only lead to angry rebuttals. Hence, these contingencies are necessarily to be dealt with by starting with the analysand's subjective reaction as a given, to be taken for granted, and then exploring the analytic transactions that precipitated it, as Schwaber (1983) advocates doing. In Kohut's (1984) terms, we have to investigate why the idealizing transference has failed to endure (or, in some extreme circumstances, even to be established).

In some cases, even the foregoing policy of caution, tact, and "empathic responsiveness" (Ornstein and Ornstein, 1990) is very difficult to carry out. Gehrie (1993) reports on a patient, Ms. B, who responded to such efforts on his part with the paranoid outburst, "You're lying, you asshole" (p. 1095). In a case conference he and I led jointly, a candidate presented an analysis (Gedo and Gehrie, 1993, chap. 5) that rapidly evolved into demands that she concur with some opinion of the patient, although she believed it was absurd. The analyst felt that she was being driven "crazy" but eventually allowed herself to be browbeaten into insincere compliance with the patient's demand. But the analysand could not allow a agreement on

---

[1] Although it is not centrally relevant to the topic of this chapter, it may be well to note here that a fad has recently developed disclaiming that analysts have any valid expertise in assessing rationality or the distorting effects of the analysand's subjectivity. This intellectual fashion (congruent with the deconstructionist epistemology imported from France as well as with feminist and Marxist critiques of the establishment) is now called the "intersubjective" viewpoint (see Stolorow and Atwood, 1992). Although the analyst's own subjectivity may, of course, interfere with valid assessments of data, this caveat does not imply that we must refrain from making judgments, as close to objectivity as possible, about a wide range of an analysand's adaptive choices. Like those of other professionals, our judgments cannot be (and need not be!) flawless, but our diagnoses of pathological behavior should be as reliable as those of radiologists or pathologists or other experts about various aspects of human biology. I shall have more to say on this subject in chapter 11.

this basis either—later in treatment, it became clear that she was literally traumatized by the pleasure of such acceptance. The analyst's "reluctant compliance" (Kohut, 1971) was immediately followed by the patient's abandonment of the position formerly so uncompromisingly insisted on. It simply is not feasible to sidestep an active negative transference by being "empathic enough."

To illustrate, Gehrie's (1993) patient (Ms. B) initially had at her disposal only two alternative modes of selforganization: either she felt helplessly controlled within an archaic mother transference, or (if she mastered this through progress to a more mature mode along the developmental axis) she achieved command of the situation in an erotic father transference in which she felt no taboo about incest. As long as the analyst resisted her sexual demands, she could only reproach him for pushing her back into the unbearable frustration of the unhappy transactions with her mother—as she put it, she could not stand the insistence of any caretaker on an agenda she did not welcome. (She was one of the passionate creatures who, according to an old adage, understand only the logic of soup, with dumplings for arguments . . .) To put this another way, this analysand declared that for her empathy was not enough; the analyst had to comply with her openly illicit agenda, as she had been forced to submit to that of her father. And the analyst was not to offer her the unsatisfactory substitute of mere words...

Gehrie demonstrates convincingly that in such a situation there is no way to avoid rekindling the traumatic frustrations of the past. From a technical perspective, archaic material encoded in a presymbolic manner (see Makari and Shapiro, 1993) cannot be clarified by following Schwaber's (1983) recommendation to stick to the analysand's subjectivity. Hence, in these circumstances, it is no more empathic to talk about the sources of the patient's demands than it is to focus on the attempted reversal of the victimization inflicted on her in the past. At these levels of regression, all words are ineffectual—a point Gehrie's analysand was trying to communicate by insisting on a wordless (sexual) transaction. Consequently, appropriate empathy should lead the analyst to intervene in some legitimate manner that does not rely principally on word meanings. Because Gehrie's (1993) account does not specify how the impasse was overcome, let me illustrate the point by citing a case of my own.

My analysand was a highly successful businessman in late middle age whose adaptive difficulties (mostly in the sphere of human relationships) resulted from covert adherence to magical thinking, in identification with his quasi-psychotic mother. Although he disavowed his belief in his own magic, he never acted in disregard of this sense of omnipotence, no matter what conclusions we reached in the analysis; the magical system was logic-proof and impervious to words—just as his mother had been when he was a child. I do not mean that the patient could not follow my statements: he knew quite well what I meant when I told him that dealing with him was like barking at the moon. (He let me bark and bark . . .) But when I began to respond to his obstinacy by imitating a dog that howls in distress, he finally got the point that he was now treating me as he had been treated as a small child. He started to plead that he was *afraid* to violate the precepts of the magical system (i.e., to defy certain superstitions), but he did not persist too long in using this alibi after I pointed out, with obvious sarcasm, that his confidence in his omniscience was worthy of a Professor of Psychiatry. In my judgment, my tactics proved to be effective, while interpretations encoded in secondary-process terms had gone unheeded, because, when the relevant developmental level was in focus, this person could process only messages primarily conveyed through affects.

The point I am trying to make through the foregoing clinical vignettes is that the analyst's responses, when they are guided by true and accurate empathy, are not necessarily "nice," warm, or gentle. (If we can make the point we need to make in a kindly way, let us by all means satisfy all concerned with an impeccable bedside manner. Unfortunately, we cannot anesthetize our analysands when the necessities of treatment prove to be painful for them.) In fact, there are clinical contingencies in which empathic responsiveness calls on the analyst to set limits firmly, to warn of dangers sharply, to oppose abuses indignantly. The emphasis in this statement should be put on the adverbs: limits can only be set *firmly*, warnings must be issued *sharply*, and (if we wish to be effective) we have to oppose abuses indignantly.

THE QUESTION OF EXTERNAL ASSISTANCE

Numerous contributors (Winnicott, 1965a; Modell, 1976, 1979; Kohut, 1977; Gedo, 1979; Stone, 1981; Gehrie, 1993) have asserted that measures "beyond interpretation" may have to be applied in certain cases as "preconditions for insight" (Blum, 1981). All these authors agree that, among the measures necessary to make analyzability possible, "empathy" is one of the most important. Only Stone (1961) acknowledged, however, that "in certain special contingencies" the analyst may have to provide "some urgently important advice" (p. 31). In *Beyond Interpretation* (Gedo, 1979), I offered an illustration of such a contingency (chap. 5): a prospective analysand needed guidance about an acceptable solution for the dilemma of suitable arrangements to finance his analysis. The issues of intrapsychic conflict that underlay his paralysis could be discerned only after considerable analytic work. Without external assistance, this person could not have permitted himself to borrow the funds he needed to salvage his life.

Although the potential need for such "parameters" (Eissler, 1953) is now widely conceded, few authors agree with my contention that, when patients are regressed enough to require such guidance, their ability to communicate in the routine manner of psychoanalytic discourse is also likely to be impaired.

Effective interventions in the "operatic" style I advocate occasionally crop up in the literature, however, without comment about their unorthodox nature. For instance, Kohut (1984, p. 74) reported that, when an analysand engaged in dangerous driving and provocativeness with the police on his way to a session, his own response was to tell the man that he was behaving *idiotically*. Exactly.

In my work as a supervisor of candidates and a consultant to colleagues puzzled by difficult analytic problems, I have frequently found that analysts are very reluctant to intervene in a forceful manner, either because they believe such behavior to contravene the *desideratum* of technical "neutrality" or because they fear to injure their patients in the process of making such "unempathic" responses. Both rationalizations are wide of the mark. I can best illustrate this point by citing a case from the seminar I conducted in collaboration with Gehrie (Gedo and Gehrie, 1993, chap. 3): when a suicidal patient decided not to seek potentially life-saving treatment for a metastatic carcinoma, the analyst insisted that she *must* do so—that he would not allow her to destroy herself through an act of omission. He shamefacedly told the seminar, however, that in doing this he had stepped out of his analytic role. Of course, he was incorrect in his belief that the technical principle of neutrality compels analysts to act indifferent about matters of life and death.

THE COMMUNICATION OF EMPATHY

At least, in the foregoing instance, nobody could accuse the analyst of any lack of empathy. In my experience, many colleagues are unable to protect themselves from being abused (not merely verbally, but even through real enactments), and this countertransference difficulty is often justified on the ground that the archaic personalities who engage in such behaviors are too fragile to tolerate the condemnation implicit in any effort to stop the abuse. The most glaring instance of this kind I have encountered was that of a supervisee who felt raped by her male patient, who "forced her" to initiate an analysis before she had agreed to work with him. This pattern of sadistic control over their transactions continued, although I repeatedly advised the candidate to put a stop to it by setting clear limits. The analyst insisted that such a course would be "unanalytic"— she felt that the only legitimate technique she could use was to find a valid interpretation of the motives for the patient's sadism that would dissolve this pattern of enactment. The impasse continued for a number of months, with more and more distress for the candidate. She finally blurted out that she could hardly expect her patient to stop his cruel behavior as long as her own analyst allowed her to indulge in similar conduct.

Although sadomasochistic transactions of this kind seem to be rather common, they are by no means the only type of dyadic enactment (Gedo, 1988, chap. 9) encountered in practice. Even in the case I have cited, there was an obvious sexual undercurrent; in many others, the erotic component is so much in the forefront that it is not immediately obvious that the analysand is being sadistic in attempting to exercise sexual power in the analytic situation. The fact that the patient is being abusive may be disguised by verbal propaganda implying that it is the analyst's lack of responsiveness that is cruel (see Gehrie, 1993, case of Ms. B). Attractive young female patients may act grossly seductive (in posture, gesture, dress, or the recounting of sexual exploits in pornographic detail), especially with male analysts. (Male analysands undoubtedly do the same with female analysts, although I imagine the seductiveness would take different forms.) In sum, the number of ways in which patients may persevere in provocative behavior, despite having been told about their motives for doing so, is almost infinite.

Theoretical understanding of clinical developments of this kind has been facilitated by Melanie Klein's (1952) concept of projective identification. I think, however, it is even clearer to look upon them as consequences of regression to a mode of organization wherein memory is focused on the subjective component of events. When these infantile transactions are relived within the transference, what is essential for reenactment is to reproduce the original feeling state— the assignment of specific roles to each participant depends on the ability and willingness of the analyst to comply with the requirements of the analysand's scenario, as Klein also postulated. Analysts are very seldom willing to play the villain of the piece, so that usually the drama can take place only if they become its victims instead. It is widely understood that analytic progress is contingent on conveying insight about the meaning of such enactments to the patient, but this may be extremely difficult to accomplish, as illustrated by Gehrie's (1993) analysand, Ms. B, because at these levels of regression verbal messages are poorly attended to.

To return to the question of the varieties of enactment in the analytic situation that require the setting of limits, perhaps the most insidious is the one wherein the analyst becomes persuaded that the patient is so fragile that he or she must be handled with kid gloves. Such a development may occur as a result of projective identification (the analyst having been assigned the role of a caretaker unable to resist unreasonable demands), but very often the analysand's communication of the irrational therapeutic prescription is made quite explicitly, generally with considerable heat. In analytic communities strongly influenced by self psychology (or the belief that a benign object relationship can provide analysands with "a new beginning" [Bálint, 1932]), it has been widely accepted that the analyst has no choice but to comply with such demands. Even the attempt to question whether such compliance with a prohibition against stating unpleasant truths is really necessary is often regarded as "unempathic."

In circumstances of this kind, analytic empathy is no longer regarded as a channel of data collection—in fact, the very effort to collect data has been abandoned, under the slogan that it is unempathic. Instead of empathically determining what the analysand actually needs at the moment, the analyst has become persuaded that the most urgent therapeutic task is to demonstrate overtly that the treatment is being carried out in an "empathic ambience" (Wolf, 1976). In my view, such a surrender of our analytic functions does not constitute the exercise of true empathy; rather, it is the transmission of the highly dubious claim that the analyst is kind, gentle, and warm.

I do not mean to imply that analytic patients are invariably able to make use of unpleasant truths; those who do not register messages carrying such information and those who, upon registering them, become traumatized or suffer further regression have to be approached in a manner that avoids creating such an impasse. In my experience, however, contingencies of that kind are extremely infrequent; it is almost always possible to reach agreement that the analysand's passionate demand not be "criticized" (or supported by some attitude that is irrational in an adult context) is in itself a highly significant analytic finding—a repetition of a patterned transaction from the infantile past. It is true that, on the way to this insight, a great deal of primitive hostility may be unleashed, and it is imperative that the analyst be able to contain such a storm without retaliation, avoidance, or giving evidence of having been damaged in the process.

A courageous colleague (Vida, 1993) has reported on a failed attempt to analyze someone whose previous analyst had unexpectedly died in midtreatment. The second analyst implicitly blamed herself for having been unable to provide an analytic ambience that could hold this patient, so that he became increasingly anxious and broke off the treatment. Although there were hints that the analysand was most concerned about magically destroying her (as he apparently thought he had destroyed the first analyst), it did not occur to the second analyst that an appropriate holding environment for such a person had to be firm and rational, rather than warm and giving.

To recapitulate, it is necessary sooner or later to stop patients from tyrannically dictating what must (or must not) occur in the analytic situation. The sooner we succeed in setting such limits, the better—and the most direct way to interfere with such an enactment is to warn the analysand emphatically that compliance with these demands would be extremely dangerous. For instance, I have found it highly effective in such circumstances to say, with as much passion and conviction as the analysand used in making the demand, "Goddam it! You don't know the first thing about it! You are going to cut your own throat!" At a minimum, patients have always given me credit, after just such an intervention, for having their best interests at heart. I believe that it is such opposition to a patient's self-destructive infantilism that constitutes true empathy with the person's desire to mature emotionally.

Conversely, to support the alleged necessity of infantile solutions does not constitute constructive "empathic responsiveness"; on the contrary, it is the arbitrary assertion of the depreciating falsehood that one's patient is nothing but a specimen of psychopathology. A case presented in my seminar on clinical impasse (Gedo and Gehrie, 1993, chap. 4) serves as a cautionary tale in this regard: A young woman began her analysis with a temper tantrum about the candidate's statement that missing analytic sessions because of other commitments would not lead to optimal results. That the patient stormed out of the office in a rage, accusing the analyst of wishing to stifle her vocational ambitions, was never alluded to by either participant, as if the topic were too hot to handle.

Toward the end of the first year of treatment, the analyst allowed her patient to intrude on her family's celebration of Thanksgiving by *returning* a phone call from that setting. This transaction was not discussed either, until years later, when the analysand happened to read the obituary of the analyst's father. In that context, she was once more enraged because the obituary discredited a secret fantasy about the analyst's family circumstances she had harbored since her Thanksgiving intrusion.[2] She embarked on a campaign of sadistic verbal abuse and uncontrolled intrusiveness within the consulting room to which the candidate was unable to make any response. After some weeks of this stalemate, the patient left treatment—with the illusion, temporarily shared by the analyst, that a "termination" had been reached. A couple of years later, the patient returned for assistance because she was back in the state that had led her to seek help in the first place.

I believe this case report demonstrates that we are being neither kind nor empathic when we treat people as too fragile to tolerate confrontation with their delinquencies, irrationalities, or destructiveness. It should be noted, however, that some members of the seminar who were committed to the viewpoint of self psychology insisted that the problem with the conduct of the analysis was that the candidate had shown insufficient empathic responsiveness, because she once responded to a phone call at 2 AM by promising to discuss what the patient wanted to tell her during the session scheduled for the next morning.

I can only say in reply that I have never received emergency phone calls from patients past my bedtime, and I have never had to tell anyone (not even schizophrenics) that these were my ground rules. I believe my attitude and bearing make it self-evident without words that I will not tolerate such abuse—or any other kind. Hence I am inclined to believe that putting up with mistreatment is very likely to be a reaction formation to the analyst's sadism. (For

---

[2] Although it is not strictly relevant to my thesis, it is very instructive to consider that the analysand's secret fantasy was that the analyst had overcome family opposition to succeed in her profession—that, as the presenter put it in the seminar, she was "a little girl from Little Rock," one who made it on Broadway. The obituary revealed that the analyst's father had been an eminent physician. In summary, almost the entire treatment consisted of an attempted identification with a fictive being, a fragile development that was entirely disrupted by the revelation that it lacked any factual basis.

introspective insight into such a countertransference problem, see Ferenczi's *Clinical Diary* [Dupont, 1988].)

Contrary to the arbitrary assumption that analysands cannot tolerate the setting of limits on their sadism or destructiveness, I have found that many patients actually *welcome* external controls to help them stop such enactments. Most people who fall into misbehaviors damaging to others are actually aware of their destructiveness and judge themselves severely as a consequence (either through guilt or shame). For example, one patient presented to me in consultation had interrupted an earlier attempt at analysis and sought out a different analyst explicitly with the hope that, unlike the first analyst, the second would be able "not to let [him] get away with anything." In practice, this proved to be difficult, for the analysand kept testing the analyst's resolution to maintain a stable framework of ground rules, but there was never any question of humiliation or trauma when the patient was confronted with the requirements of a workable treatment. (See also Gedo, 1979, p. 125, n. 4.)

Some years ago, I published a more detailed description of such a transaction (Gedo, 1981a, chap. 6, case 14). The patient, who was a pious and guilt-ridden religious fanatic, gradually developed in the analytic setting a pattern of sadistic provocativeness, consisting mostly of deliberately misconstruing what I was telling her, although she generally understood my communications without trouble. I shared with her my conviction that her provocativeness was almost never sparked by me and that it was a deeply meaningful pattern of behavior, although for the time being I found it incomprehensible. It took time for her to stop the pattern of misconstruing what I meant, but she did so as soon as I showed her that I was on the verge of getting angry. Her associations then revealed that, as a child, she had been the victim of similar sadistic teasing by her psychotic father—and that his assaults had also been incomprehensible, because they were seemingly unprovoked. The patient was very grateful that I had managed to stop her sadistic behavior, because she felt extremely guilty about her "wickedness" while she tried to torture me. Thus, she was greatly relieved to *shed* her identification with her wicked parent.

THE AVOIDANCE OF TRAUMA
THROUGH APPROPRIATE DISCOURSE

Perhaps I have now elaborated at sufficient length the point that empathic interventions may well have to create temporary unpleasantness for analysands and can now turn to a different, though related, matter. Empathy may require the analyst to refrain from interventions that produce *pleasant* reactions. We may have to avoid these not for the sake of a theoretical ideal of "neutrality," but because many patients become overstimulated by too much kindness, warmth, or intimacy. I have already cited the case (from Gedo and Gehrie, 1993, chap. 5) of one person who always made certain that she and her analyst would not reach agreement because she was (rightly) afraid that such harmony would traumatize her. A similar dilemma was recently described to me in a private seminar. In that instance, the analysand was unable to forestall the pleasurable effects she felt when the analyst showed that he understood her accurately, and she was so overstimulated by these transactions that she would lose her ability to participate in rational discourse. Instead, she made frantic retaliatory efforts to stimulate the analyst, in turn, by regaling him with pornographic tales.

Although, with analysands who have this kind of vulnerability, it is probably impossible completely to avoid traumatic incidents, it is evident that it is desirable to minimize their frequency by *empathically* restraining our tendency to promote intimacy, warmth, consensus. Sometimes less is truly more! (If a more austere analytic style succeeds in avoiding such therapeutic setbacks, it is safe to conclude that they do not constitute "negative therapeutic reactions" based on a need for self-punishment [see Moraitis, 1981].) Needless to say, I do not advocate mindlessly substituting coldness and distance, or an argumentative manner, as the proper standard for an analyst's attitude. I *am* trying to say that empathic responsiveness entails the responsibility to tailor our manner of discourse to the specific requirements of the analysand's current state.

If the foregoing principle is accepted, it follows that striving for accord, warmth, or intimacy, a kindly couchside manner, and efforts to avoid humiliating or otherwise upsetting the analysand are "empathic" only if these characteristics of the analyst's activities have been chosen because they are specifically indicated. If they are used because the analyst assumes they are always optimal, they are not empathic but formulaic. In my judgment, relatively few analysands actually require an approach characterized by such tactics. As I have already stated, they are not likely to be of much use when patients are developing an archaic negative transference. And, as we all know, tactical questions are unlikely to cause problems when the transference is focused on positively toned past transactions.

To pinpoint the specific circumstances that call for the kind of responsiveness that echoes the good-enough holding environment of a growth-promoting childhood, in my judgment such tactics are called for when it seems prudent to postpone the potential development of an archaic transference because it threatens to be unmanageable (see Gedo and Gehrie, 1993, chap. 2).[3] By establishing a new kind of object relationship, without precedent in the patient's past, it may be possible to expand the patient's repertory of basic adaptational skills (if necessary, through explicit instruction) so that, when the storms of the negative transference later supervene, it may be possible to master them (see Gedo, 1988, Epilogue). Note that I do not claim that a new relationship can overcome the pathological legacies of the past; in my view, it merely provides the proper context for promoting new learning (see Wilson and Weinstein, 1992a, b).

---

[3] In most cases, the prospect of unmanageable transference developments is merely a probability, a risk the prudent analyst will try to minimize. Such predictions have to be made on the basis of historical data about the nature of the childhood transactions that are likely to be repeated transferentially; admittedly, the data available about the childhood past are often quite unreliable. Despite this difficulty, it is not legitimate to ignore information that suggests that severely disruptive transactions in childhood resulted in the formation of ominous psychopathology that was subsequently walled off. The risks of undoing such defensive splitting must be weighed very carefully.

11 On Countertransference, Projective Identification, and the Question of Intersubjectivity

ON CORRECTIVE EMOTIONAL EXPERIENCE AND THE HOLDING ENVIRONMENT

Until relatively recently, the great majority of psychoanalysts (of most ideological persuasions) professed adherence to a single theory of technique. According to that theory, analysts should focus their activities on promoting insight, generally speaking by means of interpretations of hitherto poorly understood mental contents. Necessary interventions beyond interpretation were subsumed under the poorly defined metaphor of "working through." (For detailed discussion of this concept, see chapter 13, this volume, and Gedo, 1995b.) Differences of opinion among competing schools of analytic thought have concerned the specifics of the mental contents analytic interpretations should illuminate. Probably the best expositions of this viewpoint were the monographs on technique by Fenichel (1941) and Stone (1961).

Dissenting voices on the theory of technique have not as yet been codified in a similar manner. From a historical perspective, the publication of Sándor Ferenczi's *Clinical Diary* (Dupont, 1988) has revealed that the earliest technical experiments to initiate a lasting tradition *within psychoanalysis* (as opposed to secessionist movements such as those of Otto Rank or Wilhelm Reich) were those conducted by Ferenczi in the last decade of his life. These experiments were intended to make possible the analysis of conditions that did not yield to the technique Ferenczi outlined in *The Development of Psychoanalysis* (see Ferenczi and Rank, 1924). As I have tried to show in some detail elsewhere (Gedo, in press), this work was the culmination of Ferenczi's role as the "Grand Vizier" of Freudian orthodoxy: the technical prescriptions published by Fenichel and Stone during the next generation were only such natural extensions of this position statement as took the intervening progress in ego psychology and object relations theory into account.

Despite its conservative credentials, *The Development of Psychoanalysis* marked a decisive advance on the previously prevalent theory of treatment, that of Freud's (1911-15) "Papers on Technique." It was in the 1924 monograph that Ferenczi, for the first time, conceived of successful analytic treatment as a unitary process with an internal coherence of its own, rather than the decoding of a series of symptoms or complexes. Although he did not spell this out in the monograph, to judge by his subsequent modifications of technique, Ferenczi seems to have realized that, as a *process*, psychoanalytic treatment cannot be characterized exclusively as a function of the validity of the interpretations offered by the analyst.

As we know from the snippets of the Freud-Ferenczi correspondence from this period already published (see Jones, 1957), Ferenczi believed that the emotional ambience of the therapeutic relationship is one crucial factor that codetermines the effects of analytic interventions; basically, this was the departure from accepted theory that Freud was then unwilling to accept. Although ca. 1930 this vocabulary was as yet unavailable, what Ferenczi was recommending is the offer of a "corrective emotional experience" (see Alexander and French, 1946) by way of a novel object relationship (see Loewald, 1960). His most eloquent paper on this subject (Ferenczi, 1933), written for the 1932 Congress of the International, encountered actual censorship by the guardians of orthodoxy.

Ferenczi's *Clinical Diary* (Dupont, 1988) also reveals that, with certain troublesome analysands, he never did find a way to avoid repeating the pathological and pathogenic transactions that had characterized the patients' relationships in the past. In retrospect, we may judge that this failure stemmed from an underestimation of the stability of these analysands' structured mental dispositions. This excessive optimism about human plasticity was spelled out in an important paper written by Ferenczi's intellectual heir, Michael Bálint (1932)—presumably a task he undertook because Ferenczi was already severely affected by the pernicious anemia that was shortly to end his life. As I reviewed in chapter 9, Bálint articulated the concept that a novel relationship offered in the analytic situation will enable analysands to experience a "new beginning" of psychological maturation. This notion became most influential with the British school of object relations, in all likelihood as a result of Bálint's relocation to London a few years later, and it also influenced the "interpersonal" school in America.

In chapter 9, I also tried to differentiate instances of developmental arrest, which may indeed respond with spontaneous maturation to a constructive new relationship, from those disturbances of character that compulsively repeat dysfunctional transference patterns instead. In the context of discussing Ferenczi's work it may be most fitting to draw a parallel between these contrasting conditions and the difference between iron deficiency anemia and pernicious anemia, respectively. In other words, most analytic patients do not suffer from the consequences of some lack of essential environmental input but from an inability to make use of expectable nurture. Such an inability is based (in turn) on pathogenic early experiences of various kinds, often transactions that took place before the development of the capacity for language into reliable communications with consensual meaning.

Although the therapeutic optimism of Ferenczi and Bálint in the early 1930s was not fully justified, those who followed their implicit analytic prescription to provide a nurturing environment in the analytic situation (prominent among whom was my own teacher in Chicago, Therese Benedek) certainly obtained better results with difficult patients than did analysts who unvaryingly tailored their techniques to the resources of the rare individuals who entered analysis with a "fully intact ego"—the phrase used by Eissler (1953) when he pointed out that the so-called classical technique of psychoanalysis is suitable only for a minority of analysands. The foregoing conclusion was best summed up by Winnicott (1954) in his evocative notion that analysis, like the primary caretakers of infants, should provide a "holding environment." Unfortunately, even today we possess few operational guidelines for achieving this happy state, although nobody any longer disputes its desirability (see Modell, 1976).

Ferenczi believed (and confided to his *Clinical Diary* [Dupont, 1988]) that his inability to provide certain analysands with a holding environment was the result of his own characterological shortcomings. This was the first manifestation within psychoanalysis of the intersubjective viewpoint. Ferenczi's pathetic efforts to overcome his putative handicaps by humbling himself and through other would-be reaction formations predictably failed to solve the dilemma of therapeutic stalemates caused by analysands experiencing the psychoanalytic situation not as a benign "cocoon" (Modell's metaphor for a holding environment) but as a traumatic repetition of the worst aspects of their past. In the 60-odd years that followed, numerous followers of the tradition Ferenczi initiated have similarly blamed themselves whenever they were unable to maintain what some have called an "empathic ambience" (Wolf, 1976, 1992). To illustrate the point, let me cite Margaret Little's (1985) amazing account of her analysis with Winnicott. She claims that when, in a paroxysm of hatred, she smashed a Ming vase in the analyst's office, he left the room in tears but never spoke about the incident and replaced the precious object with another just like it. *Amor vincit omnia.*

The tendency to place the onus of responsibility for "breaks in empathy" on the analyst alone has been particularly marked within self psychology, and it has grown even stronger with the emergence of the "intersubjective" viewpoint (see Stolorow and Atwood, 1992). From that perspective, the analysand's subjective experience of treatment is principally a function of the analyst's attitudes (rather than of structured intrapsychic dispositions); consequently, unpleasant vicissitudes in the course of treatment are necessarily the responsibility of the analyst. These views endorse the claims of the analysand described by Gehrie (1993): when the analyst did his utmost to be soothing and benign, she assaulted him furiously with the transference-based reproach that he was trying to mislead her with his falsehoods!

To put all this a different way: in the realm of archaic transferences, it is not love that is likely to triumph but the compulsion to repeat. Our most difficult patients are those who are able to suck melancholy from an egg, to paraphrase Shakespeare.[1] With such people, the therapeutic task is first to demonstrate the precise manner in which they actively manage to restage the pathogenic transactions of their past and then to assist them to find better alternatives to these behaviors. In the early 1930s, when Ferenczi was struggling to solve these problems, the psychoanalytic armamentarium simply did not have tools adequate to deal with them. Lacking something better, analysts of later vintage have also been tempted simply to offer corrective emotional experiences, despite repeated reminders that "love is not enough" (see, e.g., Bettelheim, 1950).

ON COUNTERTRANSFERENCE

Do we now possess therapeutic skills, unavailable in the 1930s that can help us overcome the kinds of analytic impasse that often defeated Ferenczi? In my judgment, we have learned several new techniques that may lead to such success. Perhaps the most

---

[1] *As You Like It*, Act II, Scene 5.

important among these (although not the earliest to enter the public domain) followed the realization that countertransference attitudes are generally not attributable to the analyst's unresolved psychopathology, so that (instead of having to be eliminated as unwelcome contaminants of the analytic process) they should be closely examined as sources of potential information about crucial dynamic issues not adequately addressed by studying the analysand's verbal associations. This major technical advance was initiated more or less concurrently by several authors, among whom pride of place probably should be given to Heinrich Racker (1968; see also Tower, 1956).

Here, at long last, was a rational explanation of the phenomenon Freud (1912, p. 115), in a poetic but difficult-to-understand *façon de parler*[2] called the unconscious of one person speaking to that of another. There is nothing occult about the assembly of verbal and nonverbal cues that evoke the analyst's global responsiveness to the analysand's implicit transferential attitudes—these are simply those channels of communication that are available to young children before they begin predominantly to rely on consensual language as their principal means of discourse. It is only natural that the most archaic psychological issues, particularly if they have remained split off from other aspects of the organized personality (see Gedo, 1988, chap. 4), are likely to be encoded in a manner that does not make use of the secondary process: instead, preverbal infants communicate affects and simple needs through a language of gestures, facial expressions, and paraverbal signs. As the epigenetic view of development makes clear (see Gedo and Goldberg, 1973), the earliest basic skills are never lost, even after they have been, for most purposes, superseded by more sophisticated analogues. In other words, even while analysands are ostensibly communicating their subjective experience by means of verbal associations, they will continue to send additional messages by way of the nonverbal system of signals.

The realization that much of an analyst's responsiveness merely represents a compliant (or a defiantly noncompliant!) reply to an analysand's nonverbal communications rather than some pathological contaminant of the analytic process made it possible to use those responses as a crucial source of information about the patient's archaic transferences. (For an earlier discussion of this issue, see

---

[2] Manner of speaking—phraseology.

Gedo, 1984, pp. 121-125.) To put this differently, this insight made possible a technical innovation that has sometimes been called "interpretation based on countertransference." Of course, to make such measures feasible, it is imperative to grasp that the response does not primarily constitute part of the analyst's own system of motivations—that it is not a transference reaction on the part of the analyst. If one is reasonably certain that the response is an automatism evoked by a wish or need of the analysand, the nature of that unstated desire may be inferred from the reciprocal emotional signal (of relatively low intensity, it is to be hoped) experienced by the analyst. Clearly, it is easier to identify such a signal as a response to the analysand's motivational system if it does not happen to coincide with a response pattern of the analyst's own emotional life, especially one that occurs with some frequency. Presumably Ferenczi was unable to grasp that he was being victimized by some patients who were skilled at emotional blackmail because, from a characterological viewpoint, he was always prone to engage in masochistic enactments: witness his amazing submissiveness to Freud's manipulative interventions on the question of whom Ferenczi should marry (see the Freud-Ferenczi letters [Brabant, Falzeder, and Giampieri-Deutsch, 1993]).

As I have tried to show in detail elsewhere (Gedo, 1988, chap. 9), whenever crucial matters can be communicated by the analysand only by means of dramatic enactments, the full meaning of the message can be grasped only if every member of the dramatis personae participates by engaging emotionally in a complementary enactment. As I have already stated, the analyst cannot, in such circumstances, avoid emotional participation in a "dyadic enactment." To cite only the commonest of instances to illustrate this point: the analyst cannot simply sidestep a sadomasochistic transaction initiated by an analysand, for any effort to refrain from taking part in the enactment will be experienced by such a patient as abusive. Witness the reaction of the analysand described by Gehrie (1993)—as I have already mentioned, the analyst's "empathic" responsiveness only convinced her that he was mistreating her by engaging in some manipulative deception.

Clearly, these constraints do not imply that the analyst should engage in any *action*, other than offering the appropriate interpretation "from" the countertransference—let us say, "I feel that you are trying to provoke me to treat you in such and such a manner." It is the possibility of such a therapeutic stance vis-à-vis communications not principally encoded in words that opened the way to analyzing persons whose difficulties stem in significant degree from the preverbal era of childhood, by assisting such persons to learn for the first time a verbal code for the relevant transaction. This amounts to the offer of a truly novel relationship, whereas for the great majority of analysands mere goodness is not likely to constitute a new experience. Through this expansion of psychoanalytic technique, we have acquired a way to train patients in hitherto missing yet essential cognitive skills.

ON PROJECTIVE IDENTIFICATION

Beyond the foregoing technical advance, the most significant addition to the analytic armamentarium has been the result of understanding the phenomenon Melanie Klein (1952) labeled "projective identification." Her choice of terminology does not really do justice to the conceptual meaning of her observation, for the clinical data she described actually amount to the discovery of a whole set of hitherto incomprehensible transferences. From the genetic viewpoint (in contrast to the dynamics stressed by Klein), projective identification constitutes the repetition of early childhood transactions (generally those from the preverbal era) with the roles reversed: the analysand's childhood role is assigned to the analyst, while the patient enacts that of one of the early caretakers.

When projective identification is viewed from the perspective of its transferential significance, the difficulty of understanding its manner of operation largely disappears: it amounts to the emergence of a split-off sector of archaic mentation organized in such a primitive mode that the roles of the participants are interchangeable, because only the resultant affective reverberations are precisely noted, in the manner postulated by Hadley (1992). In other words, these are merely special instances of dyadic enactment, wherein the analyst completes the transaction by experiencing in the present something of significance that the analysand experienced as a child. Because such a response may now yield useful insights if appropriately used to reconstruct the past, some authors have assumed that the aim of projective identification is to send a message. I believe that such a teleological assumption is unwarranted: the attempt to relive a traumatic segment of the past is principally a manifestation of repetition compulsion (Freud, 1920)—it is an attempt at mastery by turning a passive experience into its active counterpart.

Understanding that there is a set of transference reactions that repeat childhood transactions by way of role reversals has greatly expanded the range of possible interpretations based on countertransference responses by including those based on counteridentification. In combination, clarification of these two sets of archaic systems of meaningful signs has made possible more accurate reconstructions of the preverbal past than those available to analysts of previous generations. It is worth recalling that, until relatively recently (see Boesky, 1982), interpretable mimetic enactments were misunderstood as "acting out." In some quarters, they were actually regarded as manifestations of resistance to the analysand's necessary commitment to the verbalization of all mental contents. Such views misunderstood various psychological disabilities as signs of malingering.

THE WIDENING SCOPE OF PSYCHOANALYSIS

As a result of the foregoing expansions of the analyst's capacity to translate nonverbal codes into consensually meaningful words, it is now possible to assist patients to learn to symbolize matters they previously could deal with only through affectomotor actions. Such symbolization will, in turn, enable these individuals for the first time to reflect about potential courses of action involving these matters. Nor are these two ways of dealing with preverbal aspects of emotional life the only significant advances in psychoanalytic technique to have become widely accepted in the past 50 years, as I have tried to indicate throughout this volume.

Suffice it to mention as one example Kohut's (1971) most important technical contribution, the caveat to give priority to the need to preserve analysands' self-esteem by taking care to avoid unnecessarily humiliating them. For that matter, the Winnicott/Modell prescription to provide patients with a holding environment (or cocoon) constitutes another crucial technical innovation devised since Ferenczi's demise. Along the same lines, I should like to mention my own technical suggestion (see Gedo and Goldberg, 1973; Gedo, 1979, 1988) to add a number of modalities of treatment to our standard technique of interpretation, each devised to deal with problems more primitive than the intrapsychic conflicts characteristic of an infantile neurosis.

It should also suffice to say, therefore, that we are now able to overcome many of the technical difficulties that defeated Ferenczi's best efforts two generations ago. Subsequent developments in psychoanalytic technique have proved that, in the disputes about optimal therapeutic procedures between Freud and Ferenczi, it was

Ferenczi's way that would become more fruitful, albeit only after careful refinement. Correction of the historical record is now greatly overdue, as some of us have been proclaiming from the rooftops for almost 30 years (see Gedo, 1967a; Gedo and Pollock, 1976). Such a belated verdict in favor of Ferenczi must not be allowed to lapse into the mindless copying of his procedures of 1930, in some misguided effort to substitute Ferenczi for Freud as a mythical ancestor figure suitable for automatic emulation. (For both appropriate and uncritical reassessments of Ferenczi's contributions, see also Aron and Harris, 1993).

Least of all should we follow those of Ferenczi's ideas that proved to be in error. Among these, the notion of intersubjectivity has recently become all too fashionable (see Stolorow and Atwood, 1992). In its modern guise, this viewpoint radically challenges the notion of analytic objectivity, as if the participants in psychoanalysis were incapable of reaching agreement. It is worth noting that in his *Clinical Diary* (Dupont, 1988), Ferenczi ultimately concluded that his readiness to accept his patients' interpretations of his unconscious motives had been excessive. It is by no means impossible for analysts to be reasonably cognizant of their own structured psychological dispositions, so that they can make proper allowances for their subjectivity in arriving at valid conclusions about that of their patients. Although it is certainly difficult to make valid inferences about the meanings of mental contents, it is entirely feasible to be objective enough about other kinds of analytic data, such as the nature of the analysand's affectivity, thought processes, communicative skills or apraxia, and so on. Functions of this kind tend to remain stable, regardless of the interpersonal situation; analysts should gain expertise in making accurate observations about them.

III Intrapsychic Communication

12 The Self As True or False, Crazy or Sane

ON SPLITS OF THE MIND

Ever since Winnicott (1954) put forward the notion that a person's predominant behavior may represent a "false self," while one's "true self" may remain largely hidden as a potentiality seldom realized in action, psychoanalysts have faced the problem of explaining how such disparate nuclei of the self (Gedo and Goldberg, 1973) might simultaneously influence the regulation of behavior. One coherent explanation was offered by Kohut (1971), who postulated a "vertical split" between contrasting mental dispositions—a defensive arrangement to be differentiated from Freud's (1915a, 1923) "secondary repression," which Freud always indicated on his graphic model of mental functioning by means of a "horizontal" barrier. Basch (1974) was the first to suggest that a vertical split is maintained by means of disavowal (*Verleugnung*, as Freud, 1927a, termed it), that is, disregard of the significance of whichever of the uncoordinated mental fragments is for the moment warded off.

When nuclei of mental functioning remain unintegrated, splitting by way of disavowal often seems to fit the clinical data of observation, but the concept does not cover every contingency of this kind. In somnambulism there is a regressive return to an archaic state of altered consciousness in which mutually exclusive alternatives are tolerated without conflict (Gedo, 1979, p. 124). When "normal" consciousness returns, the somnambulistic mental contents probably undergo repression. (For a clinical example, see Gedo, 1983, pp. 89-90). No doubt many other combinations of unusual functional arrangements will be found that maintain incoherent mental conditions. For instance, although I have had no clinical experience with patients suffering from "multiple personalities," I suspect that in these conditions, whichever of these factitious personae occupies center stage, others may either be disavowed or repressed.

Even Winnicott's choice of terminology, that of "true" and "false" selves, fails to do justice to the complexities of human behavior. This choice actually reflects Winnicott's personal predilection for privileging those mental dispositions that in early childhood defied parental expectations and therefore may have had to be hidden. It is, however, self-evident that a child's compliant behaviors cannot be equated with hypocrisy in adult life and are therefore mislabeled when they are designated as "false." This point is buttressed by the fact that, after successful analytic treatment, the behavioral repertory that Winnicott depreciated as false is never relinquished in toto—it remains available whenever it confers some kind of adaptive advantage. In other words, its use becomes a matter of voluntary choice, instead of being constrained. Thus the true-false dichotomy would be better described as contrarian-compliant. Improvement does not imply the replacement of compliance by obligatory negativism—it means the predominance of rational considerations in determining the future choice of behavior.

Moreover, major splitting of the mind does not necessarily involve a true self-false self differentiation. To cite only one other possibility, the unintegrated dispositions may be the derivatives of compliance with the mutually exclusive requirements of multiple caretakers; such were the conditions that in infancy confronted the three analysands I described in chapter 5. Among such syndromes, the one I have found most difficult to clarify conceptually is the splitting of aspects of personality that could well be designated "crazy" and "sane." These are people properly described in the celebrated phrase of Hamlet, "I am but mad north-northwest; when the wind is southerly, I know a hawk from a handsaw." (Historical records reveal that many prominent persons have displayed islands of psychosis within a productive and otherwise reasonably integrated life course. I give several examples of such eminent persons in Gedo, 1996, chap. 13.)

ON THE "PSYCHOTIC CORE"

In my psychoanalytic practice, I encountered a significant fraction of patients who responded to the iatrogenic regression induced by the analytic process with emergent psychotic ideation previously absent from their discernible mentation. I believe it is of significance that every one of the half dozen analyses I attempted that were interrupted after a considerable period of work (that is, failed efforts that were not merely brief trials of unsuccessful collaboration) came to grief because we were powerless to influence a core of delusional ideation that turned out to be a crucial determinant of the analysand's personality structure. (For accounts of these failed analyses, see Gedo, 1981a, chap. 3, and 1984, chap. 7.) In order to characterize such a syndrome, I should like briefly to summarize one of these clinical misadventures (see Gedo, 1981a, pp. 61-62, 64-68, 80, 381; and 1984, pp. 103-104).

The patient was a graduate student in the humanities who sought analysis because of a masochistic perversion but also turned out to have severe difficulties in organizing and completing the written work required in his discipline. Sometime in the second year of this man's life, his mother became incapacitated by a depressive illness, and his care was taken over by a late-adolescent sister. The patient was around five years of age when his sister got married and left the family home. Shortly thereafter, he succeeded in enmeshing his new brother-in-law in a pattern of physical exhibitionism to gain the child's admiration, a scenario that then served as the core of his masturbatory fantasies. Although in adult life these events were recollected as scenes of humiliation, we soon learned that, if I allowed myself to be trapped into exhibiting my intellectual prowess in making interpretations, the analysand felt that *he* was triumphing over me. Late in the analysis, fantasies of his being worshipped by young boys gradually emerged.

This development of insight clarified the fact that, for this person, the analytic situation per se constituted fulfillment of a lifelong, erotized fantasy of being the subject of fascinated admiration, a fantasy disavowed in the conscious version encoded in the masturbatory scenario. No verbal communication on my part ever succeeded in overcoming this illusion—only the threat of losing the treatment relationship (either through therapeutic success or through definitive failure of the analysis) would temporarily produce rage or panic and disrupt the analysand's smug complacency. Most of the time, he enjoyed teasing me by overtly espousing planlessness, impulsivity, and illogic as the proper guides to action. It took over five years of analytic work to uncover that these absurdist commitments were intended to prove that no ill could befall him, because he was divine—possibly the reincarnated Christ, in His guise as the Infant Jesus.

In other words, the core of the disavowed fantasies of being worthy of worship was a megalomanic delusion that, prior to its articulation through our joint efforts, appeared never to have been verbally encoded. I assume it is derailments of development of this kind that Kernberg (1975) chose to call "pathological narcissism." Robbins (1993) has correctly emphasized that incipient schizophrenic psychoses represent similarly wide departures, already in early childhood, from the expectable curve of psychological development.

At any rate, my analysand's delusional ideation—delusional because it proved not to be amenable to modification even after he put it into words—had not been kept out of awareness as a consequence of defensive operations. It could not previously be put into words because this sense of omnipotence had supervened in the preverbal era (presumably in reaction to the helplessness the child experienced while his mother deteriorated into psychosis), and none of the caretakers ever commented on this undesirable development. In Freud's (1915a, 1923) terminology, these intrapsychic conditions are referred to as "primary repression." Nor did the elucidation of the patient's corollary fantasy, that I possessed the power magically to transform him into an artistic genius, alter the therapeutic impasse.

Note, however, that this second delusional idea implicitly contradicted the first; in the patient's archaic mode of organization, he experienced no discomfort about holding such mutually exclusive beliefs. By sticking to my confession of inability to influence the patient, I was able to convince him that I did not possess the magical power he attributed to me; but he concluded (like the mad emperor in a celebrated Second City skit) that it was available to someone else. The incoherence of these conscious beliefs did not make this person uncomfortable, so that he had no need to disavow (or otherwise to defend against) either of the rationally incompatible alternatives. If I confronted him with the disorder of his thought processes, he was not embarrassed; rather, he was angry with me, as if I had committed blasphemy.

The same was true when I inadvertently betrayed being shocked by his report that, on his trip home from my office, he had lost bowel control on a train without toilet facilities that he had boarded despite feeling an urgent need to defecate. (My unconcealed reaction also constituted a loss of control: I was stunned because this incident first showed me that I was dealing with a personality much more primitive than I had realized.) In addition to the megalomania implicit in the patient's lack of shame, the very fact that an adult could behave as if he had no responsibility to monitor his own sphincters demonstrated that there was no defensive barrier between certain infantile impulses and their enactment as unconflicted behavior.

After a number of years of therapeutic impasse, I began to articulate that I had lost hope of effecting real changes in the patient's mental organization. For a considerable period, he attempted to persuade me that I was in error, and as a consequence his outward behavior underwent considerable alteration. He now began to deal with his megalomania through the most archaic of defenses, that of denial: he tried to prove that he did not regard himself as the Infant Jesus by having sexual relations for the first time, and he experienced humiliation because his initial attempts at intercourse did not go well. His dreams, however, consistently presented his grandiosity in an undisguised manner, like the dreams of adults in situations of extreme duress. Freud inserted such examples in his 1911 revision of The *Interpretation of Dreams* (Freud, 1900, pp. 550–572.) Kohut (personal communication, ca. 1972) was fond of recounting that, in roughly similar circumstances, one of his analysands had to confess that, although in his dreams he seemed to have his feet on the ground, he was actually still walking on air, just a few microns above street level!

It is difficult to estimate the extent of the deleterious influence of such persisting islands of madness if they have become unacceptable to the adult personality. I have occasionally found walled-off delusions of that kind in relatively well-integrated analysands who reported them as "childhood memories." Let us recall my patient, a competent archeologist, who insisted that, on a visit to the circus as a five-year-old, she had successfully walked into and out of a lion's cage. The analysis was carried to a satisfactory termination, with adaptive improvement in previously problematic areas, but this scholar committed to reason continued never to entertain any doubt about the veridical nature of her screen memory (Freud, 1899).

At any rate, the sole permanent accomplishment of the analysis of the young man with divine pretensions was to teach him that such ideas are socially unacceptable and thereby to make them "ego alien." In view of my discouragement and the exhaustion of his insurance coverage, he decided to stop treatment after six years of effort. In a casual encounter some years later, he revealed that he had had a rocky time of it but was, for the first time, gainfully employed, in a modest position. Although I have always regarded this outcome as an analytic failure, I am also convinced that it was only my consistent policy of confessing therapeutic helplessness that succeeded in causing this man to cover over his megalomania. Yet, even then, he continued to proclaim that Herbert Marcuse was correct in deploring the reality principle as an illegitimate instrument of social control.

Another way of stating the foregoing point is to call attention to this person's inability, in the depths of his being, to abandon his delusions. Such an inability to hear what Freud (1927b) called "the voice of the intellect" amounts to a thought disorder, albeit one that operates only within a particular fragment of the personality. Another analysand who abandoned treatment as soon as an advantageous adaptive compromise became feasible showed a different form of pathological thinking: When, in the analysis, he was confronted with unpalatable truths he wished to avoid, he regularly lapsed into pseudologia fantastica—that is, associative sequences consisting of transparent fictions that only he was able to believe. (For a more detailed discussion of these circumstances, see Gedo, 1984, pp. 114–115.)

A third form of underlying thought disorder came to the fore in the course of the (ultimately unsuccessful) analysis of a negativistic mental health professional who originally sought help for marital problems. It took several years of therapeutic effort to overcome the enactment of his negativism vis-à-vis his spouse, whereupon it became more evident within the analytic situation. If I succeeded in side-stepping these struggles, the patient regularly lapsed into a confusional state, accompanied by a loss of the consensual use of language, a syndrome I discuss in greater detail in chapter 2. Here I merely note that, to cover over this collapse of essential human capacities, he tended to parrot his own past ideas or even those he had heard from others, without regard for their current relevance, as if they were fresh associations. At the same time, he experienced my attempts to assist him in getting his bearings as violations of his autonomous boundaries. No wonder he eventually extricated himself from this impasse by quitting the analysis in a paranoid huff. These events occurred some 15 years ago, before I had formulated the technical strategy of giving priority to the correction of apraxic deficits [see Gedo, 1988, see esp. chapters 11–14 and Epilogue; Gedo and Gehrie, 1993]. I think the consistent application of this principle might have made it possible to treat this person more successfully.

ON THE FAILURE OF SYMBOLIZATION

Whenever primitive pathological islands of personality persist within a generally more mature self-organization not because of defensive splitting but as a result of a lack of symbolic representation, these archaic residues will continue to exert unimpeded influence on behavior despite the impossibility of articulating the purport of their motivations in consensual language. Such conditions are not to be confused with neurotic symptom formation, based on a "return of the repressed," because they do not constitute compromises, as do behaviors that result from unresolved intrapsychic conflicts. In the case of the negativistic patient I have just described, this impulsion from "unconscious" sources manifested itself in the form of grandiose risk-taking, such as gambling or the sexual exploitation of certain clients. Although he put a stop to this specific enactment as soon as I stated that I viewed such behavior as extremely rash, his dreams demonstrated that he did not really accept that in general such judgments applied to him. For instance, he might fail to seek medical attention for an acute illness. When, on one such occasion, I reminded him about the dangers of this course, he dreamt about an alligator, sitting in a tree and happily eating a bunch of Concord grapes.

His associations may be summarized as follows: The dream reminds him of Aesop's fable about the fox and sour grapes, except that Concord grapes are not sour—they are blue. He read a satire on psychoanalysis in which a tiny dog with enormous jaws swallows a much bigger opponent. The "dog's" owner admits that it is really an alligator with its tail cut off and painted white. The dream is like the famous childhood dream of the Wolf Man about wolves sitting in a tree—but an alligator could only get up a tree by magic, and grapes do not grow on trees. As a therapist, he tries not to practice magic. The day before the dream, one of the former clients, whom he had screwed, called him to avow her love for him.

We may conclude that the archaic dream-wish is to attain omnipotence—the automatic satisfaction of his needs, particularly for relief from depression or murderous hostility in response to frustration, without his having to rely on anyone else. He could then magically cure himself—something the Wolf Man could never do!—by consuming his female clients or incorporating me, like a disguised alligator. (For a more detailed account of this clinical material, including additional corroborative evidence, see Gedo, 1981a, pp. 271-275, 279-280.)

Patients whose integrative faculties are keener than were those of the foregoing analysand can sometimes rationalize primitive behaviors of this sort by finding some ideological justification for them. It is worth recalling that one of the terrorists of the Weatherman underground of the 1960s was actually in analysis at the time she was setting off explosives! The clearest instance of this kind in my own clinical experience was that of another psychotherapist who spent her entire adult life in some form of treatment. I was the fourth (but not the last) of her analysts, and we collaborated for more than a decade. From an outside observer's vantage point, while we worked together her adaptation improved in many areas, and the termination of the analysis was by mutual agreement. (I have reported on various aspects of this very instructive experience on a number of occasions: see Gedo, 1981a, pp. 98-99, 111-113, 120-126, 378-379; 1988, pp. 158-160; 1991a, p. 125, and chapters 1 and 9, this volume) Within a few years, however, she was bitterly disappointed *about me as a person* (i.e., on the basis of fantasies about my behavior after her treatment—the transaction I described in chapter 1) and entered a fifth analysis with someone known to disapprove of my views.

Because this ex-patient's "disappointment" was based on a literal misunderstanding of my position, I conclude that this transaction represented the return of chronic mental dispositions (temporarily) denied in the latter stages of our work together. When the analysis started (and for many years thereafter), she assailed me and my views on psychoanalytic technique by citing the many ways in which they differed from those of Heinz Kohut. (Of course, her persistence in a treatment she found so unsatisfactory could mean only that the situation constituted a transference of her childhood vacillation between the world-views of her dotty, Rosicrucian mother and her rigid but sober father.) This form of negative transference "disappeared" only in the last year of our work together, probably in response to increasing signs of pessimism on my part about being able to influence the patient's delusional ideas—akin to the tenets of Christian Science—about the power of properly conducted relationships to overcome all human ills, including somatic disease. In other words, this relatively poorly educated therapist's conception of self psychology was severely distorted: she attributed magical properties to "empathy," which she equated with therapeutic interventions that boosted patients' self-esteem, without regard for accuracy. (Her mother, claiming that her daughter was a princess—literally—had consistently told her that she was better than others.)

In retrospect, I did not pay sufficient attention to the fact that, when the patient stopped her ideological attacks on my therapeutic philosophy, she was still wordlessly enacting her disagreement with me by continued adherence to magical procedures in her own clinical practice. I only noted (and to some extent helped to mitigate) her hatred of those of her clients who failed automatically to thrive as a result of her therapeutic influence. As one might expect, as the intensity of this countertransference problem diminished, her work seemed to go better; this improvement undoubtedly contributed to our decision to bring the analysis to its end. I do not know what caused the breakdown of the uneasy equilibrium we had achieved—

suffice it to say that she chose her next analyst from the ranks of self psychologists. Obviously, this person did not hear her account of the transactions with me as delusional: this clever woman was more than able to discuss such matters in abstract terms that could pass muster as respectable theoretical convictions.

It is precisely the ability to fit irrational behavior into a quasi-acceptable framework that distinguishes persons who merely have an island of delusion from those who, from a nosological viewpoint, are properly classified as suffering from a psychosis. I want to emphasize that even very bizarre notions about one's "self-in-the-world" can be rationalized in this way, often by means of misusing the creed of a respected religious community. In this regard, the analysand who felt himself to be divine was *not* claiming that such an idea was compatible with his family's Roman Catholic beliefs—clearly, his vague identification with the Infant Jesus was a relatively late formulation of his delusional notion. When, in the analysis, he encoded this idea in terms required by consensual language, he started immediately to repudiate it, without surrendering the conviction of omnipotence that it had been designed to articulate. Arguably, his overall functioning could be regarded as "psychotic," at least as long as he did not feel the need to claim some socially sanctioned rationale for it.

This may also be the best place to note that it is impossible to classify the delusional and reality-adequate thinking of personalities suffering from a lack of integration ("self-cohesion," as I prefer to call it [Gedo, 1979]) in terms of Winnicott's differentiation between a true and a false self. In each of the clinical illustrations I have presented, both the delusions and their repudiation were completely genuine; neither fragment of the personality was imposed on the patient through some sort of outside pressure in childhood. In my experience with such patients, whenever delusional convictions have persisted despite their elucidation in the course of the psychoanalysis, I have gained the impression that the "voice of reason" went unheeded, albeit it was heard, because the delusions formed part of the bedrock of self-organization—they could not be relinquished without a major disruption of the personality. Such an event might best be compared to the severe disorganization suffered by certain pious adolescents if they suddenly lose their faith. In neither case does the persistence of a circumscribed delusion that was part of the "true self" mean that the person's ability to test reality about most matters is in any way "false," as Winnicott's terminology suggests, in misleading fashion.

13 Working Through as Metaphor and Treatment Modality

THE METAPHOR

When he made his only major effort to discuss technique, Freud (1914b) saw as the greatest challenge for psychoanalysis-as-therapy the propensity of analysands to reenact, rather than remember, aspects of their past. This finding forced him to conclude that resistance to change could not be overcome solely by giving patients information about their mental contents, no matter how accurate such interpretations might be! Although he failed to spell out in operational terms the additional modalities of treatment required to overcome this obstacle, Freud described the processes that lead to success by means of one of his most evocative metaphors, that of *durcharbeiten*, "working through."

I find this term unusually apt because, in its ambiguity, it seems simultaneously applicable to therapeutically successful measures in the interpersonal arena and in the intrapsychic realm. The German verb can, in fact, be used either transitively, in which case it means "to finish or perfect something," or reflexively, for "making one's way." In the first sense, we cannot assist analysands to complete the collaborative work without promoting certain intrapsychic changes (of a kind I shall later discuss more fully); in the second, the analysand cannot make his way to adaptive improvement in actual relationships without these same alterations in the intrapsychic world. Because of its evocativeness, Freud's metaphor has continued in active use; because of its ambiguity, it has served as the vehicle for the ever-competing stresses on the intrapsychic and the interpersonal.

Freud elaborated the notion of working through in his theoretical papers of the mid-1920s, and his viewpoint has been espoused by most subsequent commentators on the subject (see Stewart, 1963; Brodsky, 1967; Shane, 1979; Sedler, 1983; O'Shaughnessy, 1983; Valenstein, 1983). In *Inhibitions, Symptoms and Anxiety*, Freud (1926, p. 159) emphasized the need to overcome the resistance of the id, which he attributed to the force of the compulsion to repeat;

in *Analysis Terminable and Interminable*, Freud (1937) stressed the role of "constitutional factors" in determining analyzability. Some later authors (e.g., Stewart, 1963) have emphasized Freud's idea that working through should refer to the mastery of id resistance, conceived as a biological attribute; some (e.g., Sedler, 1983) stress a complementary notion, that the crucial biological variable is "ego strength." At any rate, in contrast to the usual psychoanalytic focus on mental contents viewed from a dynamic and a genetic viewpoint, Freud and most other writers on working through have insisted on the priority of economic and structural considerations in determining the power of accurate interpretation to alter mental functioning. The only significant dissent has been that of Brenner (1987), who asserts that working through involves nothing beyond conducting a competent analysis with the conceptual tools of ego psychology. Brenner restricts the technique of psychoanalysis to interpreting impulses and the defenses against them, with particular emphasis on elucidating transferences and defensive operations. In this version of psychoanalysis, interpretive efforts overcome resistances as an attacking force gradually overcomes the entrenched defenses of its opponents in war, and from the intrapsychic vantage point, resistance is worked through in analogy with the physics of electrical conduction. In this sense, the intensity of the transference determines how much effort is required to accomplish the work.

But most contributors on working through have followed Freud in looking upon the question of id resistance as something beyond a matter of insight. Some (Stewart, 1963; Shane, 1979) have proposed that id resistance is the antonym of maturation, so that working through should be literally regarded as the completion of development. Consequently, it has been classified as a learning experience (Ekstein, 1965) that must involve a process of gradual, cumulative change through small increments (Galatzer-Levy, 1988; Levin, 1991). These are views of working through not in terms of a military or an electrical metaphor but as the gradual substitution of a more sophisticated cognitive program for a less effective one. Levin (1991) has elucidated that repetitive behavior tends to occur whenever there is some difficulty in learning. I have espoused this viewpoint for more than 20 years (see Gedo and Goldberg, 1973; Gedo, 1979), most extensively in *The Mind in Disorder* (Gedo, 1988, chapters 11-14). In the hierarchical model I have proposed (Gedo and Goldberg, 1973; Gedo, 1979, 1988), these issues are dealt with in terms of the line of development of cognition and, implicitly, the maturation of the brain.

WHAT "WORKING THROUGH" ALTERS

Let us review the actualities of psychic life to which Freud's metaphor *durcharbeiten* ostensibly made reference. Over the years, Freud gradually refined his position on this matter. Freud (1914a) implied that most instances of repetition in the course of analysis merely signify that the analysand is reliving a transference constellation; in contemporary terms, such clinical contingencies are optimally dealt with through accurate transference interpretations. In such instances it is justified to claim that "working through" implies nothing beyond interpretation. By 1926, however, Freud was attributing the necessity for working through to biological factors that transcend mental contents.

In *Inhibitions, Symptoms and Anxiety*, Freud (1926, p. 141) described the constitutional vulnerability that leads to pathogenesis as an incapacity of the ego to tolerate states of mounting tension without experiencing anxiety and various reactive sequelae. Such a state of psychoeconomic imbalance is allegedly independent of the mental contents being processed at the time; in Freud's view, it is produced by excessive stimulation, generally of instinctual origin. Another way he put this was to state that psychoneurotic symptoms are organized around an "actual neurotic core." With this statement, Freud returned to a conceptual schema he had devised in the 1890s (Freud, 1892-99, 1895c,d) to explain the generation of anxiety in the absence of the psychic processing of stimulation. At that time, Freud still equated psychic activity with what we now term symbolically encoded ideation.

Starting with *The Interpretation of Dreams* (Freud, 1900), psychoanalysis was, for a quarter of a century, primarily preoccupied with the mental contents associated with intrapsychic conflicts. During World War I, however, analysts serving with the military were confronted with large numbers of patients suffering from posttraumatic disorders, the so-called war neuroses (see Ferenczi, Abraham, Simmel, and Jones, 1919). Freud (1920) acknowledged that their conclusions, implicating biological predispositions rather than psychodynamics in the genesis of these syndromes, played a large part in persuading him to attribute proper weight, once again, to the role of constitutional variables in producing all forms of psychopathology. In the era of ego psychology that followed the conceptual revolution of the 1920s, these variables were generally described as ego weakness, ego deficit, or ego distortion. This viewpoint was probably most clearly articulated by K. R. Eissler (1953), who claimed that the possibility of employing an exclusively interpretive analytic technique depended on the prior development of an essentially "intact" ego. At the same time, Eissler stressed that the idea of an intact ego is merely a theoretical fiction, so that the notion of an analysis relying exclusively on interpretation is never feasible. A model of the mind that includes as one of its variables the person's biological endowments requires a radical rethinking of the psychoanalytic theory of technique which had been reduced, over the years, to dealing with the problems inherent in mental contents.

To meet Eissler's ideal criteria for analyzability without "parameters"—that is, without departure from an exclusively interpretive technique—perfect analysands should be able to work through whatever propensity they have for psychoeconomic imbalance simply through a gradual process of mastering unpleasure. (Note, once again, that the notion of "mastery" is merely a metaphor!) The most dramatic reports of successful analyses that depend on the mastery of trauma concern certain survivors of concentration camps: one colleague who had been a prisoner of the Nazis for several months related to me (Rappaport, personal communication, ca. 1956) that, in his training analysis, the traumatic memories of those overwhelming experiences eventually came into sharp focus and, as a consequence, he gradually overcame the tendency to experience panic. It is particularly instructive that his analyst never commented directly on these experiences or their sequelae (see also Krystal, 1968, 1975.) In other words, in this instance, working through led to behavioral modification while the analyst confined his role to that of an empathic witness (see Gedo, 1981a, Epilogue).

It should be recalled, however, that Freud's (1926) explanation of the need for working through is focused on what he called id resistance—a term poorly applicable to instances of the kind just discussed, wherein what is at issue is avoidance of disorganizing trauma by gradually building tolerance for intense stimulation. Freud tried to clarify what he meant by id resistance through another striking metaphor, that of "adhesiveness of the libido." This notion implies that the conservative tendency to repeat even maladaptive patterns of behavior has a constitutional basis, or, as Freud (1920) put it, that it operates like an instinct. Unfortunately, Freud classified this constitutional force as a "death instinct"; this was a conceptual error, for the repetition of automatized patterns, far from leading to destruction, is in fact necessary for continuing survival. Although Freud's proposal of a death instinct proved to be a metapsychological blind alley, the concept of a compulsion to repeat explains a wide array of behaviors, including gravely maladaptive activities, that do not fit the model of compromise formations attempting to reconcile intrapsychic conflicts. As I have mentioned, perhaps the most convincing illustration of such a pattern has been provided by Valenstein (1973) in his description of a syndrome of "attachment to painful feelings." In the 1920s, Freud (1924) would have regarded such a pattern of behavior as a manifestation of a particular type of libidinal constitution, an expression of "erotogenic masochism."

Contemporary psychoanalysts are no longer satisfied with theoretical propositions framed entirely in terms of putative drives or their vicissitudes, so that any recourse to explanations on a constitutional basis has to be buttressed by reliance on data more directly borrowed from brain science. In those terms, the compulsion to repeat is simply the consequence of automatic reliance on the established organization of the brain; learning new patterns of behavior necessarily involves the development of novel organizational arrangements in the nervous system, and working through must refer to the difficult transitional process whereby reliance on former modes of behavioral regulation is gradually superseded by more effective adaptive measures.

WORKING THROUGH AS COGNITIVE MATURATION

Until relatively recently, we had apparent consensus that psychoanalytic treatment effected adaptive changes, mediated through structural reorganization, as a result of valid interpretations of previously incomprehensible mental contents. Most of us also acknowledged the necessity of working through, beyond receiving such information; but this complication has been widely regarded as relatively insignificant, as if all it implied were that analysts have to insist on the cogency of those interpretations that further investigation proves to be valid. Paradoxically, our traditional theories of mental function rightly insisted that psychology is a branch of biology; this connection was maintained in our metapsychology in the form of the economic and structural points of view. In other words, we have correctly maintained all along that the verbal interchange in psychological treatment must in some manner alter the biology of the analysand: "Where id was, there shall ego be," proclaimed Freud (1933, p. 8). In Hartmann's (1952) terms, analysis promotes the neutralization of drive energies.

But how can our words influence the energic charge of drive derivatives? For that matter, how do they even reach what we call "the id," in view of the fact that, according to the structural theory, the verbal realm is the exclusive province of "the ego"? (See Freud, 1915b, for a statement of this idea, albeit in topographic terms.) Because such questions are unanswerable within the framework of Freud's metapsychology, we simply did not ask them. We have been content, instead, to rely on the metaphor of "working through" to cover over this disjunction between our theories of therapy and our theory of mind. Some among us, discouraged by the conceptual dilemma but wedded to traditional procedures, advocate the abandonment of the biological matrix of psychoanalysis. This option would permit confining our attention to mental contents and ignoring issues of information processing, including matters encoded through affectivity and somatization, implicit in the notion of working through.

If we acknowledge that mental contents are, in principle, ineradicable and, therefore, within a theory of therapy, epiphenomenal, it follows that the principal aim of psychoanalytic interpretation is not the immediate provision of information but long-term training in the skill of more effective self-cognition—as Gardner (1983) has rightly pointed out. And if an analysand profits from treatment to the extent of his or her increased ability to think straight, it follows that the elucidation of mental contents cannot be the principal task of analysis—translation by the analyst does not alter the person's ability to process unconscious material; the analysand has to learn to read a new language. The real task of treatment can only be the identification of areas of primitive thinking (including affectivity and somatization) and efforts, by whatever means we can find, to promote the maturation of the relevant cognitive functions (see Gedo, 1988, Epilogue).[1] This is precisely what the various forms of "working through" try to accomplish.

WORKING THROUGH AS THE REPAIR OF APRAXIA

Whenever I have tried to promote self-inquiry on the part of analysands, I have encountered a variety of consequences, depending on the particular person's "psychological-mindedness." Certain analytic patients respond to a simple expression of my puzzlement about some aspect of the current material with a stream of relevant

---

[1] Needless to say, these analytic procedures have nothing in common with the naive therapeutic method called "cognitive therapy," which deals only with conscious mental contents.

associations from which they formulate seemingly valid insights, and they demonstrate this ability very soon after starting treatment. Others flounder, become blocked, start arguments about the relevance of my inquiry, accuse me of interfering with their spontaneous productions, subtly change the subject—they display the gamut of resistances to analytic methods. Obviously, sometimes the nature of our analysand's response is merely a function of the specific transference pattern uppermost at the moment, but (and this is crucial) some analysands are unable to reach their own insights, even after years of analysis and no matter what the state of the transference may be. We label such people "psychologically obtuse." With them, working through requires operations much more complex than simple self-exposure to gradually increasing intensities of unpleasure in order to master trauma.

It is sometimes assumed that an analysand's obtuseness is necessarily a function of the need for defense against insight. Whenever such failures occur *only* in the analytic situation, it is indeed legitimate to look upon them as instances of "pseudo-stupidity." In many cases, however, one discovers that the lack of psychological-mindedness constitutes a handicap in everything the patient undertakes. To illustrate: One analysand, who was a psychotherapist, was just as unable to make inductive inferences about his own patients as he was about himself. Ultimately he acknowledged, in the face of great humiliation, that he was generally unable to follow the narrative of the movies he attended; he had to rely on his wife to explain the gist of their plots. Needless to say, in his analysis, the process of working through required a great deal of intervention designed to help him to connect the data of his experience with concepts he could understand.[2]

A lack of psychological-mindedness is by no means the only kind of ego distortion (if I may use the vocabulary of a past generation) that has to be overcome in the process of working through. To mention only the most obvious of examples, patients with delinquent propensities and those who, in the course of regressive transferences, lose the ability to communicate through consensually meaningful words also present unusual challenges if these obstacles to insight are to be overcome. Of course, until relatively recently persons with such ego defects were allegedly discouraged from

---

[2] Hence, formal learning difficulties and neurocognitive problems should be added to the roster of the "psychological" causes of faulty adaptation (Levin, 1991).

undertaking an analysis. (In a letter to Edoardo Weiss, Freud [in Weiss, 1970] literally advised Weiss to arrange to exile to South America a prospective analysand with delinquent traits!) In the last 25 years, however, the scope of psychoanalysis has been sufficiently expanded to permit persons with many such handicaps to attempt analytic treatment. Instead of demanding prior guarantees of an "intact ego," many contemporary analysts accept the responsibility to assist even severely handicapped persons in working through their difficulties in processing the information relevant for their problems. Starting 30 years ago, I have been proposing a variety of interventions, each designed to address the specific handicaps caused by early derailments of development (see Gedo, 1964, 1966, 1967b, 1979, 1988, 1991a, 1993b; Gedo and Goldberg, 1973).

Let me illustrate what might be involved in working through a transference resistance consisting of serious lapses into delinquent behavior in the psychoanalytic setting proper. In the terminal phase of a tempestuous and lengthy analysis, a competent professional woman continues to proclaim that she can never change what is fundamentally wrong with her, although she looks upon these characteristics as shamefully undesirable. Her pessimism is not groundless, for she continues repetitively to reenact in the transference her destructive attacks on the work of those she envies, particularly those of brother figures. In other words, she is engaging in the familiar ploy of defeating her analyst by refusing to make progress, because she feels she would remain inferior to him even if she got well. The impasse has been very difficult to overcome because analytic interventions are invariably met with furious accusations of misconduct and other unreasonable arguments. It is very much to the point that the patient's self-contempt is largely focused on the acknowledged fact that she is a habitual liar. She avoids stating the truth whenever she can circumvent trouble or humiliation by doing so, and even in the analysis she often resorts to prevaricating in this manner. In the battles she is now waging against the analyst, she utterly disregards the obligation to articulate what she believes to be true (or at least to label her falsehoods as such). In sum, she does not meet the basic requirement for productive analytic work, that of engaging in free association: whenever she is threatened with a sense of helplessness, she regresses to an archaic identification with her abusive father and as a result her language comes to be used sadistically to manipulate the analyst.

No doubt it is in principle correct to attempt to resolve this impasse by means of repeated interpretations of the transference, but these efforts remain ineffective because the patient fails to attend to the lexical meaning of these communications. In her mind, this dialogue does not consist of messages having truth value but only of maneuvers, with no holds barred, in a wrestling match each participant is determined to win at any cost. She hears interpretations as a stream of confabulations designed to defeat her. Of course, this difficulty is merely an aspect of the very transference the interpretations are intended to bring to the patient's attention—but to work through this resistance it is imperative to depart from merely repeating, in a language the patient refuses to listen to, the analyst's understanding of the transaction. There are a number of possible solutions for such a therapeutic dilemma (see Ehrenberg, 1992); let me cite only one alternative. In such circumstances, the best chance of reestablishing one's credibility is to convey one's authentic affects. Hence, it might be effective to say, with profound indignation, "No wonder you hate yourself! You're a goddamned liar! You're cutting your own throat by mistrusting me because you imagine I'd stoop to your dirty tricks!"

Similar regressive impairments of the ability for meaningful communication may occur on the basis of transference developments of various other kinds; they are by no means confined to circumstances in which analysands reexperience primitive hostility. I have already mentioned that in certain contingencies analysands may relive archaic transference patterns that involve some degree of loss in the very ability to use words consensually. Such therapeutic regressions to conditions preceding the attainment of full linguistic competence may even occur in the context of a *positive* transference. I wish, however, to illustrate the problem by means of an incident precipitated by my failure to realize that, after several years of work, a shift to a dyadic (mother) transference was finally taking place; instead, I perseverated in making interpretations of the hostile father transference that had long held sway. (I have already described this transaction in chapter 1.)

In response to these untimely (and therefore inexact) interpretations, the analysand developed a perceptual illusion that the consulting room was permeated by a fecal odor for which he believed me to be personally responsible. I knew that, in the middle of the second year of life, this man had had an illness characterized by foul-smelling diarrhea. Hence I suspected that the new development in the transference echoed his mother's disappointment about his progress as a toddler, albeit it did so by means of a role reversal. Yet, making such an interpretation did not dispel the analysand's conviction that I had literally befouled his analysis—his concretization of a disappointment in my analytic performance into a foul smell first had to be undone. The necessary working through could not be accomplished as long as I tried to communicate through the customary channels of psychoanalytic discourse. For the moment, the patient could only process the affective content of my speech and simply did not attend to or register the meaning of my words.

The acute phase of this crisis did not prove to be too difficult to overcome by conveying the relevant information—that the analysand was in a confusional state—with urgency and emphasis, in the manner I tried to illustrate through the previous example. Instead of going into detail about the specific manner in which I chose to encode the intervention, let me stress the rationale of such a departure from the technique appropriate to deal with compromise formations stemming from intrapsychic conflicts. In this instance, the conflict created by my therapeutic error rapidly led to a catastrophic regression involving even functions that were usually stable and, in Hartmann's (1939) term, "autonomous." In the framework of the hierarchical model I use (Gedo and Goldberg, 1973; Gedo, 1979, 1988, 1991a; see also Epilogue, this volume), this shift involved reorganization from a relatively advanced mode of functioning that permitted discourse on an adult level to a primitive state wherein the meaning of another's communications could be gauged only in terms of the paraverbal aspects of speech. The resultant mode of functioning calls for an analytic response different from a technique relying on communications encoded in secondary-process terms (see chapter 8).

At any rate, getting past this temporary episode did not by itself constitute working through the patient's propensity either for concretized thinking or for trying to humiliate people before they had an opportunity to humiliate him. This is not the place to describe how such changes might be effected; suffice it to note that to accomplish such far-reaching goals, as a first step, he had to learn to make use of analytic interventions. For him, this required making certain that he truly understood what his interlocutors were trying to tell him in their every statement. In other words, he had to accept the usual ground rules of rational discourse among adults, a matter about which this very eccentric person was largely ignorant when he started his analysis. In parallel with our efforts to persuade analysands to associate freely, we have to convince them that they must not be arbitrary in interpreting our communications.

A series of procedural skills of this kind have to be learned to achieve "working through." Hence, I have concluded that this modality of treatment is best understood as an educational process (see also Ekstein, 1965; Wilson and Weinstein, 1992 a, b), or, if you will, a "technology of instruction" (Gedo, 1988, Epilogue). Analytic progress means that a wide spectrum of procedural skills have been learned, so that focal ego defects (apraxias) are overcome.

THE NEUROLOGY OF WORKING THROUGH

I have used the example of two kinds of apraxic disorders of communication to suggest that, with patients who do not meet ideal criteria of analyzability, the process of working through necessarily entails the acquisition or consolidation of modes of thought more effective than those previously available to them. It is through such after-education (Freud, 1916–17, p. 451) that the analyst's words have a mutative influence on the analysand's psychobiology. As I have already mentioned, it has been thought that analysands who bring rich ego resources to the joint endeavor do not appear to need parametric interventions by the analyst to assist with the process of working through, as do those whose psychological resources are allegedly less suited to the analytic task. It was postulated that, if we simply instruct the better prospects to free associate, and if we interpret the resulting material correctly, they metabolize the information thus provided in a manner that produces adaptive change. But we should never forget that such an ideal scenario is a theoretical fiction, never attained in actuality.

The realities of clinical practice tend to echo Freud's (1909) experience with the Rat Man, who in his very first analytic session demanded a dispensation from the basic rule. You will recall that Freud did not treat this request as simply another link in a chain of associations, to be met with expectant silence; he chose to intervene in a noninterpretive manner instead, instructing his patient to consider that assenting to the analysand's request would constitute a procedural violation that was likely to defeat their therapeutic aim. In other words, he met a resistance to adherence to the analytic compact not by an interpretation of motives for defense but by confronting the basis of the demand in poor reality testing. Powerful persuasion, indeed! This classic example demonstrates that even patients well suited for our procedures require orientation and instruction in its methods to be able to profit optimally from analysis.

Around 40 years ago, when I entered the psychoanalytic community, it was often said that, when an analysand has mastered the skill of associating freely, the time has come to plan for termination.

Today, with looser criteria for patient selection prevailing, such an aphorism may sound facetious, but in the 1950s it was arguably valid: the major resistance to be worked through with analysands who can profit from our traditional interpretive technique is the propensity to compromise the basic rule. Thus, acquiring the ability to free associate, whatever the circumstances may be, usually takes some time and much effort; but, once it *is* acquired, it does make insight through self-inquiry feasible. The foregoing notion is therefore very similar to Otto Isakower's unpublished idea, also widely discussed a generation ago, that effective analytic work presupposes that the practitioner possesses a cognitive structure Isakower named "the analytic instrument," one presumably acquired in the course of a training analysis. As I have suggested in another context (Gedo, 1993a), the crux of the matter in both cases may be the acquisition of a "self-analytic instrument."

The notion of such a cognitive apparatus involves psychological skills transcending the freedom to associate without defensive impediments; it implies, in addition, that the operator is able to understand and to articulate the crucial meanings of the associated mental contents. This ability is always contingent on overcoming the ubiquitous tendency defensively to disavow unpleasant truths, but it is equally related to the degree of the person's talent for finding hitherto unknown patterns of meaning. The specific skill most important for discerning such meanings is that of translating concrete experience impregnated with subjectivity into reasonably reliable, secondary-process terms.[3]

Although the development of thinking is a direct reflection of the maturation of the brain, we know that this process is, in turn, decisively influenced by infantile experience. Mental activities Freud (1911) called the primary process become operational earliest; the secondary process becomes additionally available after the child's symbolic capacities mature. The third phase in the development of thinking is the acquisition of the ability to correlate primary and secondary processes—a third process Bucci (1993) calls "referential activity." This is the development most vulnerable to unfavorable

---

[3] Rapaport (1940, p. 244) was aware of the significance of the symbolic transformation of memories, whereby a higher level of functioning, involving deeper self-cognition, is achieved. This transformation takes place by means of associative linkages between experience and symbol. This process corresponds to the conception of working through presented here. Concrete examples of the foregoing process can be found in chapter 14.

environmental vicissitudes. To put this differently, the acquisition of these skills is maximally dependent on stimulating environmental input. The talent for finding meanings in the data produced by free associations is a function of the degree to which referential activity has become elaborated. In other words, for psychologically obtuse persons, the process of working through necessarily involves the expansion of referential activity, that is, the actual reorganization of the relevant aspects of brain function (see also Gray, 1973).

RECAPITULATION

Let us, at this point, recapitulate the thesis presented thus far. I have postulated that adaptational change requires the abandonment of established response patterns through the facilitation of preferable alternatives by means of a gradual consolidation of the automatic use of the new patterns. Such a reorganization of neural networks is the necessarily slow process we call working through. I have offered several examples of the kind of psychological changes that may be entailed in such a reorganization: from the acquisition of hitherto missing skills in communication, through the gradual expansion of referential activity, to the consolidation of the ability to free associate, even in the face of mounting unpleasure. Whatever contributions the analyst may make in the interpersonal field to facilitate the requisite changes, lasting reorganization can take place only as a result of intrapsychic processes. Hence, it should be spelled out how the various changes included under the rubric of working through might be explained, preferably in terms of a single concept.

Let me begin with the matter of expanding referential activity so that the analysand becomes able to interpret the meanings of personal experiences—to overcome an inability to read one's own affects or to discern correctly the purport of other somatic events, for example. Such changes will, for the first time, make it possible to deliberate about alternative adaptive responses to the contingencies that produced the reactions in question. In neurophysiological terms, either cortical processing replaces automatic responses mediated in the midbrain, or the cortex and midbrain collaborate to provide better control. From a cognitive vantage point, this amounts to the acquisition of a symbolic code permitting constructive use of relevant information through timely retrieval and appropriate diffusion; prior to learning this new skill, the affected person could only emit a series of signals of gradually increasing intensity, messages that necessarily remained undeciphered.

I have chosen the specific example of the inability to recognize affects to illustrate the broader category of communicative deficits, because the task of overcoming the resistance to uninterrupted free association also depends on substituting reflection for pure affect. As I have already mentioned, Freud (1926) understood the need to inhibit desirable activities—like free associating in the analytic situation—as a function of an inability to contain dysphoria, a condition he called actual neurosis. Thus the process of mastering the potentiality for panic (or, for that matter, for lapsing into somatization or clinical depression) corresponds to the acquisition of a symbolic code to deal with contingencies that were previously processed unconsciously, producing only affective or other somatic signals to mark their cogency (see Gedo, 1991a, chap. 6; chapter 3, this volume). In other words, insofar as working through involves the mastery of affective intensities, this process (like the expansion of referential activity) actually consists of learning to *think* in a manner that can potentially solve life's problems. The ability to engage in reflection is, in itself, the best way to avoid helplessness.

The foregoing examples of working through, then, are best conceptualized as bringing into play more efficient psychical operations by developing new modes of thought or, if you will, new channels of intrapsychic communication. In this sense, they are indistinguishable from the third kind of change I have discussed, the improvement of skills in interpersonal communication, for any such change for the better in sending or receiving information greatly enhances the effectiveness of the analysand's thinking. In other words, every type of working through with which I am familiar amounts to training in the rare skill of thinking straight.

14 On Fastball Pitching, Astronomical Clocks, and Self-Cognition

AT THE WORLD SERIES

Some years ago, I was invited to deliver a Radó Lecture to the Columbia University Institute for Psychoanalytic Training and Research. This event was scheduled to take place at the New York Academy of Medicine, and my hosts insisted that I wear a tuxedo for the occasion. The night before I left for New York, I had a dream that struck me as so fitting that I decided to share it with the audience at the start of my presentation. After the lecture, more than one person complimented me on the clever joke in the form of a pseudodream they thought I had concocted. Of course, I knew that these misperceptions were trivial—I had, indeed, created the manifest dream—but I found it difficult to grasp how anyone could see these matters as comic.

In my dream, I was at Yankee Stadium. I was wearing a baseball uniform and warming up in preparation for the start of the World Series. I realized that I was the pitcher Ron Guidry, who was supposed to lead the New York Yankees to the championship. A number of sportswriters approached me, and one of them asked, "Is it true that you have the best fastball in the business?" I gave the inquiry careful consideration but remained puzzled. Finally, I answered, "I don't know. We'll see. We'll see." This answer gave me enormous pleasure.

More than 15 years have passed; I suppose I can now forgive those who found my discomfort laughable. Perhaps one cannot expect people to empathize with a successful person who has reached a pivotal moment in his life. At the time, I was totally preoccupied with the dream. It was beyond my control to disavow its significance or to stop the process of trying to discern its meaning—after all, I had even continued the effort to decipher it in the course of my lecture. It is not irrelevant that the topic of the presentation was the problem of "the choice of symptom," so that I experienced this message from the inner depths as a unique marker of my own compromises in adaptation, a key to the issues left unresolved in my personal analysis.

I do not mean to imply that I ever reached a definitive or fully satisfactory understanding of the dream; after all, it is self-evident that at this time I feel the need to review its significance once again. Although my willingness to share some of the results of my introspection with my readers is a consequence of a certain degree of confidence I have gained about understanding myself—and the belief that others will empathize with such self-inquiry (as the French say, *"Tout comprendre, c'est tout pardonner"*)[1]—I do not plan to share the putative infantile determinants of the intense ambition articulated in the manifest content of the dream. First, I do not wish to claim more self-knowledge than I in fact possess; second, about certain matters I do not intend to surrender my privacy.

I did not know, I said, whether I was then the "best in the business," but my current assignment led me to take the possibility very seriously, indeed. I once lived in New York for a decade and attended medical school there. During those years, the New York Academy of Medicine assumed for me the aura of The Castle in Kafka's fiction. My father had attended medical school in Prague and practiced in New York for many years. Yankee Stadium, Hradčany Castle, and the Academy of Medicine, where I was now a welcome personage, were inaccessible to him, a perpetual exile. Perhaps I had achieved this competitive success because my father, poor man, never gave himself the opportunity to have a psychoanalysis, and his introspective efforts—he tried, he really did!—were defeated. At any rate, a dozen years ago, Ron Guidry really did have the best fastball in the majors, and a *Times* reviewer had called my representation in a *roman-à-clef* about analysis "a wise and gentle guru. . . . "

I suspect that people were amused by the lame pun on my name involved in identifying with the Yankee player. For me, of course, other, less obvious associations were more important. I did not wish to be taken for an invader from Chicago, with its inept baseball teams—or, if you will, my psychoanalytic loyalties were with the Eastern establishment. It is my Boston friend and colleague, Robert Gardner, who is in the habit of saying, "We'll see." I was still a Yankee fan, almost 30 years after accustoming myself to spoken English by listening to radio broadcasts of the Yankees' 1941

---

[1] To understand completely is to forgive everything.

championship season. The star of 1941 had been Joe diMaggio, a son of recent immigrants; Guidry himself was a francophone Cajun from Louisiana; and I had arrived in New York from French North Africa. And so forth.

I do not report these details at this juncture because they matter in themselves; I am merely trying to illustrate the kinds of thoughts that were crowding in on me following the occurrence of the dream. Suffice it to say now that the sum of these associations pointed in the direction that I had always desired to be the very best, that nothing had thus far occurred to disabuse me of these hopes, and that I was still in painful suspense about how to evaluate my performance. This was much as I had been as a 15-year-old greenhorn, when I applied for admission to Columbia College. (I was somewhat bitter then about being rejected, although subsequently I came to realize that an Ivy League college full of prospective Navy officers [V12][2] would have been a bewildering place for a child of political refugees. Perhaps the college authorities understood that I would not fit in.) Was it arrogant of me to think that there is special merit in finishing high school that early, or in articulating a new theoretical proposal for psychoanalysis in the 1970s? We'll see; we'll see . . . In the meantime, one cannot allow Radó Lectures, tuxedos, or reporters of psychoanalytic meetings to turn one's head. (Or, I might now add, to discourage one: the Reporter of my presentation utterly misunderstood it and wrote an offensively hostile commentary. Sometimes "Kill the umpire!" is really the only proper attitude one can take!)

At any rate, the pleasure I experienced in my dream seemed to be connected to the long-delayed and still tenuous mastery of the propensity to yield to complacency or self-satisfaction. Fastball pitchers are likely to ruin their arms—this was to be the fate of Ron Guidry within a few years—and the proponents of theoretical schemata in psychoanalysis generally gather a cult following devoted to glorifying the leader. I had recently witnessed the fall of an admired colleague as a consequence of such a failure of self-criticism. As another great Yankee, Yogi Berra, always said, "It ain't over 'til it's over!"

THE SELF-ANALYTIC INSTRUMENT

In the course of my 35 years of self-inquiry (Gardner, 1983), the number of experiences as illuminating as the dream of the World

---

[2] The V12 program put Naval Cadets into colleges during WWII. Consequently, civilians were crowded out of certain schools, including Columbia.

Series could be counted on the fingers of one hand. As I recall, in every instance of that kind, some insight was attained as a result of a process set in motion without my conscious volition. Some mental content—perhaps a dream, a daydream, sometimes a parapraxis—would come back as if to haunt me, even if at first I made no effort to pay attention to it. When I had further associations to such material, they flowed easily, and I had a mounting sense of excitement and discovery.

If one can refer to the mental operations involved as an "apparatus," this equipment was automatically triggered, and, once the process started, it appeared to have a certain momentum that carried it to a more or less satisfying conclusion. In no case was the conclusion an end point: I am discussing matters of lifelong significance that do not admit of any permanent solution. In the early stages of these experiences, I was aware that the associations that arose into consciousness represented only the tip of an iceberg of mental activity. Preoccupation with the underlying problem was continuous and absorbed as much capacity as other requirements of living allowed me to spare.

I should perhaps specify that I never experienced such an episode prior to the termination of my analysis—or, for that matter, while that treatment was in progress. I have therefore concluded that this new functional capacity was one (invaluable!) benefit gained from analytic treatment—the acquisition of previously unavailable psychological skills as a consequence of new learning (Gedo, 1988, Epilogue). Although I am aware that the term has been used in a slightly different sense, I believe that Isakower's famous concept of an "analytic instrument," the availability to an analyst of certain unusual cognitive skills, may be applicable to the phenomena I have in mind. As I stated in chapter 13, perhaps we might call it the "self-analytic instrument." I suspect that certain cognitive operations, initiated in the course of a therapeutic analysis, are facilitated through practice and then become automatic as a consequence of the adaptive advantages they confer on the individual. From the viewpoint of cognitive psychology, the relevant skills have been described by Bucci (1993), who calls them "referential schemata," which connect verbal and nonverbal representations. The attainment of such abilities should be a primary goal of every psychoanalytic treatment.

It is also worth noting that these capacities are not available to me as a matter of choice; they go into operation only in case of dire necessity. Whenever I have tried to evoke them as a matter of conscious volition, the nature of the subsequent psychological processes was utterly different—not necessarily less useful, but lacking in the automaticity and unbroken impetus that characterize the more crucial episodes. The latter almost always arose in the context of fundamental problems in adaptation and not in performing the responsibilities of a psychoanalytic clinician. To cite an example that might well apply to many other people, the first of my children's marriages produced an emergent need to reexamine my sense of "self-in-the-world." In comparison, the desirability of analyzing a parapraxis committed while doing analytic work pales in significance.

All that is not to say that career issues are less likely to arouse adaptive emergencies than are family matters—after all, the illustration with which I began this chapter deals with a turning point in professional life. In fact, the very first time I experienced the availability of the processes in question was toward the end of my candidacy at the Chicago Institute, when a bitter confrontation I had with a supervisor led the powers that be to urge that I resume a personal analysis. In the face of this pressure (and the implicit threat of penalties for noncompliance), the yield of the self-analytic process emboldened me to assert that accepting the opinion of someone else in such a situation would have amounted to a self-betrayal. It is people who are unable to stand their ground who need therapeutic assistance.

On that occasion, in the very midst of my preoccupation with this dilemma, I did consult my former analyst, and it was his inability to add anything to my own thinking about the problem that convinced me that interpreting the meanings of one's associations is best performed by oneself. It was entirely clear to me that I was the only one who had at his disposal the full range of associations to my associations, so that no other person, however professionally skillful, was equally positioned to formulate the requisite interpretations. My conviction in this regard did not find confirmation in the analytic world until Robert Gardner (1983) showed me early drafts of his crucial study of this question, *Self Inquiry*. Thus, the problem of self-analysis is not the difficulty of discerning the proper interpretation, however novel that insight may be; it is the scarcity of affectively charged associative material in circumstances less emergent than are the crucial turning points I have discussed thus far. Another way to put this is that one must be strongly motivated to deal with one's routine resistance to self-inquiry, and it is strong affect, particularly *unpleasant* affect, that is most likely to provide the necessary motivation to engage in productive self-analysis. For matters of everyday significance, Freud recommended the process wittily called doing one's "analytic toilette"; as the phrase implies, this is not a pressing need.

THE ANALYST'S TOILETTE

I must admit that, on weekends and holidays, whenever I plan to stay at home, I am likely to skip shaving. I have been no more diligent about my analytic toilette—I suspect most of us regard it as a terrible nuisance, and one seldom hears about colleagues who pursue it systematically. In this regard, Calder (1980) represents the most notable contemporary exception. I require some incentive to focus my attention on poorly understood psychological issues, something like an untoward event in my consulting room or a dream charged with sufficient affect to become memorable. I do not think that the manner in which I endeavor to work on such puzzles is in any way unusual, and I shall say no more about it here: Freud's (1898) analysis of his Signorelli parapraxis may serve as the ideal prototype for such work.

What I would like to focus on, instead, is my impression that, exactly contrary to more pressing personal issues, these matters from the psychopathology of everyday life tend to involve vicissitudes in managing transference crises in the course of doing analytic work. To be more precise, in my experience, incidents that require self-analytic attention tend to arise when, in a way more subtle and insidious than usual, an analysand creates a transference enactment wherein the role of his or her childhood self is assigned to me while that of the original parent is assumed by the patient. Whenever such a constellation goes undetected for a while, one is likely to respond (countertransferentially) with complementary attitudes or activities without realizing that one has accepted a role extrinsic to one's usual motivations. The crux of the self-analytic task in such contingencies is to differentiate what is authentically one's own desire from behaviors that comply with the desires of the analysand.

To give a brief example of a temporary confusion about such matters: Some time ago, I was forced to make a slight change in my schedule, so that my appointment with a certain analysand was to begin and end ten minutes later than previously. Shortly thereafter, I realized one day that I had terminated his session six minutes early, under the sway of an illusion that I had kept him four minutes overtime. When I asked the patient whether he had noticed my error, he replied that he had only perceived that he had felt confused about when his session should have ended. I then made it clear that the error was entirely mine and that I did not yet understand its significance or even whether it had a bearing on his analysis. There matters rested for a few days, until I made an identical parapraxis. Before the patient's next session, I made a good-faith effort to take care of my "analytic toilette," and I realized that I was enacting my analysand's habitually cavalier attitude about our schedule. I began the next session by telling him that, by reversing our roles, I was sending the nonverbal message he had repeatedly sent me: that it is intolerable to be at another person's mercy with regard to that person's availability. When he perceived that he had the power to cause me the kind of discomfort he found so difficult to bear, this patient's need to convey his feelings through nonverbal channels was replaced by syntactically encoded messages. In parallel, I regained my customary ability for precision in my handling of time.

As a consultant, I have had the opportunity to observe that even colleagues with adequate self-analytic capacities tend to have particular difficulty in preventing patients from perpetuating enactments wherein the analyst is sadistically abused. Similarly, it took me many years to trust my own sense of outrage whenever I felt misused in the analytic situation—to understand such a reaction as a signal of a potentially fruitful transference-countertransference development (such as the parapraxes about time I have just described) rather than seeing it as an unmanageable reality. Yet, of course, every occurrence of this kind must call forth fresh self-analytic efforts, lest one fall from the frying pan of masochism into the fire of unempathic rigidity.

What is most difficult about handling these matters through self-analysis is the lack of opportunity to get consensual validation for one's conclusions. Perhaps the solution most frequently available to analysts is to seek consultation with a trusted colleague, either formally or informally. My own experience has been confined to the arena of informal exchanges with friends. When I have been consulted by colleagues, generally of a younger generation, they have very seldom shared with me detailed personal material; if they talked about countertransference feelings or a temporary identification with a patient, they tended to state their self-diagnosis tersely, without citing their thinking in reaching it.

The question of needing validation induced Ferenczi (Dupont, 1988, pp. 71-73) to experiment with mutual analysis, reportedly with a patient who was also a colleague. Obviously, the experiment proved only that such a procedure is unworkable. In my experience, however, it is on rare occasions quite effective to share the results of a bit of self-analysis with analysands, particularly those who have good reason to mistrust their caretakers' capacity for honest self-inquiry. (Whenever I have tried such a procedure, I have been as careful to balance the need for candor with the desirability of preserving my privacy as I have tried to be in writing this chapter.) Clearly, there is no time for serious self-analytic efforts in the course of performing an analysis for someone else, so that one should have the conclusions of a piece of self-inquiry ready-to-hand before attempting to communicate them to a patient.

In these circumstances, it should be possible to determine in advance the appropriate limits of the self-revelations one is willing to make. With my patients, I have seldom mentioned any details of my personal history or my current private life, and (in exact parallel with my policy in writing this chapter) I have shared aspects of my inner life only insofar as I felt entirely comfortable about them. But as I have grown older and better established as an analyst, I have become comfortable about more and more aspects of our common humanity.

ISSUES UNRESOLVED IN ANALYSIS

Obviously, the useful range of self-analysis may have its limits. It is important to be able to determine when it would be preferable to seek either consultation (about a clinical impasse) or further personal treatment. On theoretical grounds, I suspect that it would be extremely difficult (perhaps impossible) to deal with archaic issues against which more or less successful defenses were erected in childhood without setting in motion a systematic regressive process in a context conducive to the evocation of transferences. This is particularly true if the relevant issues have been split off from the part of the personality that came into focus in a therapeutic analysis. In other words, self-inquiry is most likely to be fruitful if one's defenses are neither too rigid nor completely unfamiliar—or, if you will, when one has overcome one's propensity to avoid threats of potential traumatization (Freud, 1926).

Obviously, none of us gets immunized against potential traumata through personal analysis, so that self-analysis remains a limited instrument for us all. I have found that I have been unable to profit from it when, in the context of some meaningful relationship, someone repeats with me those behaviors of my parents (particularly the mother-of-attachment) that proved to be traumatic in the past. In some instances, the old wounds have reopened and were healed only by the passage of time. On other occasions, I could see the traumatic potential before it reached me, and I withdrew from the situation—something I had been unable to do as a child. It is probably worth noting that neither waiting out a traumatic state nor withdrawal qualifies as self-analytic activity.

Despite these caveats, the cumulative results of continuing self-inquiry can be far reaching. In my own case, I suspect that I have changed more decisively in the decades since I terminated my personal analysis than I did during that treatment. Yet it was the experience of the analysis that made subsequent self-analysis possible for me. In some instances, I have come to believe that certain issues were misunderstood when they emerged in the analytic transference. I shall here offer only one relatively innocuous example of such an error.

A pattern of slight tardiness for analytic sessions was interpreted by my analyst as an expression of depreciation for my elders and betters. This inexact interpretation temporarily eliminated the symptom, which then recurred after termination. It was permanently overcome following a casual remark by a colleague who witnessed my distress on an occasion when I was afraid of being tardy. This casual acquaintance bluntly stated that my discomfort was entirely self-induced. Confrontation with this self-evident truth enabled me to review the transference meaning of having come late for analytic sessions. I believe it represented ambivalence about longing for maternal involvement in regulating time-related activities. (My analyst was perfectly correct in sensing my hostility but absolutely wrong in seeing *this* bit of behavior as depreciating—I believe I had been trying to fend off a wish to submit to his overwhelming influence.) I have never since become disorganized in carrying out my schedule. I assume that such a correction of an inaccurate interpretation was possible only because the defenses against experiencing unjustifiable hostility had been loosened and the entire sequence of transference reactions continued to be affectively available for reprocessing.

Perhaps the effects of dealing with issues that failed to emerge in the course of analysis have been still more striking than that of correcting minor errors of commission. In my own case, I now consider the most important omission to have been a failure to examine carefully the meanings of a commitment to a healing profession, although, to be sure, we did consider such obvious determinants of this choice as my identification with a physician father. At least, this omission is the one I have thus far found to be most regrettable. Needless to say, I have no way of identifying other sleeping dogs that subsequent events have still failed to waken, to use the metaphor Freud (1937) appropriated to characterize this issue.

Interestingly enough, I have been very slow to come to grips with my unconscious motives for becoming a clinician, despite my lifelong preference for the humanities (I should have become a historian of medieval Europe!) and a marked scholarly bent. Needless to say, this problem does not occupy the forefront as long as clinical work is going well—the secondary gains of being a successful clinician generally silence all objections. Thus I did not confront this issue until I also encountered it in family life, in what I found I expected from my grown children in return for having been a conscientious (and relatively successful) caretaker.

That I expected more than one could realistically hope for was gradually clarified, in large measure through sharing my feelings with friends at the same stage of life, many of them analysts. (I do not mean to suggest that my attitudes were significantly different from those of my peers: we all had to come to terms with the fact that adequate parenting is, in retrospect, simply taken for granted.) In the process of renouncing unwarranted expectations, I experienced moments of bitterness, and these eventually focused on some of my professional disappointments as well. In particular, I began to feel that my local colleagues did not adequately reciprocate my efforts on behalf of the analytic community. This idea was concretized in my mind in the form of the metonym that I was being used in the same way as the famous astronomical clock of Strasbourg, which goes through amazing gyrations at an appointed time, for the delectation of assembled multitudes. I was so taken with this image that I began to write a "memoir" around it, at first without realizing that the impulse to make art was taking the place of self-inquiry.

After a while, I became sufficiently aware that I was engaging in symptomatic behaviors to mention my preoccupation to a respected, older colleague, who, not at all coincidentally, reminded me of my father. We were in an informal setting, and my friend wisely fended off my communication with a joke. I mention this detail merely to suggest that the temptation to reestablish a father transference alerted me to the fact that I was struggling with archaic issues—that the culprits were neither my children nor my indifferent fellow analysts. This was the only occasion, I believe, when my effort to seek validation for my self-analytic attempts took the form of turning to a transference figure rather than an alter ego. It was also the sole instance of not finding a receptive ear when I shared something private with a fellow-analyst.

At any rate, I began to pay closer attention to the fantasy of the astronomical clock as a potentially analyzable derivative of the underlying issues. I trust it will be understood that I prefer not to spell out the details in their entirety. Suffice it to say that Strasbourg is connected with my mother, some of whose forebears were Alsatian, and that it was for her that I had first attempted to perform wonderful but dehumanizing feats. In this sense, all analysts are used, appropriately, as scientific measuring devices. In our professional capacity, we cannot expect reciprocation on a human level. All those who have paid the price of admission may take advantage of our services without giving us credit or even feeling gratitude. A person with childhood experiences such as mine should think three times before embarking on an analytic career. I have now thought about it twice, and I decided to eliminate my clinical responsibilities. It has been a salutary change!

THE POWER OF FREE ASSOCIATION

I trust that I have now provided a fair sampling of bits of my self-analysis and that these vignettes suffice to demonstrate that, albeit this process of self-inquiry appears haphazard when observed in terms of its overt (i.e., conscious) manifestations, in reality it amounts to a continuous (and therefore essentially seamless or holistic) monitoring of one's status as an individual within a specific milieu. Doubtless most of the time this process is automatic and can yield effective results without gaining conscious representation. The manner in which a skilled driver operates an automobile may be roughly analogous to the operation of routine self-analytic activities: only when one is confronted with sudden and previously unfamiliar contingencies does it become necessary to pay conscious attention to such matters.

Viewed from this perspective, the new psychological skill one acquires in the course of a personal analysis is that of systematic reliance on the process of free association. Clearly, when one resorts to this process, self-inquiry has been elevated to the level of consciousness. Endopsychic resistance to facing the truth about oneself in "one's own mind" perforce must take the form of breaking off the work of associating before it succeeds in linking words and affects. It is true that certain matters of archaic origin may never have been verbally encoded and consequently may emerge not in the form of a symbolically represented "thought" but in that of pure affect or some other bodily event. It is just as feasible, however, to observe such phenomena and draw verbally encoded conclusions about them in the course of self-analysis as it is to discuss them in discursive language in a dyadic analytic setting. In sum, the most important gain of a personal analysis proves to be the conviction one should gain about the unfailing power of Freud's procedure—paying minute attention to the yield of the free-associative effort to produce increments of self-understanding. One must learn to damn the torpedoes and think full speed ahead.

If, by reaching rational, symbolically encoded conclusions concerning one's self-monitoring, one is enabled to make reasoned decisions about one's future conduct, this acquired skill—the all but unique outcome of mastering the analytic method—should provide greater effectiveness in choosing optimal adaptive solutions. As the frequent necessity for resuming therapeutic analyses demonstrates, all too often analysands fail to master this skill during their initial exposure to the analytic situation. I believe it is worth discussing some possible reasons for this kind of failure.

My experience in performing second (or third, or fourth!) analyses has given me the impression that a certain attitude of laissez-faire has become prevalent about making certain that the method of free association is in fact followed by analysands. On one hand, it is often falsely assumed that, as long as patients keep talking, they are adhering to Freud's technical prescriptions—this laxity may lead to the neglect of associative links that are not topically related. On the other hand, it is nowadays quite common to condone the triumph of resistances vis-à-vis the obligation to report all mental activities—as if the anxiety or shame attendant on total candor were more than analysands can be expected to bear. The result of such complaisance is the encouragement of irresponsibility about the analytic task. Analytic delinquents will not acquire self-analytic skills.

One of the principal pieces of evidence that will convince me that a reanalysis is needed, if I am consulted by someone who was previously analyzed, is the report that, instead of attempting to achieve self-understanding by engaging in free association, the patient tries to fit his or her behavior into certain (more or less familiar) formulations. These formulations may be either those heard in the analysis or (in the case of mental health professionals) certain intellectualizations that may have come into fashion more recently. Although such a result may come about in a number of different ways, it is quite likely that such persons had analyses characterized by excessive interpretive activity by the therapist. Moreover, the interpretations seem often to have been chosen arbitrarily: analytic formulae used as magical incantations.

Am I implying that, if all analyses were properly conducted and completed, their outcomes would obviate the need for reanalysis because sufficient self-analytic capacity would invariably develop to deal with all subsequent adaptive challenges? I am tempted to think that this statement approaches the truth—although, to be sure, perfection in human affairs is unattainable, and it is never to be expected that any analysis will be concluded without serious flaws. There is, though, one particular constellation of circumstances that may leave an analysand unprepared to cope with future contingencies through self-analysis, however "properly" the initial treatment may have been performed. I have in mind the possibility that certain potential difficulties may be masked through the provision of symbiotic assistance by family or friends, so that the developmental deficits in question never come up for scrutiny in the first analysis. In such a case, later loss of the symbiotic mode of adaptation will leave the person unable to cope, however capable of self-inquiry he or she may be. The loss of symbiosis reveals potentialities for traumatization that were previously warded off by the assistance of the symbiotic partner.

In this regard, it is relevant to recall that Kohut (1984) ultimately came to believe that the very effort to engage in self-analytic activities is a pathological disavowal of our eternal need for "self-objects" (i.e., that it is healthier to turn for assistance to another person than it is to attempt to cope by using one's own resources!). I hope it is clear that such an opinion reflects assumptions about the human condition that I do not share. No stigma should be attached to the need for several periods of analysis to deal with different sets of pathological deficits. In principle, however, the primary task of every analysis is to enable the analysand to conduct effective self-inquiry, thus freeing the person of the necessity to use therapeutic assistance. Incidentally, when Kohut first communicated his clinical discoveries about what he called "narcissistic" transferences, he proudly shared with his friends his conviction that they were the fruits of his self-analytic activities. Pathological or not, the process of self-inquiry may be fruitful!

IN PRAISE OF SELF-INQUIRY

In a celebrated letter to Wilhelm Fliess, Freud (in Masson, 1985, p. 281) stated that self-analysis is actually not feasible—that in his own case, he had succeeded only in applying the insights accumulated in his analytic work with his patients to the material of his associations. My personal experience has been different. Although it is ever tempting to resist self-understanding by falling back on intellectualizations, in the manner Freud mentioned, for me such defensive operations obstruct self-inquiry only when I am going through the motions, pro forma. It must not be forgotten that Freud made his pessimistic assessment without the benefit of a personal analysis—or, if you will, at a time when systematic ego analysis was more than a generation away. Once an analysand has learned to identify his or her defensive operations and consequently masters the capacity volitionally to forego using these capacities in the service of resisting self-cognition, some measure of self-inquiry does become feasible.

If the results of self-analysis tend to be underplayed, nonetheless, I suspect that this prejudice may stem from the widespread conviction that personality change is most likely to occur as a consequence of transference interpretation. Whenever the problem represents a transference repetition of more or less archaic behavior patterns, it is, of course, quite true that transference interpretation is most likely to lead to insight, and such circumstances are unlikely to arise in a self-analytic context.[3] It is quite erroneous, however, to assume that useful self-knowledge can be gained only about transference repetitions. In my experience (Gedo, 1988, chaps. 11–12), it is equally crucial to gain insight into the precise limits of one's psychological skills, thereby enabling oneself to fill the lacunae in one's repertory. In the realm of overcoming one's apraxic deficits, the potentialities of self-analysis are limitless.

---

[3] Such contingencies are by no means unknown. One colleague shared with me his experience of developing a crucially meaningful transference to the analyst of his spouse, a process he was able to turn to good account through self-analytic efforts.

Epilogue

THEORIES OF MOTIVATION

To achieve a coherent theory of mental functioning, psychoanalysis cannot continue to explicate its clinical observations through the "complementary" use of multiple models, each based on differing premises (see Gedo, 1979).[1] The current profusion of plausible theories in psychoanalysis is, moreover, unmanageably prolix (Gedo, 1991b). This is true in spite of the principle that the psychoanalytic theory of mind must account for the complexity of frequent shifts in the adaptive devices currently in use from one developmental level to another. In accord with the epistemological principle of "Occam's razor," that is, the imperative of choosing the simplest possible hypothesis among those available to explicate a given set of data, our theory of mind must account for these shifts in terms of the laws of development accepted within theoretical biology as these apply to the theory of motivation.

Although there is general consensus that psychoanalysis is a science of motivations, there is much less agreement about how "motivation" should actually be defined. According to the dictionary, the word refers to whatever impels a person to act—or, more narrowly, to act volitionally. In Freud's metapsychology, the focus shifted to mental acts, and motivation became the force that sets the mental apparatus in motion, what psychoanalysis viewed from the "dynamic" viewpoint. This conceptualization presented depth psychology in the language of physics, particularly that of the late 19th-century science of electricity. In parallel with measurements in terms of volts, ohms, and amperes, Freud relied on concepts of

---

[1] Not every theoretician within psychoanalysis has concurred with the desirability of postulating a single, internally consistent theoretical system. Among others, Kohut (1977, pp. xvii–xviii), Modell (1983, unpublished), and Pine (1990) have explicitly endorsed simultaneous resort to incompatible but complementary theoretical fragments. Admittedly, adherence to values of classical order or to those of romantic chaos is a matter of subjective preference (see Gedo, 1986). Yet only a yearning for order and simplicity will motivate psychoanalysts in the Einsteinian quest for a single general theory.

forces, resistances, and energies. In other words, a dynamics of motives implicitly required complementary concepts of structure and intensities. Freud outlined such a theoretical schema between 1892 and 1900, from "Sketches for the Preliminary Communication of 1893" to chapter VII of *The Interpretation of Dreams*.

For two decades thereafter, Freud tried to define the nature of behavioral phenomena he attributed to a "repetition compulsion." Hartmann's heirs have also failed to note that, once we have abandoned the assumption that drive theory must apply to the entire range of motivated behaviors, it is no longer necessary to accept Freud's a priori postulate that narcissistic motivations are fueled by a special kind of libido. Thus, for the past generation or more, psychoanalysis has not had a coherent theory of motivation.

To fill this vacuum, Joseph Lichtenberg (1989) has made an extensive effort to classify those universal human goals that can be presumed to have constitutional roots. Largely on the basis of behavioral observations in the psychoanalytic situation, he has listed a set of five independent, preprogrammed biological patterns of motivation. Lichtenberg calls these biological systems attachment, aversion, active exploration, sensuality/sexuality, and the maintenance of physiological equilibria. In a chapter appended to Lichtenberg's (1989) *Psychoanalysis and Motivation*, June Hadley (1989) reviews the neurophysiological data available through 1989; she confirms that structures mediating behaviors serving the aims listed by Lichtenberg do exist in the brain. Neither author excludes the possibility that neural structures subserving further organismic goals may yet be found, so that it is possible that additional preprogrammed motivations may have to be added to such a list. It must be kept in mind that the ultimate decision on this matter should be made on the basis of neurophysiological data: the functional definition of motivational systems, which are necessarily wired into the brain, does not constitute theory construction *within* psychoanalysis. Thus the identification of a physiological blueprint for exploration/assertion, for example, is a matter entirely different from postulating an "aggressive drive." And it is illegitimate to assert the operation of any drive for which brain mechanisms cannot be found (see Hadley, 1989; Levin, 1991; Levin and Vuckovich, 1987). At any rate, Lichtenberg's schema does take cognizance of "self-preservative" aims, as well as sexual and aggressive ones.

If we face the implication of Freud's greatest scientific contribution—the conclusion that most mental activities remain unconscious—it should be acknowledged that the organismic needs subserved by the motivations wired into the brain are generally pursued automatically, without self-awareness; their current status can be inferred only from the shifting affective reactions generated in response to relative success or failure in meeting these manifold needs. The aphorism that man is a thing of shreds and patches can refer only to the kaleidoscopic alterations in these affective states. At any rate, the difficult-to-discern blueprint of organismic needs is rendered into a recognizable image only when it has been given coloring by affectivity (see Basch, 1976).

Basic human motivations are constant from the cradle to the grave; psychological development consists of the acquisition (either through the unfolding of constitutional potentialities or through learning by means of environmental input) of ever more complex skills that expand the possibilities of success in fulfilling organismic needs. Acquisition of such skills as the consensual use of language, rational thought, reality testing, and the capacity to recognize one's own affects and those of others is the prerequisite of what psychoanalysis calls "emotional maturation." Note that these basic constituents of being human-among-humans can come into being only if the child has the requisite capacity to process the information provided by its environment (see Freedman, 1984), including symbolically encoded information and direct perceptual input.

Most of the basic skills necessary for adaptation are learned so thoroughly that they remain available in almost any circumstance. Some acquired skills can remain in the person's repertory only under certain specific environmental conditions. Whenever these conditions seem to be unavailable, other features of the behavioral repertory become manifest. In a clinical context, we tend to describe such contingencies as the emergence or predominance of a previously splitoff (or sequestered) sector of the personality. Alternatively, it is possible to conceive of these events as results of a regression that leads, at least temporarily, to the reestablishment of a mode of functioning more archaic than the one apparently characteristic for that person. If, however, a skill has been permanently acquired, we call this state of affairs the accretion of mental structure.

THE LIMITS OF PREPROGRAMMED PATTERNS

Whether or not it is satisfactorily inclusive (a question to be discussed later in this Epilogue), Lichtenberg's (1989) theory of motivation has entirely abandoned the matrix of Freud's metapsychology. Lichtenberg's motivational systems are not conceived as drives pressing for discharge or as forces, presumably bound to encounter structural resistance and characterized by measurable intensities. His theory is not an extrapolation from the physics of an electrical apparatus; rather, it is an example of cybernetics. As such, it relies on a much more sophisticated understanding of the operations of neural control than did Freud's theories of motivation, which were based on the brain science of the 1890s. It should be noted that Freud also had to rely on additional biological models that seem inadequate today; thus his notion of *Trieb* echoed the operation of urinary excretion: something was steadily produced, it accumulated and built up pressure and urgency, and after a period of resistance it was discharged, with satisfaction and relief.

The set of preprogrammed biological patterns listed by Lichtenberg is available at all times through the life cycle; each is evoked by the adaptive requirements for which it is appropriate. In other words, sexual or aggressive motives come into play in response to specific stimuli, not because of built-up drive pressures. Once a child becomes capable of creating fantasies, this potentiality makes it possible to stimulate sexual (or aggressive) responses autochthonously, without external cues. (In this connection, it should again be noted that Freud did not postulate an aggressive drive; what he did assume in his late work was the drive-like operation of primary masochism [Freud, 1924]—a notion crucial for Melanie Klein's, 1984, theories.) Insofar as sexuality does operate in accord with a preprogrammed "blueprint," this state of affairs can prevail only in infancy, before this bit of patterned behavior is integrated into more complex hierarchies of motivation. (I have discussed this issue in similar terms and in greater detail in Gedo, 1988, chap. 15.)

The greatest advantage of Lichtenberg's proposal is that, once we are freed of the constraint of having to devise a theory of motivation that is at the same time a drive theory, it becomes possible to extend the definition of motivation beyond the realm of the preprogrammed patterns essential for survival. Let us take the example of a Roman Catholic nun who, according to her spiritual advisor, has pursued the ideal of belonging to an "aristocracy of goodness." In her analysis, it comes to light that she developed this ambition to overcome a sense of being a monster of badness. This reaction formation marked the resolution of a predominantly negative oedipal struggle through the internalization of rigid superego standards. This woman has now derived most of her satisfaction in life from pursuing the paths of virtue (as these are understood in her community) for some four decades. How are we to understand her motivation for so doing?

In clinical terms, most of us would attribute her gratification to increased self-esteem due to living up to an ideal, as well as the feeling of competence involved in doing anything well. We might wonder about the possibility that some of the satisfaction could be masochistic, but further consideration of the analytic material revealed nothing of the kind: rather, this person was merely *inhibited* with regard to her sexuality, which remained fixated on certain infantile aims. In other respects, she was able nonmasochistically to lead a life rich in a variety of ways. It seems that what started out as mere reaction formation had, in Hartmann's (1939) terms, undergone a change of function: being virtuous remained this woman's primary goal even after she was relieved of her sexual inhibitions through the analysis.

I do not see how this set of priorities could be determined by any preprogrammed pattern wired into the brain. These are precisely the circumstances that impelled Freud (1914a) to postulate the existence of "narcissistic libido"—a desperate conceptual tour de force designed to apply drive psychology to behaviors lacking direct connections to man's presymbolic world. In considering matters involving abstractions such as "good" and "bad," we are dealing with a symbolic universe much more complex than that of inborn patterns of organismic response—whether such programs are conceived of as drives or as broad adaptive requirements such as the "motivations" postulated by Lichtenberg. This is not to say that human ideals are disembodied, but that, with regard to such "higher" functions (n.b.: "superego"), what is built into the nervous system is the capacity to regulate behavior on the basis of manipulating abstract symbols.

Perhaps it would, in fact, be misleading to equate capacities preprogrammed to subserve adaptation *qua* motivations with the power of abstract ideas to propel human behavior. Moreover, attaining conceptual clarity is complicated by the operation of the principle of multiple function (Waelder, 1936): every behavior simultaneously serves several purposes. It is entirely possible to aspire to an aristocracy of virtue in order to fulfill some aversive goal, for example—let us say, to distance oneself from a despised parent—while, at the same time, this ambition satisfied a wish for moral excellence. Hence I prefer to approach complex matters of this kind by applying to them a hierarchical schema (see Gedo and Goldberg, 1973; Gedo, 1979, 1988; Wilson and Gedo, 1993).

A HIERARCHICAL VIEW OF MENTAL FUNCTIONING

Hierarchical concepts entered my theoretical views in the late 1960s, when, in collaboration with Arnold Goldberg, I made an attempt to reexamine the competing models of mind then in use. We concluded that the clinical data elicited in the psychoanalytic situation were then optimally explicated through appropriate resort to a minimum of five different theoretical subsystems (Gedo and Goldberg, 1973). Three of these, the topographic theory of 1900, the structural theory of 1923, and the 1900 model of the "reflex arc," were introduced by Freud; the other two, the theory of object relations (see, e.g., Fairbairn, 1954, Winnicott, 1958, or Bowlby, 1969) and that of archaic mentation prior to the development of symbolic capacities (see Barry, 1987), were introduced later to complement the Freudian models.

In contrast to Freud's consistent use of the libido theory to bind together his entire conceptual system like an underlying armature, the foregoing models are five fully independent constructs. Before our effort of 1973, they had never been adequately correlated. As Rapaport (1967, pp. 599, 750) was the first to note, the two post-Freudian models are not based on the libido theory. To create a supraordinate model that could legitimately use all five of the foregoing theoretical fragments, Goldberg and I (1975) were therefore obliged to relinquish libido theory as the central organizing principle of the system.

We felt confident about this choice because Freud's (1920) own theoretical work on archaic mentation found the concept of libido to be too narrow to deal with the phenomena of the "compulsion to repeat." Freud tried to preserve the internal coherence of psychoanalytic theory by inventing a new drive psychology broad enough to accommodate all analytic findings. To do this, he had to make his concepts so abstract and generalized that they failed the test of clinical relevance: through sheer disuse, the theory of life versus death instincts has become a historical relic. A generation later, Hartmann (1948) tried to breathe new life into the dual-instinct theory by counterposing libido and aggression. In doing so, he created an admirably tidy but grossly reductionistic system that leaves phenomena referable to the compulsion to repeat unaccounted for. Hartmann's version of "ego psychology" has been rejected by the great majority of analysts because of its neglect of derivatives of the earliest phases of development (see Klein, 1984).[2]

---

[2] Of course, Klein's rejection of Hartmann was paralleled by her continued use of the death instinct concept; as I have discussed elsewhere (Gedo, 1986, chapter 6), she bent this in a manner Freud could not have accepted because of its overt vitalism.

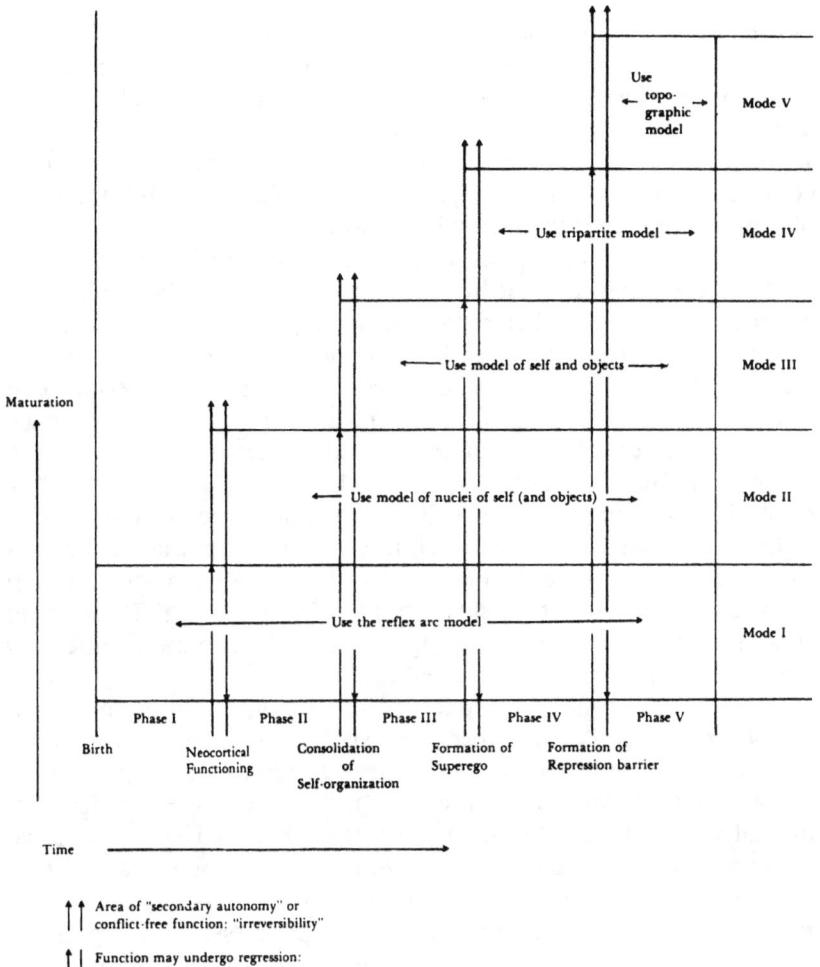

Figure 1. The Hierarchical Model: Modes, Phases, and Appropriate Subordinate Models of the Mind (after Gedo and Goldberg, 1973)

By devising a hierarchical schema (Figure 1), instead of relying on drive theory, Goldberg and I (1973) proposed a model able to accommodate a series of subsidiary theoretical schemata by ordering them in a sequence presumably duplicating the serial occurrence of typical developmental nodal points in the course of childhood. It is well to remember that we made no claim that by juxtaposing the five clusters we had culled from the literature of psychoanalysis we had satisfactorily covered all contingencies. Quite the contrary: if the evolution of clinical experience should begin to highlight typical developmental patterns underemphasized in previous psychoanalytic discourse, these changes of focus would necessitate the insertion of additional phases into the hierarchical schema, yielding an even more complex map of the modes of functioning available in adulthood and observable in the psychoanalytic situation.

Another signal of caution to be observed about the hierarchical model is the reminder that human behavior need not be exclusively governed by the characteristics of a single developmental level. Contrary to such a schematic ideal of global developmental regression or progression, clinical observation reveals that people can selectively use functional capacities from various modes of organization (that is, developmental levels) simultaneously (Gedo, 1988, chapter 3). This differential regression in various "ego functions"—a blessed inconsistency, if you will—has generally been described as a "splitting" of the mind. The term is not felicitous, for it falsely implies that the normal state is necessarily that of adaptation through consistent adherence to a single mode of functioning. There is no reason to suppose that such a simple state of affairs would confer any advantages on anyone constrained to live by it.

At the same time, the aspects of psychological functioning that are of greatest clinical interest—the psychopathology that forms the subject matter of our clinical theories—do tend to be organized in terms of various modes that are age-appropriate at specific developmental phases in childhood (Figure 2). Hence, from a conceptual viewpoint, the clinical theory of psychoanalysis should focus not on distinctive syndromes but on the protean human capacity to respond to changing aspects of the milieu with progressive or regressive movements along the developmental axis. These movements constitute organized shifts in behavior that give the *appearance* that clinical entities are emerging or dissolving.

The adaptive devices currently available to an individual originated at various developmental levels; clinical theory must account for the shifts among these devices and levels of psychic organization. In this view, adaptation involves the attempt to fulfill as many as possible of the person's lasting motivations by selecting from a repertory of patterned modes of behavior the particular alternatives that have the best chance to attain the desired goals in the context of current circumstances. (In this view, maladaptation consists in being constrained to make unfortunate choices in this regard, for instance, through unthinking reliance on precedents poorly applicable in the present.) Let us now consider how the human motivational system can be illuminated by means of a hierarchical schema.

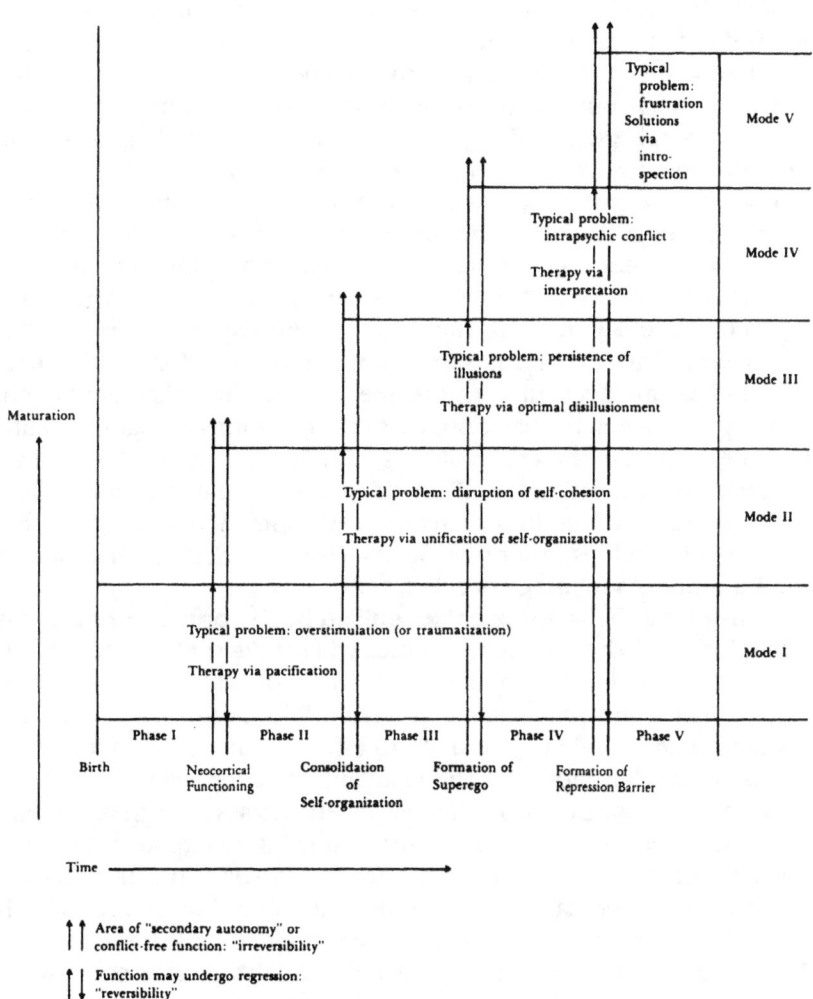

Figure 2. Hierarchical Schema of Problems Typical for Specific Modes of Functioning and Their Therapies

THE HIERARCHY OF MOTIVATION

Insofar as a set of inborn programs for action are present from birth, the simplest and most basic system of human motivations is in force only as long as these biological potentialities operate in pure culture, unmodified by actual experience. (These are the conditions I have called "mode I" in the various hierarchical schemata I have proposed.) The influence of nurture makes itself felt by means of remembered patterns of affective responses that were typically evoked by various contingencies. It is important to note that affects are also preprogrammed organismic responses; according to Tomkins (1970), they are called forth by various patterns of events within the nervous system. But *memories* of previously experienced affects may serve as signals about the expectable consequences of various behaviors. Whenever a system of such signals becomes operative, the organism has acquired a second order of motivations—what Freud (1911) variously termed the pleasure principle or that of "unpleasure." The latter term is the more appropriate, for it is the threat of unpleasant affects that is more likely to override other motivations. At any rate, when the basic organismic motivations are supplemented by the guidance of memory-signals, conditions may be classified as a more differentiated mode (II). Incidentally, for the moment we have no evidence about how early in development such signals may become conscious, nor do we know whether they can motivate the child without attaining consciousness.

Insofar as behavior becomes guided by the principle of avoiding "unpleasure," the resultant activities will *on the surface* appear to be aversive; that is, they will seem to be motivated in terms of the preprogrammed schemata of "aversion." It is true, of course, that these functions will be recruited to effect the necessary actions, but *at bottom* what motivates the resultant behavior is a preference for one affective state over another. Psychoanalysis is a depth psychology precisely because it is never content with surface explanations alone. The neonate appears to look for interesting novelty because exploratory schemata are wired into the brain, but before long the infant will engage in exploratory behaviors because he or she has previously found them to be pleasurable. Such a change corresponds to the progressive organization of the central nervous system for ever more complex functioning: as Hadley (1989) put this, a neurophysiological subsystem "which supplies both positive and negative motivations depending on the outcomes of the matching process and the addition of affect" (p. 337) is activated in the course of development.

Psychoanalysts have long had consensus about the privileged role of affective experience—the need to keep its intensity within prescribed boundaries and, from a qualitative point of view, to promote the occurrence of certain preferred emotional experiences and to avoid those for which the person has an aversion. In putting this matter in quasiphysiological terms (as Freud, 1895a, did), I am, at the same time, linking this kingpin of the theory I propose with Stern's (1985) emphasis on the crucial role of affective attunement between infant and mother *prior* to the full maturation of any symbolic capacity (see also Emde, 1980). In my judgment, the quantitative and qualitative parameters of the affective patterns established in a privileged position during the preverbal era form the core of those aspects of experience human beings are compelled to repeat, at any cost, in order to maintain a sense of their own continuity (Gedo, 1979, pp. 146–147; 1981b).[3]

It is especially important to note that it is never self-evident whether any specific type of activity will evoke pleasure or unpleasure, even if, were it to occur in isolation, its effects would be experienced in some particular way by everyone. In other words, in vivo no activity occurs in isolation but only in the context of a variety of complex transactions with the milieu. Thus infants with unusual experiences may learn that exploratory behavior is followed by very unpleasant consequences or that temporary spells of unpleasure are rewarded by long-term satisfactions. Whenever an individual is consistently subjected to paradoxical results of this kind, the system of affective signals will produce seemingly maladaptive motivations capable of overriding "expectable" motivational schemata.

Nor does the evolution of motivational complexity stop with the acquisition of this second layer of causation for behavior. Repetition of patterns of activity and their characteristic affective coloring will relatively quickly result in the formation of a model of self-in-the-world, probably in some medial structure like the cerebellum (see Levin, 1991). This is the process I have proposed to call self-

---

[3] In later life, the occurrence of lasting unfavorable affective reactions is almost always the consequence of intrapsychic conflict. Clinical experience has revealed that conflicts about sexuality and aggression are not the only relevant ones in this regard: Modell (1965) has called attention to conflicts about affiliation and attachment; Kohut (1971) highlighted those related to a whole series of ambitions and the need for idealized others; my own clinical contributions have focused on conflicts generated by failure to acquire essential psychological skills—conditions I call apraxic (Gedo, 1988). There are doubtless still other kinds.

definition; when the model is firmly in place, it forms a self-organization (Gedo, 1979). As Hadley (1989) has pointed out, repetitions of behavior are measured by comparator mechanisms that signal their attainment by means of neurochemical changes that produce subjective "satisfactions." These are the neural functions corresponding to the phenomena psychoanalysis has attributed to the repetition compulsion. When self-organization has become stable, the rate of tolerable change is greatly reduced, so that the need to maintain this rate within the boundaries of comfort becomes a third type of motivating force for human behavior. These are the conditions characteristic of mode III in the hierarchical model.

Among unceasing motivations clinicians are actually confronted with, the need to preserve the integrity of self-organization—to resist any impingement on one's primary identity, to use an alternative vocabulary—is the most fundamental. In contrast, preprogrammed schemata are engaged on an ad hoc basis, and, as rational and social considerations gradually gain more and more influence on behavioral choices, even the operation of the pleasure/unpleasure principle becomes merely episodic. Another way to put this is that the formation of a stable self-organization is equivalent to the integration into a single hierarchy of aims of the disparate biologically determined motivations of the infant. Henceforth the maintenance of this macrostructure assumes a supraordinate role for the individual.[4]

This enduring state of affairs is then greatly complicated by the transformation of the child from an organism regulated by biological automatisms and by affectomotor cues from the caretakers to a being capable of symbolic operations, including consensual language (at worst, if the child is deaf, sign language). These cognitive gains enable the child to grasp whatever increases or decreases his or her value in the estimation of the parents and to accept the standards implicit in such judgments. At this stage of development, children also become capable of learning a system of symbols to represent various affects; as a result of this cognitive advance, they are enabled to achieve emotional self-awareness. Henceforth, verbal transactions are mediated by way of affective responses along a pride-shame axis—or, if you will, a new pathway for motivating behavior becomes available, that of pleasure-unpleasure in response to conceptual

---

[4] According to Hadley (1989), the repetition compulsion corresponds to the neurophysiological mechanism that underlies *all* motivation, namely, "the maintenance of familiarity of neural firing patterns" (p. 337).

categories (such as good and bad). This development initiates the fourth phase in the elaboration of the motivational hierarchy.

Another way to conceive of this watershed in development is to focus on the child's new-found ability to experience conflict about a wish. This change is a result of an increasing tendency simultaneously to keep in mind representations of other wishes with which the initial wish is incompatible (Barry, 1987). The need in such circumstances to avoid painful affects gives rise to defensive operations, such as disavowal of the significance of the wish or forgetting its ideational content—"repression," as Freud (1915a) called it. Achievement of the ability to avoid distress by forestalling danger through defensive maneuvers greatly increases the child's power to pursue most of its organismic goals, albeit at the price of frustrating certain wishes. This is the achievement I call the attainment of self-regulation. Before it is reached, the child is unable, when left to its own devices, to maintain behavioral integration; it is at the mercy of caretakers to establish priorities on its behalf. Henceforth, it turns into a creature of self-awareness, able to establish priorities among its wishes on the basis of the remembered affective consequences of their fulfillment or frustration.

Clinical experience has taught us that embarrassment—even humiliation—is sometimes insufficient to override motivations stemming from the need to maintain the stability of the self-organization. We see this most clearly in those instances where the stability requires some kind of symptomatic behavior that induces shame but is endlessly repeated in spite of this emotion. One common example is that of compulsive self-mutilation. If, however, the conflict between ideals and the need for stability arises in early childhood in a particularly intense and prolonged manner, this irreconcilable and potentially traumatic circumstance often leads to defensive splitting and a permanent division of the personality into unreconciled and contradictory "nuclei" (see Gedo and Goldberg, 1973).

Are we justified in classifying motives that arise as a result of the onset of shame and pride (or, at a somewhat later stage, the analogous operation of guilt) as independent sources of behavioral initiative? When, in clinical work, we rashly undertake to treat people whose development was arrested at such a primitive level that they remain functionally shameless (or, a more common circumstance, if we deal with a patient whose capacity for shame is split off from the dominant fragment of the personality), our difficulties soon teach us the importance of the availability in childhood of culturally acceptable behavioral standards, enforced through shame or guilt and promoted by example. Thomas French (1952) once suggested that we call these "acquired" reasons for human action "countermotives"; this is another way of indicating that these are motivations arising as a consequence of superego formation.

One way to conceive of felicitous development is that it requires a self-organization flexible enough in rate-of-change to assimilate the countermotives learned from the caretakers, without inducing defensive splitting. If a child is able to make such an accommodation, superego standards become hierarchically dominant, and the four classes of motivation thus far discussed are smoothly integrated into one single assembly.

If the motivations newly acquired during this fourth phase of development represent the functional entity Freud (1923) named "super-ego," those remaining to be added in the course of later development are the motives-for-action related to the functions that Hartmann (1939) conceptualized as the aspects of the "ego" subserving optimal adaptation. In a discussion of the requirements of civilized existence, Freud (1927b) referred to such motivations as the soft "voice of the intellect." The voice of reason and "common sense" gradually gains more and more influence on the individual's behavior as that person becomes less and less dependent on caretakers to monitor his or her decisions. Hence the timing of the acquisition of these motivations is widely variable: some children learn to rely on their own judgment as early as the age of latency; most people seem to assume these burdens in the course of adolescence; still others do so only sometime in adult life—or never at all.

CLINICAL ILLUSTRATION AND SUMMARY

Perhaps a clinical illustration may help to illuminate what it means not to develop autonomous motives to achieve satisfactory adaptation and, simultaneously, it may clarify the nature of the need to plan behavior on a rational basis. I can offer the example of a middle-aged professional man who had always used therapists, with greater or lesser frequency, since he discovered the availability of such services when he was in college. He was sophisticated enough to obtain competent help at all times and, with this assistance, was able to master his discipline and manage a career of some distinction. It was only when his mother died, when the patient was around 50 years old, that we discovered that what had appeared to be vocational ambition was merely compliance with a demanding parent's desire for narcissistic satisfaction from her talented son.

In private life, this man led an isolated existence devoted to the pursuit of momentary satisfactions: gluttony, masturbation with fantasies of perverse enactments, penny-ante gambling, sadistic provocations vis-à-vis powerless strangers (such as waitresses or cabdrivers), entertainment he could enjoy passively and in privacy. However disastrous such a way of life turned out to be, he responded to the very idea of expanding his horizons with aversion. Ultimately, he came to the realization that clinging to this primitive agenda represented a desperate loyalty to his "true self" (in Winnicott's, 1954, sense of the term), just as his professional activities had initially constituted a "false" one. Because success as such was, of course, very satisfying for him, the patient eventually adopted as his own what had originally been his mother's ambitious goals for him. His self-esteem came to depend on his vocational achievements instead of remaining tied to his mother's positive responses to him.

When this man entered analysis, the mother transference took the form, in large part, of looking to me for approval—and disapproval. One might characterize these responses as a "mirror transference" in Kohut's (1971) terms. In these circumstances, the patient projected onto me the ideals he had absorbed from his mother. Because she had been a very bizarre lady, some of these standards were rather odd: for example, the highest good was to be a successful trickster by means of glib and misleading pronouncements. Nonetheless, it did come to light that this stunted personality did possess some motivations stemming from a system of ideals he had made his own in childhood. However, we never detected any evidence of genuine guilt.

When this analysis entered the termination phase, we encountered tenacious resistances to the completion of treatment. The analysand overtly articulated the wish to perpetuate my availability indefinitely because he felt too deficient in judgment to manage his own life without provoking fresh adaptive difficulties. Closer examination of these issues confirmed that, with regard to practicalities, he was still childlike, unable to formulate a plan, and dependent on external guidance; he was grossly "apraxic."

What I found most surprising, however, was this highly intelligent person's inability even to imagine an alternative to extracting symbiotic assistance from a therapist. It is true that, in this sense, the self-organization was based on the premise of a psychic merger with an enslaved caretaker—like Aladdin commanding his genie—so that any change in these adaptive arrangements could take place only very gradually. At the same time, the very notion of *coping* was utterly alien to this man. The relevant adaptive functions were missing; he was never motivated to do anything simply because long-term advantages might follow. To give one concrete example, he was unable in a consistent way to keep his car in working order and respectable shape, although he was utterly humiliated if people who knew him professionally detected the state of its disarray.[5]

I hope I have provided enough detail to show that the absence of motivations stemming from the side of an "organ of adaptation" (in this case because of an overriding need to preserve a state of psychic merger) creates a crippling handicap to adult adjustment. Whenever a person, such as the foregoing analysand, "chooses" a regressive solution, we would do well to consider very seriously the probability that he or she does not have the psychological skills requisite for a progressive one. We may expect to find that the challenges of the relevant developmental phase could not be met because the outcome of all previous developments left the person with a certain deficit, or "apraxia."[6] Apraxias may come about as a result of constitutional deficiencies, unsuccessful nurture, or (most frequently, I suspect) a combination of both.

On the basis of such data, I conclude that adequate development implies the integration of motives stemming from the following sources:

Mode I: the inborn, preprogrammed motivations proposed by Lichtenberg (1989)

Mode II: the differentiation of the pleasure-unpleasure gradient

Mode III: the overarching importance of a stable self-organization

Mode IV: the internalization of ideals (and imperatives)

Mode V: the learned requirements of adequate adaptation

---

[5] The psychogenesis of this unusual character structure is not germane to the thesis of this discussion, but, for those interested, it may be summed up as an upbringing in which the mother forced a psychic merger on this, her youngest child. Only the clarification of the genesis of his need to enslave a caretaker (as a reversal of his emotional position as a child) could lead to a wish on his part to learn to manage for himself. Although this process was necessarily slow, it did not present any major difficulty, and the analysis was eventually successfully terminated.

[6] Should this claim sound too radical, recall that Freud (1926) continued to assert that every unresolved neurotic conflict is based on an underlying "actual neurotic" core—that the inability to tolerate the anxiety generated by an unacceptable wish is caused by a deficit in affect tolerance.

Epilogue

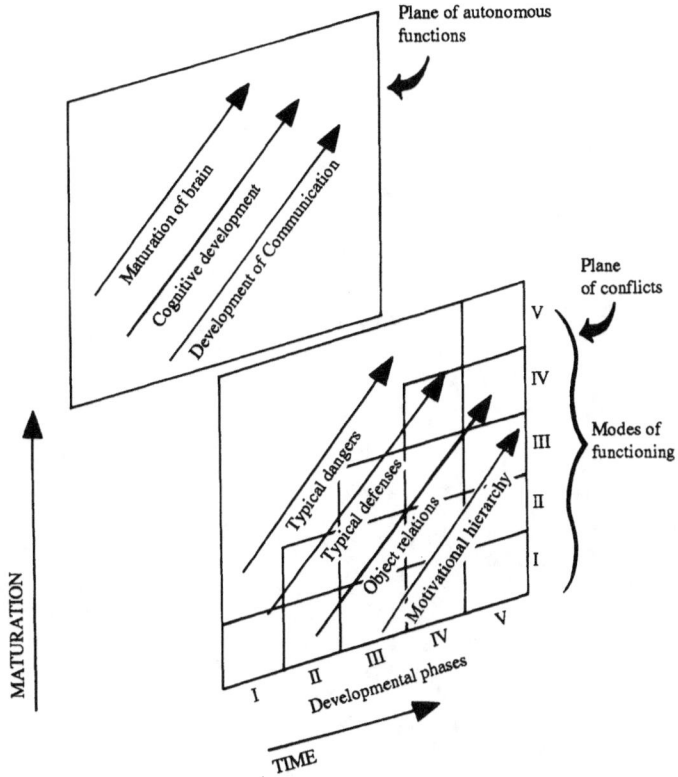

Figure 3. The Lines of Development of the Revised Hierarchical Model

This line of development may be entered on the hierarchical model, as in Figure 3. A great deal, however, remains to be learned about the manner in which these complex motives are optimally integrated or come into conflict with each other and produce maladaptation.

References

Abraham, K. (1924), A short study of the development of the libido viewed in the light of mental disorders. In: *Selected Papers on Psycho-Analysis.* London: Hogarth Press, 1942, pp. 418-449.

Alexander, F. (1950), *Psychosomatic Medicine.* New York: Norton.

———— (1956), *Psychoanalysis and Psychotherapy.* New York: Norton.

———— & French, T. (1946), *Psychoanalytic Therapy.* New York: Ronald Press.

Aron, L. & Harris, A., eds. (1993) *The Legacy of Sándor Ferenczi.* Hillsdale, NJ: The Analytic Press.

Bacon, K. & Gedo, J. (1993), Ferenczi's contributions to psychoanalysis: Essays in dialogue. In: L. Aron & A. Harris, eds., *The Legacy of Sándor Ferenczi.* Hillsdale, NJ: The Analytic Press, 1993, pp. 121-139.

Bálint, M. (1932), Character analysis and new beginnings. In: *Primary Love and Psychoanalytic Technique.* London: Maresfield Library, 1985, pp. 151-164.

———— (1967), Sándor Ferenczi's technical experiments. In: G. Wolman, ed., *Psychoanalytic Techniques.* New York: Basic Books.

Barry, V. (1987), Maturation, integration, and psychic reality. *The Annual of Psychoanalysis*, 15: 322. New York: International Universities Press.

Basch, M. (1974), Interference with perceptual transformation in the service of defense. *The Annual of Psychoanalysis*, 2:87-97. New York: International Universities Press.

———— (1976), The concept of affect: A reexamination. *J. Amer. Psychoanal. Assn.*, 24: 759-777.

———— (1983), The perception of reality and the disavowal of meaning. *The Annual of Psychoanalysis*, 11;125-154. New York: International Universities Press.

Bettelheim, B. (1950), *Love Is Not Enough.* Glencoe, IL: Free Press.

Blum, H. (1981), Some current and recurrent problems of psychoanalytic technique. *J. Amer. Psychoanal. Assn.*, 29:47-68.

Boesky, D. (1982), Acting out: A reconsideration of the concept. *Internat. J. Psycho-Anal.*, 63:39-55.

Bowlby, J. (1969), *Attachment and Loss*, Vol. 1. New York: Basic Books.

Brabant, E., Falzeder, E. & Giampieri-Deutsch, P., eds. (1993), *The Correspondence of Sigmund Freud and Sándor Ferenczi*, Vol. 1. Cambridge, MA: Belknap Press/Harvard University Press.

Brenner, C. (1987), Working through: 1914-1984. *Psychoanal. Quart.*, 56:88-108.

Breuer, J. (1895), Anna O. In: *Studies on Hysteria. Standard Edition*, 2:21-47. London: Hogarth Press, 1955.

———— & Freud, S. (1895), *Studies on Hysteria. Standard Edition*, 2. London: Hogarth Press, 1955.

Brodsky, B. (1967), Working through: Widening aspects of its metapsychology. *Psychoanal. Quart.*, 36:485-496.

Bucci, W. (1993), The development of emotional meaning in free association: A multiple code theory. In: A. Wilson & J. Gedo, eds., *Hierarchical Concepts in Psychoanalysis*. New York: Guilford, pp. 3-47.

Calder, K. (1980), An analyst's self-analysis. *J. Amer. Psychoanal. Assn.*, 28:5-20.

Demos, V. (1992), The early organization of the psyche. In: J. Barron, M. Eagle, & D. Wolitzky, eds., *Interface of Psychoanalysis and Psychology*. Washington, DC: American Psychological Association, pp. 200-232.

Dupont, J., ed. (1988), *The Clinical Diary of Sándor Ferenczi*. Cambridge, MA: Harvard University Press.

Edelman, G. (1987), *Neural Darwinism*. New York: Basic Books.

Ehrenberg, D. (1992), *The Intimate Edge*. New York: Basic Books.

Eissler, K. (1953), The effect of the structure of the ego on psychoanalytic technique. *J. Amer. Psychoanal. Assn.*, 1:104-143.

Ekstein, R. (1965), Working through and termination of analysis. *J. Amer. Psychoanal. Assn.*, 13:57-78.

Emde, R. N. (1980), Toward a psychoanalytic theory of affect. In: *The Course of Life. Vol. 1: Infancy*, ed. S. I. Greenspan & G. H. Pollock. Madison, CT: International Universities Press, pp. 165-191.

Fairbairn, W. R. D. (1954), *An Object-Relations Theory of the Personality*. New York: Basic Books.

Fenichel, O. (1941), *Problems of Psychoanalytic Technique*. Albany, NY: The Psychoanalytic Quarterly.

Ferenczi, S. (1912), On transitory symptom constructing during the analysis. In: *Sex in Psychoanalysis*. New York: Basic Books, 1950, pp. 193-212.

———— (1913), Stages in the development of the sense of reality. In: *Sex in Psychoanalysis*. New York: Basic Books, 1950, pp. 213-239.

———— (1933), Confusion of tongues between adults and the child. *Final Contributions to the Problems and Methods of Psychoanalysis*. New York: Basic Books, 1955, pp. 156-167.

———— Abraham, K., Simmel, E. & Jones, E. (1919), *Psychoanalysis and the War Neuroses*. London: International Psycho-Analytic Press, 1921.

———— & Rank, O. (1924), *The Development of Psychoanalysis*. New York: Nervous & Mental Disease.

Fonagy, I. (1983), *La Vive Voix*. Paris: Payot.

Freedman, D. (1984), The origins of motivation. In: *Psychoanalysis*, Vol. 1, ed. J. Gedo & G. H. Pollock. New York: International Universities Press, pp. 17-38.

French, T. (1952), *The Integration of Behavior*, Vol. 1. Chicago: University of Chicago Press.

Freud, A. (1965), *Normality and Pathology in Childhood.* New York: International Universities Press.

Freud, E., ed. (1960), *The Letters of Sigmund Freud, 1873-1939.* New York: Basic Books.

Freud, S. (1891), *On Aphasia.* New York: International Universities Press, 1953.

———— (1892), Sketches for the "preliminary communication" of 1893. *Standard Edition*, 1:147-154. London: Hogarth Press, 1966.

———— (1892-99), Extracts from the Fliess papers. *Standard Edition*, 1:177-280. London: Hogarth Press, 1966.

———— (1895a), Project for a scientific psychology. *Standard Edition*, 1:283-391. London: Hogarth, 1966.

———— (1895b), The psychotherapy of hysteria. *Standard Edition*, 2:253-306. London: Hogarth Press, 1955.

———— (1895c), On the grounds for detaching a particular syndrome from neurasthenia under the description "anxiety neurosis." *Standard Edition*, 3:87-115. London: Hogarth Press, 1962.

———— (1895d), A reply to criticisms of my paper on anxiety neurosis. *Standard Edition*, 3:121-140. London: Hogarth Press, 1962.

———— (1898), The psychical mechanism of forgetfulness. *Standard Edition*, 3:287-300. London: Hogarth Press, 1962.

———— (1899), Screen memories. *Standard Edition*, 3:303-322. London: Hogarth Press, 1962.

———— (1900), *The Interpretation of Dreams. Standard Edition*, 4 & 5. London: Hogarth Press, 1953.

———— (1909), Notes upon a case of obsessional neurosis. *Standard Edition*, 10:153-250. London: Hogarth Press, 1955.

———— (1911), Formulations on the two principles of mental functioning. *Standard Edition*, 12:218-226. London: Hogarth Press, 1958.

———— (1911-15), Papers on technique. *Standard Edition*, 12:85-171. London: Hogarth Press, 1958.

———— (1912), Recommendations to physicians practicing psychoanalysis. *Standard Edition*, 12:110-120. London: Hogarth Press, 1958.

———— (1914a), On narcissism: An introduction. *Standard Edition*, 14:73-102. London: Hogarth Press, 1957.

———— (1914b), Recollecting, repeating and working through (further recommendations on the technique of psycho-analysis, II). *Standard Edition*, 12:146-156. London: Hogarth Press, 1958.

———— (1915a), Repression. *Standard Edition*, 14:146-158. London: Hogarth Press, 1957.

———— (1915b), The unconscious. *Standard Edition*, 14:166-204. London: Hogarth Press, 1957.

———— (1915c), Observations on transference love. *Standard Edition*, 12:157-174. London: Hogarth Press, 1958.

———— (1916-17), *Introductory Lectures on PsychoAnalysis. Standard Edition*, 15. London: Hogarth Press, 1957.

———— (1920), Beyond the pleasure principle. *Standard Edition*, 18:3-64. London: Hogarth Press, 1955.
———— (1923), The ego and the id. *Standard Edition*, 19:12-59. London: Hogarth Press, 1961.
———— (1924), The economic problem of masochism. *Standard Edition*, 19:159-170. London: Hogarth Press, 1961.
———— (1926), Inhibitions, symptoms, and anxiety. *Standard Edition*, 20:87-182. London: Hogarth Press, 1959.
———— (1927a), Fetishism. *Standard Edition*, 21:149-157. London: Hogarth Press, 1961.
———— (1927b), The future of an illusion. *Standard Edition*, 21:3-57. London: Hogarth Press, 1961.
———— (1933), New introductory lectures on psycho-analysis. *Standard Edition*, 22:3-182. London: Hogarth Press, 1964.
———— (1937), Analysis terminable and interminable. *Standard Edition*, 23:216-253. London: Hogarth Press, 1964.
Galatzer-Levy, R. (1988), On working through: A model from artificial intelligence. *J. Amer. Psychoanal. Assn.*, 36:125-152.
Gardner, R. (1983), *Self Inquiry*. Hillsdale, NJ: The Analytic Press, 1989.
Gedo, J. (1964), Concepts for a classification of the psychotherapies. *Internat. J. Psycho-Anal.*, 45:530-539.
———— (1966), The psychotherapy of developmental arrest. *Brit. J. Med. Psychol.*, 39:25-33.
———— (1967a), The wise baby reconsidered. In: J. Gedo & G. Pollock, eds., *Freud: The Fusion of Science and Humanism. Psychological Issues*, Monogr. 34/35. New York: International Universities Press, 1976, pp. 357-378.
———— (1967b), On critical periods for corrective experience in the therapy of arrested development. *Brit. J. Med. Psychol.*, 40:79-83.
———— (1975), Forms of idealization in the analytic transference. *J. Amer. Psychoanal. Assn.*, 23:485-505.
———— (1977), Notes on the psychoanalytic management of archaic transferences. *J. Amer. Psychoanal. Assn.*, 25:787-803.
———— (1979), *Beyond Interpretation*. (rev.). Hillsdale, NJ: The Analytic Press, 1993.
———— (1981a), *Advances in Clinical Psychoanalysis*. New York: International Universities Press.
———— (1981b), Measure for measure: A response. *Psychoanal. Inq.*, 1:286-316.
———— (1983), *Portraits of the Artist*. Hillsdale: NJ: The Analytic Press, 1989.
———— (1984), *Psychoanalysis and its Discontents*. New York: Guilford.
———— (1986), *Conceptual Issues in Psychoanalysis*. Hillsdale, NJ: The Analytic Press.
———— (1988), *The Mind in Disorder*. Hillsdale, NJ: The Analytic Press.

———— (1991a), *The Biology of Clinical Encounters*. Hillsdale, NJ: The Analytic Press.

———— (1991b), Between prolixity and reductionism: Psychoanalytic theory and Occam's razor. *J. Amer. Psychoanal. Assn.*, 39:71–86.

———— (1993a), On fastball pitching, astronomical clocks, and self-cognition. In: J. Barron, ed., *Self-Analysis*. Hillsdale, NJ: The Analytic Press, pp. 133–146.

———— (1993b), Zur Form psychoanalytischer Interventionen. *Psyche*, 47:130–147.

———— (1993c), Empathy, new beginnings, and analytic cure. *Psychoanal. Rev.*, 80:507–518.

———— (1995a), Working through as metaphor and as a modality of treatment. *J. Amer. Psychoanal. Assn.*, 43:339–356.

———— (1995b), Encore. *J. Amer. Psychoanal. Assn.*, 43:384–392.

———— (1995c), Channels of communication and the analytic setup. *Psychoanal. Inq.*, 15:294–303.

———— (1995d), On the psychobiology of motivation. *Psychoanal. Inq.*, 15:490–480.

———— (1995e), The pragmatics of empathy. *The Annual of Psychoanalysis*, 23:1-12. Hillsdale, NJ: The Analytic Press.

———— (1996), *The Artist and the Emotional World*. New York: Columbia University Press.

———— (in press), Ferenczi as the orthodox vizier. *Psychoanal. Inq.*,

———— & Gehrie, M. (1993), *Impasse and Innovation in Psychoanalysis*. Hillsdale, NJ: The Analytic Press.

———— & Goldberg, A. (1973), *Models of the Mind*. Chicago: University of Chicago Press.

———— & Pollock, G., eds. (1976), *Freud: The Fusion of Science and Humanism. Psychological Issues*, Monogr. 34/35. New York: International Universities Press.

Gedo, P. (1991), Kris's good hour revisited: The good segment in psychoanalytic sessions. Presented to Division 39, American Psychological Association, Chicago, April.

Gehrie, M. (1993), Psychoanalytic technique and the development of the capacity to reflect. *J. Amer. Psychoanal. Assn.*, 41:1083–1111.

Grand, S., Feiner, K. & Reisner, S. (1993), The level of integrative failure in borderline and schizophrenic pathology. In: A. Wilson & J. Gedo, eds., *Hierarchical Concepts in Psychoanalysis*. New York: Guilford, pp. 48–75.

Gray, P. (1973), Psychoanalytic technique and the ego's capacity for viewing intrapsychic activity. *J. Amer. Psychoanal. Assn.*, 21:474–494.

Greenson, R. (1967), *The Technique and Practice of Psychoanalysis*, Vol. I. New York: International Universities Press.

Grotjahn, M. (1979), New insight into the life and work of Sigmund Freud: An overview of the literature since 1975. *J. Amer. Acad. Psychoanal.*, 2:299–313.

Gunther, M. (1984), The prototypic archaic transference crisis: Critical encounters of the archaic kind. In: J. Gedo & G. Pollock, eds., *Psychoanalysis: The Vital Issues,* Vol. 1. New York: International Universities Press, pp. 69-96.

Hadley, J. (1989), The neurobiology of motivational systems. In: J. Lichtenberg, *Psychoanalysis and Motivation.* Hillsdale, NJ: The Analytic Press, pp. 337-372.

―――― (1992), The instincts revisited. *Psychoanal. Inq.,* 12:396-418.

Hannett, F. (1964), The haunting lyric: The personal and social significance of American popular songs. *Psychoanal. Quart.,* 33:226-269.

Hartmann, H. (1939), *Ego Psychology and the Problem of Adaptation.* New York: International Universities Press, 1958.

―――― (1948), Comments on the psychoanalytic theory of instinctual drives. In: *Essays in Ego Psychology.* New York: International Universities Press, 1964, pp. 69-89.

―――― (1952), The mutual influences in the development of ego and id. In: *Essays in Ego Psychology.* New York: International Universities Press, 1964, pp. 155-181.

―――― & Loewenstein, R. (1962), Notes on the superego. In: H. Hartmann, E. Kris, & R, Loewenstein, *Papers on Psychoanalytic Psychology. Psychological Issues* Monogr. 14. New York: International Universities Press, 1964. pp. 144-181.

Haynal, A. (1989), *Controversies in Psychoanalytic Method.* New York: New York University Press.

Jackson, H. (1884), Evolution and dissolution of the nervous system. In: J. Taylor, ed., *Selected Writings of Hughling Jackson.* New York: Basic Books, 1958.

Jones, E. (1953), *The Life and Work of Sigmund Freud,* Vol. 1. New York: Basic Books

―――― (1957), *The Life and Work of Sigmund Freud,* Vol. 3. New York: Basic Books.

Karush, A. (1967), Working through. *Psychoanal. Quart.,* 36:497-531.

Kernberg, O. (1975), *Borderline Conditions and Pathological Narcissism.* New York: Aronson.

Klein, M. (1952), Some theoretical conclusions about the emotional life of the infant. *The Writings of Melanie Klein,* Vol.3. New York: Free Press, 1984, pp. 61-93.

―――― (1984), *The Writings of Melanie Klein.* New York: Free Press.

Kohut, H. (1957), Observations on the psychological functions of music. In: *The Search for the Self,* ed. P. Ornstein. New York: International Universities Press, 1978, pp. 233-253.

―――― (1959), Introspection, empathy, and psychoanalysis. *J. Amer. Psychoanal. Assn.,* 7:459-483.

―――― (1971), *The Analysis of the Self.* New York: International Universities Press.

_____ (1977), *The Restoration of the Self*. New York: International Universities Press.

_____ (1984), *How Does Analysis Cure?*, ed. A. Goldberg & P. Stepansky. Chicago: University of Chicago Press.

_____ & Levarie, S. (1959), On the enjoyment of listening to music. In: *The Search for the Self*, ed. P. Ornstein. New York: International Universities Press, 1978, pp. 135-158.

Kris, E. (1952), *Psychoanalytic Explorations in Art*. New York: International Universities Press.

_____ (1956a), On some vicissitudes of insight in psychoanalysis. In: *Selected Papers*. New Haven, CT: Yale University Press, 1975, pp. 252-271.

_____ (1956b), The personal myth: A problem in psychoanalytic technique. In: *Selected Papers*. New Haven, CT: Yale University Press, 1965, pp. 272-300.

Krystal, H. (1968), *Massive Psychic Trauma*. New York: International Universities Press.

_____ (1974), The genetic development of affects and affect regression. *The Annual of Psychoanalysis*, 2:98-125. New York: International Universities Press.

_____ (1975), Affect tolerance. *The Annual of Psychoanalysis*, 23:179-219. New York: International Universities Press.

Leavy, S. (1980), *The Psychoanalytic Dialogue*. New Haven, CT: Yale University Press.

Levin, F. (1980), Metaphor, affect, and arousal: How interpretations might work. *The Annual of Psychoanalysis*, 9:231-249. New York: International Universities Press.

_____ (1991), *Mapping the Mind*. Hillsdale, NJ: The Analytic Press.

_____ & Vuckovich, M. (1987), Brain plasticity, learning, and psychoanalysis: Some mechanisms of integration and coordination within the central nervous system. *The Annual of Psychoanalysis*, 15:49-96. Hillsdale, NJ: The Analytic Press.

Lichtenberg, J. (1983), *Psychoanalysis and Infant Research*. Hillsdale, NJ: The Analytic Press.

_____ (1989), *Psychoanalysis and Motivation*. Hillsdale, NJ: The Analytic Press.

Little, M. (1985), Winnicott working in areas where psychotic anxieties predominate: A personal record. *Free Associations*, 3:9-42.

Loewald, H. (1960), On the therapeutic action of psychoanalysis. *Internat. J. Psycho-Anal.*, 41:16-33.

Ludowyk-Gyömröi, E. (1963), The analysis of a young concentration camp victim. *The Psychoanalytic Study of the Child*, 18:484-510. New York: International Universities Press.

Mahler, M., Pine, F. & Bergman, A. (1975), *The Psychological Birth of the Human Infant*. New York: Basic Books.

MacGregor, J. (1989), *The Discovery of the Art of the Insane*. Princeton, NJ: Princeton University Press.

Makari, G. & Shapiro, T. (1993), On psychoanalytic listening: Language and unconscious communication. *J. Amer. Psychoanal. Assn.*, 41:991-1020.

Masson, J., ed. (1985), *The Complete Letters of Sigmund Freud to Wilhelm Fliess*. Cambridge, MA: The Belknap Press/Harvard University Press.

Modell, A. (1965), On having the right to a life: An aspect of the superego's development. *Internat. J. Psycho-Anal.*, 46:323-331.

―――― (1976), The holding environment and the therapeutic action of psychoanalysis. *J. Amer. Psychoanal. Assn.*, 24:285-307.

―――― (1979), Character structure and analyzability. *Bull. Assn. Psychoanal. Med.*, 19:97-103.

―――― (1983), The two contexts of the self. Presented to the 50th Anniversary Symposium, Boston Psychoanalytic Society & Institute, October.

―――― (1990), *Other Times, Other Realities*. Cambridge, MA: Harvard University Press.

Moraitis, G. (1981), The analyst's response to the limitations of his science. *Psychoanal. Inq.*, 1:57-79.

―――― (1988), A reexamination of phobias as the fear of the unknown. *The Annual of Psychoanalysis*, 16:231-249. New York: International Universities Press.

―――― (1991), Phobias and the pursuit of novelty. *Psychoanal. Inq.*, 11:296-315.

Morgenthaler, W. (1992), *Madness and Art*, Vol. 3. Lincoln: University of Nebraska Press.

Muller, J. (1995), *Beyond the Psychoanalytic Dyad*. New York: Routledge.

―――― & Richardson, W. (1982), *Lacan and Language*. New York: International Universities Press.

Noy, P. (1968), The development of musical ability. *The Psychoanalytic Study of the Child*, 23:332-347. New York: International Universities Press.

―――― (1969), A revision of the psychoanalytic theory of the primary process. *Internat. J. Psycho-Anal.*, 50:155-178.

―――― (1972), About art and artistic talent. *Internat. J. Psycho-Anal.*, 53:243-249.

Ornstein, A. & Ornstein, P. (1990), The process of psychoanalytic psychotherapy. *Rev. Psychiat.*, 9:323-340.

O'Shaughnessy, E. (1983), Words and working through. *Internat. J. Psycho-Anal.*, 64:281-290.

Petitto, L. & Marentette, P. (1991), Babbling in the manual mode: Evidence for the ontogeny of language. *Science*, 251:1493-1496.

Pine, F. (1990), *Drive, Ego Object, Self*. New York: Basic Books.

Racker, H. (1968), *Transference and Countertransference*. New York: International Universities Press.

Rapaport, D. (1940), *Emotions and Memory*, 2nd ed. New York: International Universities Press, 1950.
―――― (1951), *Organization and Pathology of Thought.* New York: Columbia University Press.
―――― (1959), *The Structure of Psychoanalytic Theory, Psychological Issues*, Monogr. 6. New York: International Universities Press.
―――― (1967), *The Collected Papers of David Rapaport.* M. Gill, ed. New York: Basic Books.
Reich, W. (1930), *Character Analysis.* New York: Orgone Institute Press, 1945.
Renik, O. (1992), Use of the analyst as a fetish. *Psychoanal. Quart.*, 61:542-563.
Robbins, M. (1993), *Schizophrenia and the Human Sciences.* New York: Guilford.
Rose, G. (1980), *The Power of Form*, rev. Madison, CT: International Universities Press, 1992.
―――― (1995), *Necessary Illusion.* Madison, CT: International Universities Press.
Rosen, V. (1977), *Style, Character, and Language.* eds. S. Atkins & M. Jucovy. New York: Aronson.
Rosenfeld, H. (1987), *Impasse and Interpretation.* London: Tavistock.
Sandler, J. (1989), Unconscious wishes and human relationships. In: *Dimensions of Psychoanalysis*, ed. J. Sandler. Madison, CT: International Universities Press, pp. 65-82.
Schore, A. (1994), *Affect Regulation and the Origin of the Self.* Hillsdale, NJ: Lawrence Erlbaum Associates.
Schwaber, E. (1981), Empathy: A mode of analytic listening. *Psychoanal. Inq.*, 1:357-392.
―――― (1983), Psychoanalytic listening and psychic reality. *Internat. Rev. Psycho-Anal.*, 10:379-392.
Sedler, M. (1983), Freud's concept of working through. *Psychoanal. Quart.*, 52:73-98.
Shane, M. (1979), A developmental approach to "working through" in the psychoanalytic process. *Internat. J. Psycho-Anal.*, 60:375-382.
Stern, D. (1985), *The Interpersonal World of the Infant.* New York: Basic Books.
Stewart, W. (1963), An inquiry into the concept of working through. *J. Amer. Psychoanal. Assn.*, 11:474-499.
Stolorow, R. & Atwood, G. (1992), *Contexts of Being.* Hillsdale, NJ: The Analytic Press.
Stone, L. (1954), The widening scope of indications for psychoanalysis. *J. Amer. Psychoanal. Assn.*, 2:567-594.
―――― (1961), *The Psychoanalytic Situation.* New York: International Universities Press.
―――― (1981), Notes on the noninterpretive elements in the psychoanalytic situation and process. *J. Amer. Psychoanal. Assn.*, 29:89-118.

Tomkins, S. (1970), Affects as the primary motivational system. In: M. Arnold, ed., *Feelings and Emotions.* New York: Academic Press, pp. 101-110.

Tower, E. (1956), Countertransference. *J. Amer. Psychoanal. Assn.*, 4:224-255.

Valenstein, A. (1973), On attachment to painful feelings and the negative therapeutic reaction. *The Psychoanalytic Study of the Child*, 28:365-392. New Haven, CT: Yale University Press.

_____ (1983), Working through and resistance to change: insight and action. *J. Amer. Psychoanal. Assn.*, 31:353-374.

Vida, J. (1993), Ferenczi's *Clinical Diary*: Roadmap to the realm. of primary relatedness. *J. Amer. Academy of Psychoanal.*, 21:623-635.

Waelder, R. (1936), The principle of multiple function. *Psychoanal. Quart.*, 5:45-62.

Warren, M. (1961), The significance of visual images during the analytic session. *J. Amer. Psychoanal. Assn.*, 9:304-318.

Weiss, E. (1970), *Sigmund Freud as a Consultant.* New York: Intercontinental Medical Books.

Wilson, A. & Gedo, J., eds. (1993), *Hierarchical Concepts in Psychoanalysis.* New York: Guilford.

_____ & Passik, S. (1993), Explorations in presubjectivity. In: A. Wilson & J. Gedo, eds. (1993), *Hierarchical Concepts in Psychoanalysis.* New York: Guilford, pp. 76-128.

_____ & Weinstein, L. (1992a), An investigation into some implications for psychoanalysis of the Vygotskian view on the origins of mind. *J. Amer. Psychoanal. Assn.*, 40:357-387.

_____ & _____ (1992b), Language and the clinical process: Psychoanalysis and Vygotskian psychology, Part II. *J. Amer. Psychoanal. Assn.*, 40:725-759.

Winnicott, D. (1952), Psychoses and child care. In: *Collected Papers.* London: Tavistock, 1958, pp. 229-242.

_____ (1954), Metapsychological and clinical aspects of regression within the psychoanalytic setup. In: *Collected Papers.* London: Tavistock, 1958, pp. 278-294.

_____ (1958), *Collected Papers.* London: Tavistock.

_____ (1960), On the theory of the parent-infant relationship. In: *The Maturational Processes and the Facilitating Environment.* New York: International Universities Press, 1965, pp. 37-55.

_____ (1965a), *The Maturational Processes and the Facilitating Environment.* New York: International Universities Press.

_____ (1965b), A clinical study of the effect of a failure of average expectable environment on a child's mental functioning. *Internat. J. Psycho-Anal.*, 46:81-87.

Wolf, E. (1976), Ambience and abstinence. *The Annual of Psychoanalysis*, 4:101-115. New York: International Universities Press.

———— (1992), On being a scientist or a healer: Reflections on abstinence, neutrality, and gratification. *The Annual of Psychoanalysis*, 20:115-130. Hillsdale, NJ: The Analytic Press.

Zetzel, E. (1965), The theory of therapy in relation to a developmental model of the psychic apparatus. *Internat. J. Psycho-Anal.*, 46:39-52.

Index

A

Abandonment, perceived, 17
Abraham, K., 48, 136, 181, 182
Acting out, 121
Activity, repetition of patterns of, 173
Adaptation, 94, 140n, 152, 170, 178
Adaptive changes, 138
Adaptive emergencies, 152
Advice, analyst's providing, 106
Affect(s), 172
   infant communication through, 47
   inner experience and, 80
   isolation of, 8
   language of, 13
   memories of, 172
   motor activities of, 36
   painful, 175
   paraverbal indications of, 14
   recognition of, 165
      inability in, 147
   somatic concomitants of, xii
   vocalization of, 78
Affective conditions, 23
Affective experience, 173
Affective patterns, 173
Affective reactions, 33
Affective state, 79
   preference for, 172
Affective tones of speech, 90
Affectomotor actions, 121
After-education, 144
Aggression, 164, 166, 168
Alexander, F., 27, 28, 62, 97, 115, 181
   concept of corrective emotional experience, 62

Alexithymia, 8
Ambiance
   analytic, 109
   empathic, 59, 62-63, 116-117
   therapeutic, 59
Analysand
   associations, 11
   male, 107
   nonverbal communications of, 118, *See also* Nonverbal communication
   provocative behavior of, 107
   psychoanalytically obtuse, 140
   psychobiology of, 144
   reaction to treatment, 102
   regression of, 22-23, *See also* Regression
   response of, 140
   semiotic codes used by, 15
   sexual power of, 107
   speech production, tempo of, 23
   state of mind, 37
   subjective experience of, 117
      communication of, 118
   subjective viewpoint of, 81, 102, 103n
   temporary identification with, 154
   verbal skills of, 59
   as victim, 42
Analysis, *See* Psychoanalysis
Analyst
   abuse of, 106-107
   as adversary, 39
   affectivity of, xii, 14
      communication of empathy, 106-111

pragmatics of empathy, 102-105
analysand's looking at, 11
appropriate attitude of, 84

articulations, mistrust of, 37
assault of, 39, 43
availability of unusual cognitive skills to, 151
communicative repertory of, 11-12, 78
countertransference potential, 96
as dispassionate technician, 82-84
female, 107
as fetish, 96
humane attitudes of, 93
language of, 84
male, 107
manipulation of, 37
meaning, 11
misleading of, 38
position of chair, 73
professional hypocrisy, 91, 99
provocation of, 42, 43
reciprocal emotional signal experienced by, 119
reincarnation as traumatically unempathic caretaker, 103
reluctant compliance by, 104
responsiveness of, 118
lack of, 107
role of caretaker assigned to, 108
sadism of, 110
as sadistically abused, 154
system of motivations, 119
theoretical strategies, 85
voice of, 58, 63-64
Analyst-patient dyad, 60-61, *See also* Shared language
Analyst-patient transactions, communication of, 58

Analytic communications, encoding of, 78
Analytic failures, 99
Analytic instrument, 145, 151
Analytic interventions
affect-laden, 84-87, 89
analyst as dispassionate technician, 82-84
analyst as the voice of the patient, 77-82
confusion of tongues in the analytic situation, 88-90
effective, 106
encoding of, 82
ill-timed, 90
Analytic setup, channels of communication and analysis and the language of gestures, 73-76
use of couch: pro and con, 68-73
Analytic situation, proper handling of, 92
"Analytic toilette," 153-155
Analyzability
determining of, 135
Eissler's criteria for, 137
Anna O, 57
Anxiety, 30
Appeasement, consistent policy of, 81
Apraxia(s), x, 100, 161, 178
communicative, somatization as, 34-36
lack of sense of humor, 99-89
repair of, working through as, 139-144
Archaic material, 104
Archaic personalities, 107
Archaic psychological issues, 118
Archaic transference, *see* Transference
Aron, L., 122, 181
Assault, speech as, 39-41
Assertion, 164

INDEX

Associations, *See also* Free association
   meanings of, interpretating of, 152
Asthma, hysterical, 28
Attachment, 164
Attention, focus of, 89
Atwood, G., 103n, 117, 122, 189
Auditory cues, 73
Autonomic nervous system, 28
Autonomous functions, regression involving, 143
Autonomous volition, 65
Aversion, 164
   preprogrammed schemata of, 172

B
Babbling, 18
   signbabbling, 20
Bacon, K., 92, 181
Bálint, M., 63, 82n, 63, 92, 108, 115, 181
   view of Ferenczi, 91
Barry, M., 168, 175, 181
Basch, M., 48, 125, 165, 181
Behavior, *See also* specific type of behavior
   avoiding unpleasure and, 172
   causation of, 173
   differentiation of, 48
   regulation of, 23, 48, 49, 125
      modes of, 45, 46, 50
   repetition of, 174
   shifts in, 170
   transitional, 32
Behavioral modification, 137
Behavioral observations, 164
Benedek, T., 69, 116
Bergman, A., 65, 187
Bettelheim, B., 117, 181
Bilingualism, 80
Biological patterns, preprogrammed, 166
Bladder control, loss of, 20
Blathering, blatherer, 19, 20, 71

Blum, H., 105, 181
Bodily functions, 29-30
Bodily symptoms, 28-29
Body, language of, xii, 15, 26-36
   developmental line concerning, 31-34
Boesky, D., 121, 181
Borderline syndrome, 8, 95
Bowel training, 18
Bowlby, J., 168, 181
Brabant, E., 119, 181
Brain, 49, 164, *See also* Neuroscience
   maturation of, 135, 145
   progressive organization of, 49
Brenner, C., 135, 181
   view on working through, 135
Breuer, J., 26, 51, 57, 182
Brodsky, B., 134, 182
Bucci, W., 99, 145, 151, 182
Budapest school, 91

C
Calder, K., 153, 182
Candor, 159
Caretaker, *See also* Parent
   behavior, 66
   enslaved, 177
   need-satisfying, 96
   original, loss of, 66
   unavailable, 96
Caretaker-infant transactions, 61
Central nervous system
   functional organization of, 8
   maturation and hierarchical organization of, xiii
   progressive organization of, 172
Cerebral hemispheres, defense mechanisms and, 48
Change, resistance to, 134
Character, disorders of, 37
   repetition and, 95-97
Charcot, J. M., 20

Child, children, *See also* Infant; Newborn; Toddler
    atypical language development, 66
    channels of communication available to, 118
    cognitive gains of, 174
    conflicts about wish, 175
    crisis of rapprochement, 65
    psychoanalysis of, 93
    symbolic operations of, 174
Childhood
    early events, enactment of, 16
    recovery of memories from, 76
Childhood transactions, repeated transferentially, 113n, 120-121
Cocoon, 116, 121, *See also* Holding environment
Cognition, development of, xi, 46, 135
Cognitive maturation, working through as, 138-139
Cognitive operations, 151
Cognitive psychology, 46
Cognitive repertory, ix
Cognitive therapy, 139n
Colitis, 29, 30, 33
Collaboration, therapeutic, use of couch and, 69
Common sense, voice of, 176
Communication
    ability for, 100
        regressive impairments of, 10, 142
        channels of, and the analytic setup, *See* Analytic setup
    disorders of, 7-11, 38, 98-100
    interpersonal, xii
    intrapsychic, xii
    manipulative, 42, 44
    metaphoric, 8
    miscarriage of, 88

modes of, 4, 13-14
    primitive, 24
    musical, 10
    nonverbal, *See* Nonverbal communication
    paraverbal aspects of, 61
    state of harmony in, 62
    symbolic, 13
    syntactically and lexically comprehensive, 19
    verbal, *See* Verbal communication
Competitiveness, angry, 81
Complacency, 149
Complex skills, acquisition of, 165
Compromise formations, 138
Concealment, speech as, 39-41
Concentration camp survivors, mastery of trauma by, 137
Conflict
    interpersonal, 48
    intrapsychic, timing of, 48
Confusion of tongues in the analytic situation, 88-90
Confusional state, 130
Consciousness
    altered states of, 35, 50, 51, 52, 53
    clouding of, 20
    problem of, 49-53
Consensual language, 7, 17, 130, 133, 174
    ability to use, 15
    acquisition of, 64
    misuse of, 66
Consensus, promotion of, 112
Consultation, 154, 155
Consulting room, 76
Control, loss of, 128
Conversion hysteria, 26-27, 30, 32
    differentiated from other kinds of somatization, 27-28
Conversion reaction, 15, 32
Convulsions, 20

INDEX

Coping, 177
Corrective emotional experience, 62, 96, 114-117
    Ferenczi's view on, 115
Couch
    leaving of, 75
    as place of exile, 72
    use of, 11, 73
        gestures and, 74
        pro and con, 68-73
        reluctance in, 71-72
Counteridentification, 64, 88
Countermotives, 176
Countertransference, 64, 106-107, 117-120
    interpretation based on, 91, 119
    problems, 96
    responses, 121
    unrecognized, 88
Countertransference feelings, 154
Crisis, 82, 84
Cues, verbal and nonverbal, 118
Cultural differences, patient-therapist, 59

D

Danger, 46
    forestalling of, 175
Data collection, 108
Death instinct, 137
    Freud's proposal of, 137-138
Defense(s)
    in early childhood, 35
    self-inquiry and, 155
Defensive operations, 46, 128, 135, 161, 175
    relaxation of, 23
Delusion(s), 42, 99, 129, 132
    abandoning of, inability in, 129-130
    isolated, 42
    lack of integration and, 133
    megalomanic, 126
Demos, V., 46, 182
Denial, 129

Depersonalization, sense of, 18
Depression, 23, 30
    clinical, 147
Dermatitis, 32-33, 34
Destructiveness, setting limits on, 111
Development
    adult pathology and, 49-50
    epigenetic view of, 118
    lines of, x, 145-146, 170, 179, 179f
        five-stage, 47-48
        oedipal stage, 48
        oral stage, 48
        phallic stage, 48
        postoedipal stage, 48
    psychoanalytic theory of, xi
    psychological, *See* Psychological development
    working through and, 135
Developmental arrest, 35, 91-95, 115-116, 175
    correction of, 93
Dialogue
    internal, 79
    therapeutic, harmonious, 63
Diarrhea, 20, 29
Different language, transactions encoded in, 80
Disappointments, 99
Disavowal
    defense mechanisms of, 48
    splitting by way of, 125
Discourse
    appropriate, avoidance of trauma through, 111-113n
    archaic modes of, xii
    psychoanalytic, x
    standards of, 3
Disgust, 33
Dissociation, 95
Distress, avoiding of, 175
Dramatic enactments, 119
Dream(s), dreaming, 19

in failure of symbolization, 131
occurrence of speech in, 19, 22
Dream-wish, archaic, 131
Drive energies, neutralization of, 138
Drive theory, 166
Dual-instinct theory, 168
Dupont, J., 62n, 92, 97, 111, 114, 115, 116, 122, 154, 182
Dyadic enactment, 87, 107, 120
emotional participation in, 119
Dying, 31
Dysphoria, containment of, 147

E
Edelman, G., 49, 182
Educational process, working through as, 144
Ego, 138, 139
intact, 116, 137, 141
regression in the service of, 22
Ego deficit, 136
Ego distortion, 140
Ego functions, differential regression in, 170
Ego psychology, Hartmann's view on, 168
Ego strength, 135
Ego weakness, 136
Ehrenberg, D., 42, 142, 182
Eissler, K., 106, 116, 136, 137, 182
criteria for analyzability, 137
Ekstein, R., 135, 144, 182
Eliot, T. S., 24
Emde, R. N., 173, 182
Emergency phone calls, 110
Emotion, unconcealed, 17
Empathic responsiveness, 103, 112, 119
insufficient, 109
Empathy, 22, 96, 105, 112, 132

breaks in, 77-78, 117
communication of, 106-111
pragmatics of, 102-105
Endocrine mechanisms, 28
Energies, concept of, 164
Evasiveness, 3
Excitement, 33
Experience, *See also* specific type of experience
three registers of, 13
unnamable and unimaginable aspects of, 13
External assistance, question of, 105-106
External controls, 111

F
Face-to-face psychotherapy, 69
Facial expressions, 11, 14, 74, 118
changing of, 73
Fairbairn, W. R. D., 168, 182
Falzeder, E., 119, 181
Fantasy(ies), creating of, 166
Feeling state, inchoate, 20
Feiner, K., 46, 185
Fenichel, O., 114, 182
Ferenczi, S., x, 26, 45, 68, 92, 96, 101, 111, 114, 115, 116, 119, 122, 136, 182
contributions of, 91, 92
counteridentification with patients, 96
differences with Freud, 92
mutual analysis, 96, 154-155
technical approach of, 92-93
views
on corrective emotional experience, 115
on holding environment, 116
on successful analytic treatment, 115
Fonagy, I., 16, 182
Forces, concepts of, 164
Free association, 37, 144
ability for, 145, 146

abuse of, 37-38, 39
engaging in, 141
method of, 159
power of, 158-160
provocation of analyst and, 43
transferential vissitudes and, 61
uninterrupted, 147
Freedman, D., 165, 182
French, T., 62, 97, 115, 176, 181, 182
Freud, A., x, 93, 94, 183
Freud, E., 57, 183
Freud, S., x, 3, 15, 19, 21, 26, 35n, 40, 45, 51, 53, 69, 77, 81, 84, 100, 101, 115, 118, 119, 120, 125, 129, 134, 135, 136, 137, 138, 139, 141, 144, 145, 147, 153, 155, 157, 164, 167, 163, 168, 172, 175, 176, 178n, 182, 183
  "analytic toilette" and, 153-155
  Ferenczi's differences with, 92
  metapsychology, 165
  preanalytic pressure technique, 68
  proposal of death instinct, 137-138
  repetition compulsion and, 164, *See also* Repetition compulsion
  theory of motivation, 166
  tripartite model, 79
  views
    on self-inquiry, 160-161
    on working through, 134-135, 136, 137, *See also* Working through
Functional capacity, 22, 151
Functioning
  levels of, shifts in, 22-25

specific modes of, hierarchical schema of problems typical for, 171f

G
Galatzer-Levy, R., 135, 184
Gardner, R., 4, 77, 80, 139, 149, 150, 152 184
Gedo, J., v, x, xi, xii, 4, 6, 8, 9n, 10, 14, 15, 16, 17, 23, 24, 27, 28, 29, 30, 31, 32, 33, 34, 35, 38, 41, 45, 48, 63, 63n, 71, 74, 75, 78, 80, 82, 84, 87, 88, 89, 91, 92, 93, 94, 99, 100, 102, 103, 105, 106, 107, 109, 111, 112, 113, 114, 118, 119, 121, 122, 125, 126, 127, 130, 131, 132, 133, 135, 137, 139, 141, 143, 144, 145, 147, 151, 161, 163, 163n, 166, 167, 168, 169n, 170, 173, 173n, 174, 175, 181, 184, 190
Gedo, P., 77, 184
Gehrie, M., 38, 92, 102, 103, 104, 105, 106, 107, 108, 109, 112, 113, 130, 117, 119, 184, 185
Gesture(s), 4, 11, 15, 24
  infant's, 47
  language of, 47, 69, 118
  analysis and, 73-76
Giampieri-Deutsch, P., 119, 181
Goals, universal, 164
Goldberg, A., x, 14, 23, 24, 27, 31, 45, 92, 118, 121, 125, 135, 141, 143, 167, 168, 169n, 169, 175, 184
"Good analytic segments," 77, 81
"Good character," 37
"Good hour" concept, 77
Grand, S., 46, 185
Grande hystérie, 95
Grandiosity, 98, 129
Gray, P., 146, 185

Greenson, R., 14, 185
Grief, 30
Grotjahn, M., 7, 185
Guidry, R., 148, 149, 150
Guilt, 30, 79, 175
Gunther, M., 6, 103, 186

H
Hadley, J., 49n, 53n, 120, 164, 172, 174, 174n, 186
Hallucination, olfactory, 60
Hannett, F., 3, 186
Harris, A., 122, 181
Hartmann, H., 94, 138, 143, 167, 168, 176, 186
    view on ego psychology, 168
Hate speech, 39
Hatred, outburst of, response to, 39
Haynal, A., 91, 92, 101, 186
Helplessness, 33, 141
Holding environment, 23, 59, 62, 63, 95, 96, 102, 116, 121
Hostility, 142, 156
Humiliation, 175
Humility, 96
Hypochondriasis, xii, 30-31, 32
Hypocrisy, professional, 91, 99
Hypomania, 23
Hysteria, 26, 28
    conversion, *See* Conversion hysteria

I
Id, 138, 139
Id resistance, 137
    working through and, 1135
Idea, ego alien, 129
Ideation, 126, 127, 136
Imaginary register, 13
Impasse, analytic, 96, 99, 109
    overcoming of, 117
Imposture, speech as, 41-42
Impulses, interpreting of, 135
Infant, *See also* Newborn
    communication by, 118
    communicative repertory, xi
    exploratory behaviors, 172, 173
    mental operations of, 46
    vocalization of, 20
Infant-mother attunement, effective, 173
Infantile experience, 145
    use of couch and, 69
Infantilism, self-destructive, 109
Inner experience, 20, 80
Inner world, sharing of, 39
Insight(s)
    analytic, 80
    defense against, 140
    preconditions for, 105
Instruction, technology of, working through as, 144
Integration, lack of, 133
Integrative faculties, 131
Intellect, voice of, x, 130, 176
Intellectualization, 161
Interpersonal sphere, punishment in, 32
Interpretation, 135, 139
Intersubjective viewpoint, 103n, 116
Interventions, *See* Analytic interventions
Intimacy, 65, 112
Intrapsychic conflicts, 32
    mental contents associated with, 136
    reconciling of, 138
    unresolved, 131
Irony, 85, 85
Isakower, O., 145
    concept of analytic instrument, 151

J
Jackson, H., 45, 186
Jargon, professional, 59
Jones, E., 57, 115, 136, 182, 186

K
Kernberg, O., 127, 186

INDEX

-201-

Klein, M., xi, 97, 107, 108, 120, 166, 169, 186
   view on projective identification, 120-121, *See also* Projective identification
Kohut, H., 3, 77, 78n. 82, 96, 102, 103, 104, 105, 106, 121, 125, 129, 160, 163n, 173n, 177, 186
Kris, E., 22, 42, 77, 187
Krystal, H., 35, 137, 187

L

Lacan, J., 13
Language(s), 13
   choice of, 85
   consensual use of, 78, 165, *See also* Consensual language
   loss of, 130
   emotional charge of, 11
   misuse of, 38
   neuropathology of, 13
   private, lapsing into, 18
   shared, *See* Shared language
   spoken, *See* Spoken language
   syntactically organized, 14
   variety of, 66
Laughing, 78
Learning difficulties, 135, 140n
Learning experience, working through and, 135
Learning situation, 15
Leavy, S., 15, 187
Levarie, S.., 3, 187
Levin, F., xi, 8, 13, 32, 46, 47, 48, 74, 76, 84, 135, 140n, 164, 173, 187
Lexical message, 10, 11
Libido, 48, 137, 167, 168
Lichtenberg, J., 15, 31, 46, 164, 178, 187
   view on motivation, 164, 167
Limits, setting of, 108, 109, 111
Little, M. 117, 187
Loewald, H., 115, 187

Loewenstein, R., 6, 7, 94, 186
Loneliness, repetition of, 95
Ludowyk-Gyömröi, E., 92, 93, 187

M

MacGregor, J., 16, 188
Magical thinking, adherence to, 98, 104-105, 132
Mahler, M., 65, 187
Makari, G., 104, 188
Maladaptation, 46, 170-171
Maladaptive motivations, 173
Manipulation, 40
   speech as
      abuse of free association, 37-38
      speech as assault or concealment, 39-41
      speech as imposture, 41-42
      speech as provocation, 42-44
Marentette, P., 20, 188
Masochism, erotogenic, 138
Masochistic behavior, 79
Masochistic proclivities, 40
Masson, J., 160, 188
Mastery, 137
Maturation, 94, 115, 135, 165,
Meaning, 11, 19
Megalomania, 126, 128, 129
Memory(ies), 129
Memory signals, 172
Mental contents, 139, 139n
   archaic, 74
   elucidation of, 139
   interpretation of, 114
   patient's refusal to discuss, 41
   repressed, 68
   unconscious, 63
Mental dispositions, chronic, 132
Mental function, functioning
   hierarchical view of, 167-171
   split-off nucleus of, 98
   traditional theories of, 138

Mental operations, 45
Mental state, primitive, 8
Mentation
  archaic, 9, 168
  secondary-process, 19, 98
  split-off realms of, 32
Messages
  lexical meaning of 58
  nonverbal, 3-7
Metaphor(s), 9
  employment of, 84-85
  working through as, 134-136, 139, 146-147
Metapsychology, 165
Mind, 49, See also Neuroscience
  agencies of, 79
  hierarchical model of, 31
  psychoanalytic theory of 163
  splits of, 125-126, 170
Miscommunication, 89-90
  archaic problems causing, 64
  painful episodes of, reenactment of, 65
Mistreatment, 99
Misunderstanding, 59, 89
Modell, A., 59, 77, 80, 102, 105, 116, 163n, 173n, 188
Moraitis, G., 101n, 112, 188
Morgenthaler, W., 16, 188
"Mother tongue," acquisition of, 15
Motivation
  biological patterns of, 164
  defined, 163
  Freud's theory of, 166
  hierarchy of, 171, 172-176
    clinical illustration and summary, 176-179
    fourth phase, 175, 176
    mode I, 172
    mode II, 172
    mode III, 174
  preprogrammed, 164
  theories of, 163-165, 166
Motivational schemata, expectable, 173

Motivational systems, 171
Motor acts, involuntary, 20
Muller, J., 13, 20, 22, 57, 188
"Multiple personalities," 125
Music, 14, 15
  of affectivity, 30
  metaphorical use of, 8
  nonverbal communication and, 3, 4-5, 6, 8
Musical associations, 22
Musical communication, misinterpretation of, 10
Musical meanings, as transference enactment, 5-6
Mutual analysis, 96, 154-155
Myth, personal, 42

N
Nacherziehung (reeducation), 77
Narcissism, pathological, 127
Narcissistic libido, 167
Narcissistic motivations, 164
Narrative(s), 14, 47
Needs, automatic satisfaction of, 131
Negative therapeutic reaction, 63, 100n, 112
Negativism, 17, 18, 65, 131
  emergency defense of, 71
  reenactment of, 130
Neural control, maturation of, xi
Neural functions, 174
Neural networks, reorganization of, 146, See also Working through
"Neurasthenia," 33-34
Neurocognitive problems, 140n
Neurophysiological subsystem, 172
Neuropsychological data, 164
Neuroscience, 45-49
  problem of consciousness, 49-53
Neurosis
  actual, 147
  transference, 26, 69
  traumatic, chronic, 95

Index

Neurotic core, actual, 136, 178n
Neurotic symptom formation, 130
Neutrality
   analytic, 14, 78
   technical, 106
New beginning, 91-95, 96, 101, 108
   shared language as, 62-64
Newborn, *See also* Infant
   communication through affects, 47
Nonverbal codes, translation of, 121
Nonverbal communication, 118, *See also* Gestures
   clinical implications of, 11-12
   communicative deficits, 7-11
   interference with, 73
   nonverbal messages, 3-7
Nonverbal representations, 151
Noy, P., 3, 188
Nurture, influence of, 172

O

Object, need-satisfying, 40
Object loss, 93, 96
Object relations, 46, 93, 113, 168
   benign, 108
Observation, empathic, 102, *See also* Empathy Obsessional syndrome, 8
Oedipal struggle, negative, 166
Oedipal wishes, 98
Omnipotence, 105, 131, 133
Ontogenesis, 45
Opisthotonos, 20
Organismic needs, fulfilling of, 165
Orgasm, spontaneous, 20
Ornstein, A., 103, 188
Ornstein, P., 103, 188
O'Shaughnessy, E., 134, 188
Overstimulation, 75

P

Painful feelings, attachment to, 100n, 138
Panic, 95, 147
Pantomine, communication in, 87
Pappenheim, B., 57-58
Paraverbal communication, impact of, 79
Paraverbal signs, 118
   infant's communication of, 118
Parent, *See also* Caregiver
   behavior of, traumatic, 155
   role of, 153
Parent-child dialogue, derailment of, 11
Passik, S., 46, 190
Passivity, 71
Pathological thinking, 130
Pathology, intractable, 98-101
Patient, *See* Analysand
Personal analysis, 155, 159
Personality, splitting of, 35, 126
Personality organization, nuclei of, 23
Personality structure, 4
Personalization, 33
Petitto, L., 20, 188
Phenomes, articulation of, 16
Physiologic equilibiria, maintenance of, 164
Piano, The (film), 5
Pine, F., 65, 163n, 187, 188
Planning, 100
Pleasure, evoking of, 173
Pleasure principle, 172
Poetry, 16, 17
Pollock, G., 122, 184
Preprogrammed patterns, limits of, 165-167
Preprogrammed schemata, 174
Presentational symbols, infant's use of, 47
Preverbal era, experiences of, 8
Preverbal past, reconstruction of, 121
Preverbal state, 18
   regression to, 22
Pride, onset of, 175
Primary process, 3, 15, 145

elements, latent meanings encoded within, 59
Primitive behavior, 131
Primitive personality, 128
Priorities, organizing of, 100
Procedural skills, acquiring of, 48
Professional life, turning point in, 148-150, 152
Projective identification, 97, 120-121
    concept of, 107-108
    transferential significance of, 120
Protolinguistic framework, 13
Protolinguistic modes of communication, 59
Protolinguistic phenomena, in psychoanalysis, xi, 15-20
    emergence of, 24
    shifts in levels of functioning, 22-25
    silence, 20-22
Provocation, speech as, 42-44
Provocativeness, sadistic, 111
Pseucocyesis, 29
Pseudologia fantastica, 130
"Pseudo-stupidity," 140
Psyche, primitive, 26-36
Psychic activities, bodily symptoms caused by, 34
Psychic functioning, hierarchical model of, x
Psychic organization, 16-17
    levels of, 170
Psychoanalytic setting, xii
"Psychoanalytic situation," 68
Psychoanalysis, 46, 63, 78
    art of, 90
    compared with other forms of psychotherapy, 61
    classical technique of, 116
    failed, 126
    Ferenczi's view on, 115
    issues unresolved in, 155-158
    protolinguistic phenomena in, See Protolinguistic phenomena, in psychoanalysis
    rhetorical dimensions of, x, 13-15
    semiotics of, 14
    theories in, 114, 163
    as the voice of the patient, 77-82
    widening role of, 121-122
Psychoanalyst, See Analyst
Psychoanalytic psychotherapy, 16
Psychobiological functioning, 63
Psychoeconomic imbalance, 136, 137
Psychological development, x-xi, 165
Psychological functions, quasi-stationary status of, 50
Psychological mindedness, lack of, 140
Psychological resources, 144
Psychological skills
    acquisition of, 151
    deficits in, x, 100, See also Apraxia
    limit of, 161
Psychoneurotic symptoms, 136
Psychopathology, 81, 170
Psychosis, 126, 133
    schizophrenic, 127-128
"Psychosomatic medicine," 27
Psychosomatic occurrences, significance as communication, 32-33
Psychotic core, 42, 98, 126-130
    persistence of, xii

R
Racker, H., 118, 188
Rage, 30, 79
Rank, O., 114, 182
Rapaport, D., 14, 50, 98, 137, 145n, 168, 189
Rapprochement, crisis of, 65
Rat Man, 144
Raynaud's phenomenon, 34

INDEX

Reaction formation, 166, 167
Reality
    distorting of, 103
    shared, 77
    testing, 42, 85, 133
    unmanageable, 82
Reanalysis, 159, 160
Reason, voice of, 176
Referential activity, 145
Referential schemata, 151
"Reflex arc," model of, 168
Regression, 22-23, 35, 78n, 88, 89, 97, 126, 155
    developmental, 170
    differentiating of, 49
    fear of, 71
    involving autonomous functions, 143
    psychological, 45, 50-51
    therapeutic, 91, 95, 142
"Regression in the service of the ego," 22
Regressive developments, revelation of, 90
Regressive movement, undetected, 89
Regressive solution, 178
Regressive states, 14
Reich, W., 27, 114, 189
Reisner, S., 46, 185
Renik, O., 96, 189
Repetition, 82, 136
    characterological problems and, 95-97
Repetition compulsion, 100, 100n, 101n, 117, 120, 137-138, 164, 168, 174, 174n
Repressed patient, successful communication with, 11
Repression, 48, 125, 128, 175
Resistance(s), 3, 4, 63, 64, 159
    concepts of, 164
    endopsychic, 81
    "to getting into analysis," 72
    nonverbal associations and, 7
    overcoming of, 147
    silence and, 20
    working through and, 135
Responsibility, denials of, 103
Retaliation, fear of, 27
Rhetoric, 10, 85
Richardson, W., 13, 188
Risk-taking, grandiose, 131
Robbins, M., 127, 189
Role
    hysterical enactment of, 37
    reversals, 120-121
Rose, G., 16, 189
Rosen, V., 14, 189
Rosenfeld, H., 14, 189

S

Sadism, 40, 86, 86n, 107, 110, 111
Sandler, J., 83, 189
Satisfaction, subjective, 174
Schizophrenia, symptomology of, 15
Schizophrenic persons, 16
Schizophrenic psychosis, 127-128
Schore, A., 53, 189
Schwaber, E., 81, 82, 102, 103, 104, 189
Scientific exposition, objective, 82
Secessionist movements, 114
Secondary process, 3, 15, 16, 58, 59, 69, 98, 145
Sedler, M., 134, 135, 189
Self
    childhood, 86, 153
    crazy, 126
    false, xii, 125, 126, 133, 177
    sane, 126
    subjective sense of, loss of, 18
    true, xii, 125, 126, 133, 177
Self-accusations, 97
Self-analysis, xii, 152, 154, 155, 160, *See also* Self-inquiry
Self-analytic instrument, 145, 150-153
Self-awareness, 35, 174, 175
Self-blame, 79
Self-cognition, 139

Self-cohesion, lack of, 32, 133
Self-contempt, 93
Self-criticism, 149
Self-definition, 173-174
Self-eroticism, 38
Self-esteem, analysand's, 121
"Self-in-the-world," 133, 152, 173
Self-inquiry, 77, 80, 145, 150, 152, 155, 158, 160-161 *See also* Self-analysis
Self-knowledge, 161
Self-monitoring, 159
Self-objects, 96, 160
Self-observation(s), 21
Self-organization, 23, 24, 34, 66, 100, 104, 174, 175, 176, 177
Self-preservative aims, 164
Self psychology, 102, 108, 110, 117, 132
Self-punishment, need for, 112
Self-reflection, 35
Self-regulation, 45, 175
Self-satisfaction, 149
Self-understanding, 159, 161
Semantic problems, sources of, 59
Semiotic capacities, line of development of, 13
Semiotic codes, assembly of, 15
Semiotics, xiii, 11, 46
Sense of humor, lack of, 88-89
Sensuality/sexuality, 164
Separateness, sense of, 65
Separation-individuation, 65
Sexual demands, analyst's resistance to, 104
Sexual exploitation, 131
Sexual inhibitions, 167
Sexual transaction, 104
Sexual undercurrent, 107
Sexuality, 164, 166
Shakespeare, W., 117
Shame, 30, 128, 175
Shane, M., 134, 135, 189
Shapiro, T., 104, 188
Shared language, 80, 99
communicating in, 66
development of, treatment as, 57-62
complications, 64-67
establishment of, 99
as a new beginning, 62-64
Sign language, 7, 174
Signbabbling, 20
Silence, 20-22
Simmel, E., 136, 182
Soma, 29-30
Somatic symptoms, 30, 33
Somatization, 26-27, 36, 58, 147
as communicative apraxia, 34-36
conversion hysteria, 26, 27-28
developmental line concerning, 31-34
hypochondriasis and, 30
transitional, 31
Somnambulism, 125
Somnolence, 33
Sonic intensity, 14
Spasms, muscular, 27
Speech, 13
as manipulation, *See* Manipulation
music of, 14
paraverbal aspects of, 10, 23, 24, 74, 143
transient episodes of, 16
Splitting, 37, 176
Spoken language, 8
Spoken message, lexical meaning of 10
Spouse, analyst of, transference to, 161n
Stalemate, *See* Impasse
Stern, D., 46, 61, 173, 189
Stewart, W., 134, 135, 189
Stolorow, R., 103n, 117, 122, 189
Stone, L., 14. 70, 102, 105, 114, 189
Stress, 29, 31

Index

Structural reorganization, shared language and, 63
Structural theory, 168
Structured mental dispositions, 115
Subjectivity, 82, 99
Suicide, 42, 95-96
Superego, 166, 167, 176
Symbiosis, 93, 160
Symbiotic experiences, 15, 65
Symbol(s)
    abstract, processing of, 22
    communication by means of, 32, 64
    system of, 7, 99, 174
    nonverbal, 7
Symbolic meanings, 29, 30
Symbolic operations, 174
Symbolization, 121
    failure of, 130-133
Symptom
    formation, 32
    transference meaning of, 33
Syndrome, symbolic meaning of, 29
Synecdoche, 85
Syntactic language, 76
Syntactically encoded messages, 154
Syntax, 79
    use of, 50

T

Talking cure, ix, 57-58
Tantrums, 18
Tardiness, 156
Teaching-learning situation, 15
Tension, 136
    regulation, 100
Termination, 96, 98, 144
Terror, 29, 33
Therapeutic alliance, 59, 63, 102
Therapeutic enterprise, regression in service of, 22
Therapeutic impasse, *See* Impasse, analytic

Therapist, *See* Analyst
Thinking, development of, 145
Thought, 19, 35, 36, 37
Thought disorder, 129-130
Tics, xii, 15, 31, 32
Time, handling of, 154
Time-related activities, regulating, 156
Toddler, 64, 65
Tomkins, S., 172, 190
Topographic theory, 168
Tower, E., 118, 190
Transference, 4, 26, 80, 82, 84, 135, *See also* Countertransference
    affect-laden analytic interventions and, 85-86
    archaic, 14, 18, 60, 86, 103, 113, 113n, 117, 118
    assaultiveness through speech and, 40
    brother, 86, 86n
    of characterological problems, 95
    dyadic (mother), 142
    evocation of, 155
    father, 89, 104, 142
    hostile, 27
    idealizing, 103
    merger, 78, 96, 99
    mirror, 177
    mother, 10, 90, 104, 177
    narcissistic, 160
    negative, 18, 104, 112, 132
    other and, 85
    positive, 142
    protolinguistic phenomenon emerging in the context of, 23
    regressive, 140
    selfobject, 103
Transference constellations, repetition of, 136
Transference-countertransference development, 154

Transference crises, managing of, 153
Transference demands, 84
Transference figure, 157
Transference interpretation, 97, 103, 136, 141, 161, 161n
Transference patterns, 116, 142
Transference reaction, 38, 86
Transference repetition, 82, 100, 161
Transference resistance, 81
    working through of, 141
Transitory symptoms, maturity of, 27
Trauma, traumata, 31
    avoidance of, through appropriate discourse, 111–113n
    early, 92
    mastery of, 137
    parental behavior related to, 155
    potential, 155–156
Traumatic experiences, 95
Traumatic incidents, minimizing frequency of, 112
Traumatization, 155
Treatment relationship, loss of, threat of, 127
Trieb, 166
Tropes, 85
Truth, facing of, endopsychic resistance to, 158

U

Unconscious material, processing of, 139
Unconscious mental activities, 164
Underlying problem, preoccupation with, 151
Unempathic responses, 106, 108
Unpleasure, 172, 173
Unpleasure principle, 172
Utterances, 59

V

Valenstein, A., 100n, 134, 138, 190

Validation, need for, 154
Vasomotor instability, 33
Verbal associations, 4, 34
Verbal codes, consensual, 35
Verbal communication
    couch and, 69
    misleading, 43
Verbal intelligence, ix
Verbal language, 47
Verbal pyrotechnics, 41
Verbal representations, 151
Verbal system, 8
Verbalizations, processing of, 37
Victimization, reversal of, 104
Vida, J., 109, 190
Visceral symptoms, 29
Visions, 4
Visual observation, 73
Vocabulary, 79
    alternative, 174
Vocalization(s), 14
    earliest, regression to, 16
    music of, 74
Vomiting, 20
Vuckovich, M., 164, 187

W

Waelder, R., 167, 190
War neurosis, 136
Warren, M., 3, 190
Weinstein, L., 77, 113, 144, 190
Weiss, E., 141, 190
Wilson, A., 45, 46, 48, 77, 113, 144, 167, 190
Winnicott, D., 59, 68, 93, 95, 98, 102, 105, 116, 125–126, 133, 168, 177, 190
    Little's analysis with, 117
Wish, conflicts about, 175
Withdrawal, 33
Wolf, E., 59, 62, 108, 116, 190
Wolf Man, 131
Word(s)
    encoding of, 74
    inner experience in, 19
    metaphorical use of, 8
"Word salads," 15

Working through, 114
  as cognitive maturation, 138–139
  learning of, 143–144
  metaphor of, xii, 139
  as metaphor, 134–136, 146–147
  neurology of, 144–146
  as repair of apraxia, 139–144
  as treatment modality, 136–138

Written messages, exchanging of, 58

Z
Zetzel, E., 59, 102, 191

For Product Safety Concerns and Information please contact our EU representative GPSR@taylorandfrancis.com
Taylor & Francis Verlag GmbH, Kaufingerstraße 24, 80331 München, Germany

www.ingramcontent.com/pod-product-compliance
Lightning Source LLC
Chambersburg PA
CBHW070606300426
44113CB00010B/1422